The Land of CANAAN

HISTORIES BY ISAAC ASIMOV

THE GREEKS

THE ROMAN REPUBLIC

THE ROMAN EMPIRE

THE EGYPTIANS

THE NEAR EAST

THE DARK AGES

THE SHAPING OF ENGLAND

CONSTANTINOPLE

THE LAND OF CANAAN

The Land of CANAAN

BY ISAAC ASIMOV

HOUGHTON MIFFLIN COMPANY BOSTON
1971

To Arthur C. Clarke
first in science fiction
second in science
by the Treaty of Park Avenue

FIRST PRINTING W

LIBRARY OF CONGRESS CATALOG CARD NUMBER 70-155557
ISBN 0-395-12572-3
PRINTED IN THE UNITED STATES OF AMERICA

CONTENTS

1 BEFORE ABRAHAM

2 AFTER ABRAHAM

3 ISRAEL

The Land of CANAAN

1

BEFORE ABRAHAM

THE FERTILE CRESCENT

In western Asia, in the nation of Iraq (ee-rahk′), there are two rivers that flow from the Turkish mountains to the Persian Gulf. They are the Tigris River (ty′gris) and the Euphrates River (yoo-fray′teez). These two rivers are an unfailing source of water so that the land around them and between them is particularly suitable for agriculture. It is a fertile land, with mild weather, rainy winters and dry summers. Its fertility is all the more noticeable because to the northeast are the rugged mountains of Iran (ee-rahn′) and to the southwest the dry Arabian desert.

This strip extends from the Persian Gulf northwestward up the rivers to the borders of Turkey. It stretches to the west across southeastern Turkey and northern Syria, then follows the Mediterranean coastline southward, including not only the coast of Syria, but also Lebanon, northern Israel, and western Jordan.

The area, extending from the Persian Gulf to central Israel, is shaped like a large crescent. An American historian, James Henry Breasted, called it the Fertile Crescent and that name is now commonly used.

South of the western horn of the Fertile Crescent is a dry and barren bit of land called the Sinai Peninsula (sy′ny), which is the connecting link between the vast continents of Asia and Africa. Immediately to the west of the Sinai Peninsula is the long Nile River, which flows from east-central Africa, north to the Mediterranean Sea. On either side of the northernmost stretch of the river is another strip of land suitable for agriculture, with desert on either side of the strip. Sometimes the Nile Valley is included as part of the Fertile Crescent by historians, but usually it isn't.

The most important human fact about the Fertile Crescent and the Nile Valley is that, as far as we know, civilization began there. It was in or near those regions that agriculture was first developed, pottery was first made, animals were first tamed, cities were first built, and writing was first invented.

Individual cities were first combined into large regions ruled by a central authority at the extreme ends of these areas. About 2800 B.C., along the lower reaches of the Tigris and Euphrates, the Sumerian civilization was in full swing,* while, at the same time, along the Nile River, the Egyptian civilization was flourishing.† Both eventually formed large empires.

The two civilizations were fortunate in that they were so far apart they could not interfere with each other in hostile fashion. For two thousand years after the two civilizations had formed there was no direct military contact. Neither one had to fight off the other; neither one had the opportunity to destroy

* For a history of the various cultures of the Tigris-Euphrates region, see my book *The Near East* (Houghton Mifflin, 1968).

† For a history of the Egyptian civilization, see my book *The Egyptians* (Houghton Mifflin, 1967).

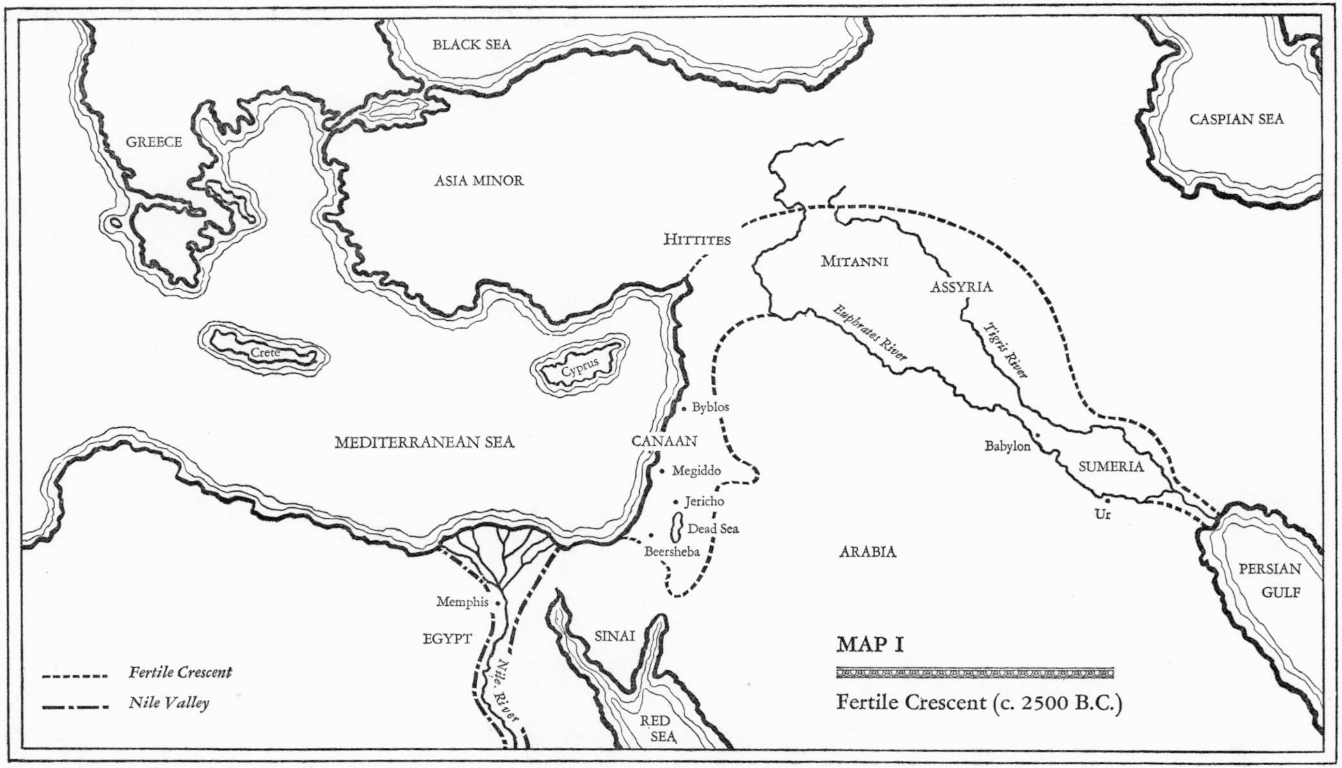

MAP I

Fertile Crescent (c. 2500 B.C.)

or the chance to be destroyed. There was, however, trade between the two across the gap between them and that helped both.

But what about the section of fertile area between Sumeria and Egypt? What about the western half of the Fertile Crescent? The western half is smaller than the eastern half and not quite as fertile; it is also smaller and less fertile than the Nile Valley. Nevertheless, in the very earliest days of civilization, that western half was as advanced as the other portions.

It was, however, in between. It could never expect the peace that comes with isolation. The civilizations of the Tigris-Euphrates always reached westward in the hope of dominating the Mediterranean coast, and the civilization of Egypt as persistently reached northward.

Caught in the middle, the Mediterranean coast could have no opportunity to develop an empire. It remained a collection of city-states and small, weak nations. Through all its history it was dominated by its neighbor empires — with the exception of one small gap in time about 1000 B.C.

Most history books tend to pay a great deal of attention to large empires, their great victories and defeats. The little cities and nations that never form empires or loom large in war tend to be skipped over. The western part of the Fertile Crescent is therefore usually taken up in connection with the various empires that dominated it at one period or another in history.

And yet the western end of the Fertile Crescent has, for its size, contributed more to modern western civilization than did all the mighty empires of the Nile Valley and of the Tigris-Euphrates. Just to mention two items, it was from the strip of land bordering the eastern Mediterranean that the modern alphabet arose. It was there, also, that a religion developed that, in various forms, now dominates Europe, the Americas, western Asia, and northern Africa.

For these two contributions alone the western part of the Fertile Crescent deserves a history book of its own, one that concentrates on the events that took place in that small but extremely important portion of the world.

It would be helpful, though, to have a name for the entire area, since "the western part of the Fertile Crescent" is a clumsy phrase which is too long to be used all the time. No one nation occupies the whole area now — it is split up among Syria, Lebanon, Israel, and Jordan — so we can't use one particular modern name. In the past, it was also split up among different nations — Moab, Edom, Ammon, Judah, Aram, and so on.

In ancient times one name that was used for at least part of the area was Canaan (kay′nan). It is a name that is familiar to the modern people of the west because it is used in the Bible. For convenience' sake, then, we will call the strip of Mediterranean coast that makes up the western end of the Fertile Crescent the land of Canaan.

THE NEW STONE AGE

Agriculture ties human beings to the land. As long as men hunted game or gathered fruit in the wild, they could wander freely. Indeed, they were forced to wander, whether they wanted to or not, in their search for food. Once they began to cultivate plants, however, they had to remain in the vicinity of their growing crops in order to tend them and to protect them from foraging animals and from other men.

For safety's sake, farmers tended to cluster together and to build houses in some spot that might be easily defended. In this way cities came into existence. Among the earliest of such cities was one which eventually came to be known as Jericho (jehr′ih-koh). It is even possible that Jericho is the oldest city ever to exist, in which case the very notion of cities was first invented in Canaan.

Jericho is located in the valley of the Jordan River, which runs southward through Canaan, about fifty miles from the coast, and flows into the Dead Sea. Jericho is about five miles west of the river and six miles north of the Dead Sea.

It is not an inviting area in general. The Jordan River is a short and twisting river that is not navigable and flows through a very hot and humid valley located below sea level. The Dead Sea is a lake of extremely salty water in which nothing lives. Nevertheless, the area on which Jericho was established had its advantages.

The site is on a low hill, which made it easier to defend. (Enemies would have to cast rocks or spears upward, while the defenders would throw them downward, so that gravity was on the side of the defense.) What's more, on the site of Jericho, the water table beneath the soil was high enough so that there were unfailing wells of water. In dry lands the presence of wells or springs are crucial, for there can be no defense without water, and no agriculture or grazing without water for irrigation either. High land and unfailing water made the site of Jericho a favorite gathering ground first for hunters and then for farmers seeking safety.

The oldest traces of human habitation in Jericho have been dated back to 7800 B.C., nearly ten thousand years ago. At first, there may have been nothing but small huts making up the city, but these gave way eventually to more substantial houses. By 7000 B.C., the city was surrounded by a strong stone wall that enclosed ten acres and included at least one tower that was thirty feet high and from which a sentry could keep efficient watch for the approaching enemy. Ten acres may not seem like much by modern standards, but in those days houses were small and the people huddled together; even without skyscrapers the city may have held over two thousand people.

Jericho spent some three thousand years in the Stone Age, a

period in which stone was the only material for making heavy-duty tools and weapons. In fact, there was a thriving flint industry there at this time, flint being a hard rock that could be easily fractured into sharp-edged flakes suitable for use.

This was a time, however, of more rapid change than mankind had yet seen. The coming of agriculture had gathered men together and increased the population. With more people and more communication among them, more ideas popped up and were put into practice. The changes produced what is called the New Stone Age, or the Neolithic Age. ("Neolithic" is from Greek words meaning "new stone.") So much change took place after the beginnings of agriculture, in fact, that it is customary to speak of the Neolithic Revolution.

For instance, containers were needed to carry grain from the fields to the cities. Very little could be carried in cupped hands, and while animal skins would hold more, they were not conveniently shaped and were difficult to use. A way of making a container more quickly and with less trouble suggested itself. Reeds were woven together to form a container that was light, tough, and porous. It could be shaped in any convenient fashion as it was woven and it could be carried easily, together with its grain content. In short, baskets were invented.

Though baskets could hold grain, fruit or pebbles, they could not hold water. One way of making baskets watertight was to daub them with moist clay. When the water evaporated, the fine particles of clay clung together, and such a clay-covered basket would not leak.*

Clay-covered baskets could easily spring leaks when bits of the clay were knocked off. It was easy to patch them, of course,

* The Bible tells the tale of how Moses' mother arranged to hide her baby from those who might kill him. ". . . she took for him an ark of bulrushes, and daubed it with slime and with pitch, and put the child therein; and she laid it in the flags by the river's brink." — Exodus 2:3. The bulrushes were reeds and the ark was a basket woven large enough to contain a baby. Then it was made waterproof with pitch so that it would float.

but eventually something better was discovered. Perhaps the discovery was made when such a basket was accidentally placed too near a fire. It turned out that the clay was hardened by heat to almost the consistency of stone.

It must then have occurred to someone to forget about the basket itself. Suppose some clay could be fashioned into the shape of a basket and was then fire-hardened. The result would be a pot that would be heavier than a basket, to be sure, but would be much stronger and both waterproof and fireproof in addition.

Hardened clay, or "pottery" — because pots were made out of it — was a kind of artificial stone. Pots could be carved out of stone but that would be hard work indeed. In the time it took to carve a stone pot, hundreds of pieces of clay could be shaped and hardened. When methods for reaching high enough temperatures were developed, the outer surface of the clay was made glossy and nonporous. The addition of colors and designs made pots into works of art that satisfied man's cravings for the beautiful as well as the useful.

The use of the potter's wheel, a horizontal wheel that could be set to turning with a lump of clay in its center, made the shaping even easier. As the turning of the wheel forces the clay outward, the touch of the potter's hand can shape it into roundness, making it squat and flat, or tall and thin, or any of a variety of more complicated shapes.

Inventions such as basketry and pottery were as important in deciding the way of life in Neolithic times as agriculture itself. For instance, a pot of fired clay could be placed directly over a fire. If it held water, that water would be heated to boiling without the pot cracking. This meant a new way of cooking — boiling instead of roasting.

The Neolithic Revolution did not occur everywhere at once. Only a few spots on earth were experiencing its beginnings in 7000 B.C., while most of mankind remained in various Paleolithic ("Old Stone Age") cultures, some parts nearly down to the present time. Canaan, however, was in the forefront of the revolution. It is possible, for instance, that pottery was first invented in Jericho. If so, this is another great advance for which we can give credit to Canaan.

Another remarkable invention of Neolithic times was the weaving of textiles. Instead of the coarse reeds used to weave baskets, thin fibers, like the woolly hair of sheep or the strands of linen derived from the flax plant, were woven together. The result was not the thick, stiff basket stuff, but a very thin and flexible material which could be draped over the body. The transition from skins to textiles meant that clothing became lighter and more comfortable. Since textiles were porous and easily washable, it meant that human beings would be cleaner and would smell sweeter — and it probably meant they were healthier, too.

By 5000 B.C. Jericho was quite an elaborate town, made up of individual houses containing several rooms each, with floors of plaster rather than of packed earth. There were probably other towns in Canaan, too, by then.

Canaan must have prospered not only because it was fertile enough for agriculture, but because it was a midway point. (Being in the middle has advantages as well as disadvantages.) The civilization that was growing more and more elaborate in the Tigris-Euphrates manufactured objects that were not manufactured in the Nile Valley, and vice versa. Canaan could receive objects from both and serve as a center of exchange. There were lands to the north in the peninsula of Asia Minor that also contributed articles for trade.

Naturally, the people of Canaan did their best to pass on articles at the price of a substantial profit to themselves. They became traders, in other words. The very name "Canaan" may have come from a word in the language of these ancient people that means "trader."

Traders are generally prosperous and, what's more, generally advanced in civilization. Handling the products of numerous cultures, they can pick and choose among them and profit by all. This was certainly true of the land of Canaan, which did well for itself in the Neolithic Age.

THE BRONZE AGE

One type of product that clearly entered Canaan from outside was metal. A few metals are sometimes found in that form in nature. Nuggets of copper, silver, and gold can be found, as well as occasional lumps of iron where meteorites have fallen. Gold was pretty, but it was very rare, and too soft to use as anything but an ornament. Silver wasn't much better and wasn't nearly as pretty. Iron was too hard to shape easily by the techniques of the Neolithic Age. Copper, however, was soft enough to hammer into a spear point and hard enough to serve for a while before being blunted (after which it could be hammered sharp again).

People began to use bits of hammered copper along with stone. Cultures where this was done are said to be in the "Chalcolithic Period" (from Greek words meaning "copper and stone"). The Chalcolithic Period arises in those places where nuggets of copper are likely to be found. The more common the nuggets, the earlier the period occurs.

We don't know exactly where and when the use of copper first arose but there is some evidence that it first appeared in the Sinai Peninsula and perhaps as early as 4500 B.C. In any case, tribesmen who possessed the Chalcolithic culture entered Canaan not long after 4000 B.C.

Their traces were first detected in excavations at a site called Teleilat el Ghassul, just east of the Jordan River and about nine miles southeast of Jericho. For that reason, these Chalcolithic people are called Ghassulians.

The Ghassulians seem to have concentrated in southern Canaan, and sites have been excavated near Beersheba (bee″ur-shee′buh), which is the southernmost town of importance in Canaan. There, traces have been found of a regular copper-working industry.

Such an industry involves more than the mere use of nuggets. Somehow it was discovered that certain blue rocks, if strongly heated — perhaps a charcoal fire was built over them — would yield copper. Ruddy bits of the metal would be found among the ashes afterward and eventually someone made the connection. The stone, actually a copper-containing ore, was much more common than copper nuggets were, so that the copper supply increased many times over.

The use of copper from copper ores introduced complications, for the copper was not always of the same quality. From some ores, copper was produced that was reddish and not very hard; from others, it might be more nearly yellow and brittle, or reddish but quite hard. A particular type of copper was particularly good for weapons and tools because it was unusually hard and held a sharp edge for a long time. Eventually the reason was discovered. The ores that produced it were impure and contained the metal tin as well as copper. When copper was formed with some tin present, the mixture — bronze — was far better than either alone.

Eventually, men learned to search for tin ore in order to add it deliberately to the copper ore before heating it. Bronze came into common use and for two thousand years it was employed for tools and weapons in preference to any other material. This period is known as the "Bronze Age." The Bronze Age began about 3100 B.C. and it penetrated Canaan at once. (The use of bronze spread slowly outward. It wasn't till 2000 B.C. that western Europe entered the Bronze Age, for instance.)

The Bronze Age made intensified wars possible. Bronze weapons were more effective than stone ones and defensive measures had to grow more efficient, too. With the beginning of the Bronze Age, the cities all over Canaan came to be surrounded by more and more elaborate walls. Each city placed as much of the surrounding farmland as possible under its own jurisdiction and guarded its boundaries. A city which considers itself an independent entity with a military apparatus of its own is a "city-state." By 2500 B.C. Bronze-Age Canaan was a conglomerate of such city-states.

In this period the civilizations of Egypt and Sumeria were becoming more elaborate. Sumeria had, by about 3100 B.C., developed the art of writing, a kind of picture code in which everyone agreed to let certain markings stand for certain words or ideas. The notion of writing was quickly picked up by the Egyptians, but they invented their own code, one that was much prettier than that of the Sumerians.

Writing was so convenient a way of keeping records and passing on instructions that it tended to catch on wherever it impinged upon a culture from outside. (What's more, the notion occurred independently at several places on the globe. The Chinese invented writing on their own, as far as we know; so did the Mayan Indians in Central America.) The mere existence of writing heightened civilization and made greater development possible. As Sumeria and Egypt developed a more and more elaborate culture, they produced a greater variety of desirable objects and an increased readiness to trade for those objects that were not available at home. The midway house — Canaan — flourished accordingly.

Some of the larger Canaanite cities now covered an area of twenty-five to fifty acres. To protect the city of Megiddo (mee-gid′oh), a wall that was twenty-five feet thick was built. Some of the Canaanite cities of the period were located on the sea, and that was a most important fact.

Water is a much better medium for trade than land is. Land is rough and uneven, and to drag heavy weights across it is an arduous and slow task. To make land trade possible at all, roads have to be built, needing sections of land smooth enough and level enough to make the task feasible. Even then, wheeled vehicles must be used to cut down friction, and animals must be used to pull the vehicles.

Water, on the other hand, is flat and smooth. Wooden rafts will float on it even if quite heavy weights are piled on board. The rivers first used for this purpose were the Nile and the Euphrates, the current in them automatically carrying the raft and its cargo downstream. Getting upstream is harder, though sails can do the trick if there is a wind in the right direction, or rowing if there isn't. Ships of various sorts, large curved structures, were more efficient than flat rafts, could carry heavier weights without sinking, and were easier to move by wind or oar.

One great danger to shipping were the storms that might strike. Rain and wind could destroy even the strongest ships. The chance wasn't too great on the rivers, however. Storms did not often strike the Euphrates and virtually never struck the Nile. In any case, if there were trouble of any sort at all, a river ship could make for the nearby shore at once.

It is different in an open sea like the Mediterranean. There the storms are much more severe than on rivers, and waves can act as battering rams. What's more, it is possible for a ship to be many miles from the nearest land when it sails the broad expanse of the sea. When a storm comes, the ship may not manage to make it safely to shore; or if it does, it may reach an unhospitable stretch and be driven to destruction on the rocks.

In short, ships used to sail the sea had to be more carefully designed and run greater risks than those used to sail rivers. It is not surprising that sea travel lagged far behind river travel and at last when ships ventured out into the sea, they tended to hug the shore cautiously.

Yet the temptation to venture out to sea was great, too. Egypt, for instance, had great use for wood as a structural material, but even as long ago as 3000 B.C. the forests had been cut down and there was little or no wood in the land. There were, however, beautiful cedar trees in the mountain ranges of Canaan. Their trunks were unusually tall and straight and could serve as pillars to support roofs. The Egyptians could and did carve stone pillars for the purpose, but wood was much lighter, cheaper, and easier to handle.

Still, how could the cedar trees be brought down to Egypt? They could be dragged down the length of Canaan and across the Sinai Peninsula, but the difficulties would be tremendous. How much easier it would be to drag them to some convenient place on the Canaanite shore, load them onto ships, and sail or row them across the sea to Egypt and the mouth of the Nile.

At least one convenient place was the city of Byblos (bib′los).* Located on the Mediterranean coast 170 miles north of Jericho, Byblos seems to have been founded as a city at least as far back as 4500 B.C. It is not as old as Jericho, but there have been periods in history where the site on which Jericho stands was uninhabited. This is not true of Byblos, and some historians suspect that Byblos is the oldest continually inhabited city on the face of the earth.

Byblos was the closest seaport to the forests where the cedar trees grew. Once in Byblos, the wood could be loaded onto ships and taken to the mouth of the Nile. This was 250 miles southwestward, but since the ships carefully followed the curve of the shore, the journey was more like 400 miles.

* Byblos is the name by which this city was known long after this early period of the Bronze Age; it was a name used by the Greeks. Most of the familiar versions of ancient names are Greek. The Egyptians seem to have called it Kubna and the Sumerians called it Gubla. In the Bible it is called Gebal, and that is probably closer to what the people of the city called it themselves. Today there is a small town on the spot in modern Lebanon that is called Jubayl. In this book I will use the most common form of names, as they occur in the Bible or in Greek histories, without worrying whether these names were actually used by the inhabitants themselves, or what the modern name might be. The pronunciations I give are those used in English and are not necessarily those used in the original language.

The ships did not return empty. The cedars were exchanged for Egyptian goods that were brought back to Byblos and sold. One commodity that Egypt had in plenty was a reed that grew along the banks of the Nile. These reeds were cut and the fibrous pith at the center of the long stem was removed. The lengths of pith were laid side by side, then more pith was laid over them crosswise. Several layers were placed alternately longwise and crosswise.

The layers were soaked in water, pressed together, then allowed to dry in the sun. The result was a thin, smooth sheet on which it was easy to write. There was nothing cheaper or more convenient as a writing surface in the ancient world than this product of Egyptian reeds which the Greeks later called "papyrus." (The word "paper" is derived from this, although modern paper is made by an entirely different process from an entirely different source.)

Naturally, as the use of writing spread over the ancient world, the demand for papyrus grew greater. In later centuries, Byblos was a center for the papyrus trade, to the point where the Greeks began to call papyrus "biblos" and a piece of writing on a long roll of papyrus a "biblion." The plural of the word, for a collection of such rolls, was "biblia," and our own word "Bible" comes from that.

The Canaanites, who guided their delicate shore-hugging boats between Canaan and Egypt, would sometimes be driven away from shore by storms. If they survived, they might make it to nearby islands. Two large islands in the eastern Mediterranean which they probably reached in this manner are those now known as Cyprus (sy′prus) and Crete (kreet). Cyprus is a little over 100 miles west of Byblos, while Crete is 530 miles west.

Cyprus definitely shows traces of Canaanite influence from an early period. Once it was reached, it proved a most desirable place to visit further, for it was rich in the copper ore on which the Bronze Age depended. In fact, copper (which is "kyprios" in Greek) seems to have derived its very name from Cyprus ("Kypros" in Greek).

As for Crete, the Greeks, at a much later period in history, had a myth concerning the manner in which Crete was settled. They said that their chief god, Zeus, fell in love with a princess of a city on the Canaanite shore. He took the form of a white bull and enticed the princess into climbing on his back. With the girl still on his back, he plunged into the sea and swam to Crete, which was then populated by the descendants of the two. The princess's name was Europa and that, according to the myth, was how Europe got its name. This myth may represent a vague memory of the fact that Canaanite traders, landing in Crete, helped contribute to the developing civilization on the island. The first form of writing developed on Crete is still undeciphered but it seems to have been in a language related to the Canaanite.

At any rate, by 3000 B.C. the Bronze Age was beginning to reach Crete, from Egypt as well as from Canaan, and the island became the site of the earliest European civilization. It, too, became a land of traders and it eventually competed with the Canaanites for control of the sea.

INVASION

Trade would seem to be a peaceful pursuit, benefiting everybody. And so it is, if everyone is content with a fair share. But is everyone content with a fair share? And what is a fair share anyway? A trading city buys and sells. It buys as cheaply as it can and sells as dearly as it can, for the difference is its own profit. The city may feel justified in this, for it takes the responsibility of transportation and the risk of loss between the buying and the selling.

Those who deal with the city may feel cheated, however. They may feel they get too little for what they produce and pay too much for what they need. There is a temptation, then, for some strong land of producers to take over the trading city, do their own buying and selling and keep the profits for themselves.

About 2615 B.C. Egypt had grown into a strong nation which we call the Old Kingdom. Among other things, it had developed military power. It had a well-equipped army which could travel the distance between the Nile Valley and the Canaanite cities.

Presumably Egyptian armies were sent northward and, during the time of the Old Kingdom, Canaan was under Egyptian influence. This meant that the Canaanite cities had to pay tribute to Egypt, handing over a fixed amount of goods each year in order to keep the Egyptian armies from inflicting destruction on the cities. In effect, the Egyptians were cutting themselves in on the trading profits.

Naturally, the Canaanite cities would resent this. At any time that they felt strong, or considered Egypt to be weak, they might refuse to pay tribute. In that case, Egypt might attempt to punish them. If the Canaanite estimate of the situation was correct, Egypt might be unable to do so and the cities would be free of tribute for a longer or shorter time. If the Canaanite estimate was wrong, Egypt might wreak destruction on them and then inflict a still larger tribute. The first word we have of such a situation dates back to about 2300 B.C. when the Old Kingdom was already past its peak and Pepi I (pay′pee) was king of Egypt.

In the reign of Pepi I, an expedition was sent against the people of Canaan (or the Sand-Dwellers, as the Egyptians of the time called them because they lived far from the Nile) under an Egyptian general, Uni (oo′nee). Uni left an inscription on his tomb which describes the great military feat of his life. One column of the Egyptian army marched into Canaan overland, another column was carried there by sea.

The sea-transported column naturally made better time and landed at a promontory called Antelope's Nose. This may be at Mount Carmel (kahr′mel), which is on the sea coast about 100 miles south of Byblos, and which juts out into the sea in a shape that might be thought to be an antelope's nose. The Egyptian army did all the damage it could, knocking down walls, burning houses, uprooting crops, and so on. They eventually returned to Egypt with all sorts of valuables which they had looted and, undoubtedly, with a promise from the chastened cities that they would pay their tribute faithfully henceforward.

The cities of Canaan did not have to worry only about Egypt, however. There were also the uncivilized tribesmen outside the Fertile Crescent. These were always a danger, for the cities had much that the tribesmen were glad to take. The cities not only controlled herds of animals and productive farms outside their walls, but accumulated pottery, metal ornaments, and other luxuries inside the walls. The tribesmen had very little in comparison and had no techniques or resources for producing what the city men had. A simple solution to that problem was merely to sweep into the civilized areas and take what they wanted. They might then even settle down there, making themselves rulers of the cities and reducing the earlier inhabitants to slaves.

The Fertile Crescent curves up and around the huge peninsula of Arabia. Except for certain coastal areas, this peninsula is dry, largely desert, and cannot support a large population. When the population increases, some of the tribesmen must starve or leave. Usually, some left.

Thus, the Ghassulians had entered Canaan from the south about 4000 B.C. Then about 3000 B.C. another group of people, later called the Phoenicians (fee-nish′unz) by the Greeks, occupied the coastal cities of Canaan. Very likely such incursions were accompanied by considerable violence and bloodshed, but details of these early invasions are lacking.

We know more about a later invasion. Some time before 2000 B.C. still another group of tribesmen flooded out of the Arabian peninsula, moving east and west against both horns of the Fertile Crescent. It would seem to be a larger movement of peoples than had taken place at any time earlier. From the standpoint of the peoples of the Tigris-Euphrates, these wild invaders were coming from the west, and they were called Amurru or "westerners." We know that name best in the Biblical form — Amorites.

The Amorites gradually took over most of the Fertile Crescent. In the east they put a final end to the Sumerian culture. In the west they took over Canaan. When the early books of the Bible speak of the inhabitants of the land of Canaan, it is these Amorites they mean.

The peoples of Arabia spoke closely related varieties of a language family we now called Semitic.* People who speak Semitic languages are sometimes referred to, in brief, as Semites. The Amorites were Semites, and the language they spoke was an early form of the one we now know as Hebrew.

The Old Kingdom in Egypt had come to an end by then and the land had broken up into feudal fragments in which different individuals struggled for power. Egypt was in no position to make a united effort and it could not protect Canaan from the Amorite invaders. Canaan went through a dark period, therefore, in which the various cities were looted and destroyed.

Eventually, though, the Amorites settled down (as wild invaders usually do) and learned that there is more to be had, in the long run, by allowing centers of civilization to carry on nor-

* We use this word because some of the peoples speaking varieties of the language are described in the Bible as having been descended from Noah's son Shem (or Sem).

mally and taking a reasonable tribute than by trying to grab everything and leaving a desolation behind that cannot produce more goods or engage in further trade.

Slowly, the cities of Canaan revived, but they were under Amorite control now, for the names of the kings that are to be found in surviving records after 2000 B.C. are distinctly Semitic in form.

2

AFTER ABRAHAM

ABRAHAM

The people who dominated Canaan about eight centuries after the Amorite invasions preserved legends of ancestors who had entered Canaan at that time. It is hard to tell how far the legends are based on fact, but the people who made the claim carefully preserved them because, in part, it served to legalize their sovereignty over the land.

They spoke of an ancestor named Abram (and later Abraham) who was born in the city of Ur in Sumeria and who wandered the length of the Fertile Crescent till he came to Canaan. In Canaan he was described as having made a covenant (that is, a legal agreement) with God, by which, in return for worship, God granted all of Canaan to the descendants of Abraham. This tale is recorded in chapters 12 to 15 in the Book of Genesis in the Bible.

Those who counted themselves as Abraham's decendants believed this and considered the tale as granting them legal title to Canaan.

Associated with the tales and legends that were later collected concerning Abraham and his immediate descendants, Isaac and Jacob, were a number of ancient Canaanite cities. These were, reading from north to south: Shechem (shee′kem), Bethel (beth′el), Salem (say′lem), Hebron (hee′brun), and Beersheba.

Shechem, which lies thirty miles northwest of Jericho, is located in a narrow valley, not more than a hundred yards wide, between two mountains. The roads from the Jordan River to the sea and from southern Canaan to the north both pass through it. This gave Shechem an advantage in trading and made it prosperous. Even after it declined politically and economically, it remained an important religious center.

Of the five cities mentioned, Salem was perhaps the least important. It was located thirty miles south of Shechem and was notable chiefly because, like Jericho (fifteen miles to its east) it was built on a hill that had an unfailing water supply. It was therefore particularly easy to defend and the time would come when, with its name slightly altered to Jerusalem (jeh-roo′suh-lem), it was to become the most important city of the region and, eventually, one of the most famous in the world.

The Biblical tale of the wanderings of Abraham tells of his entry into Egypt during a period of food shortage in Canaan. His experiences in Egypt were not altogether happy and that was, perhaps, to be expected, for the Egyptians could scarcely have had much friendly feeling for the Amorite invaders who had wiped out the profitable Egyptian occupation of Canaan.

The Egypt into which Abraham entered (possibly about 1900 B.C.) was peaceful and prosperous, however, for the chaos that had succeeded the decay of the Old Kingdom had finally come to an end. Egypt, under a new series of kings, was once again united into what is called the Middle Kingdom. That took place about 1990 B.C., not very long after the Amorite fury fell on the Fertile Crescent.

It is surprising that the Amorites, having taken over the Fertile Crescent, did not fall upon Egypt as well. Perhaps they were planning to, and perhaps advance raiding parties even reached the Nile Delta. (The tale of Abraham's descent into Egypt may be a kind of vague memory of that.) What may have prevented such raiding parties from becoming a full-fledged invasion was the fact that the Amorite kingdoms established in the Fertile Crescent fought among themselves.

The Tigris-Euphrates had been the scene of great empires, and the greatest of these had been built up about 2300 B.C. by Sargon the Akkadian, king of a Semitic people who had entered Sumeria centuries before the Amorite invasion. Later traditions stated that his kingdom stretched over the northern arch of the Fertile Crescent and touched the Mediterranean Sea.

After the Amorite invasion, however, the Tigris-Euphrates region had broken up into separate, independent districts that fought each other and were not generally dangerous to outsiders. Once in a while, though, some of them might unite in order to carry on some profitable raid.

In the fourteenth chapter of Genesis, there is the tale of such a raid that took place, perhaps, about 1900 B.C. The raiders swooped across the Fertile Crescent and descended southward east of the Jordan River to take over the more exposed and weaker Amorite kingdoms that had been established in Canaan. Opposing the raiders from the east were five "cities of the plain" of which the two largest were Sodom (sod′um) and Gomorrah (goh-mor′uh). Apparently, these cities were located in the general region of the southern end of the Dead Sea.

The Dead Sea, which receives the waters of the Jordan River, is about 47 miles long and not more than 10 miles wide. Its area is 370 square miles, only slightly larger than the five boroughs of New York City. Its surface is 1286 feet below sea level, which makes its shores the lowest land area in the world.

Despite this it is deep, 1310 feet deep in some spots.

The Dead Sea has no outlet to the ocean so that the salts that are brought in by the Jordan do not wash out; they merely accumulate. The Dead Sea now contains a dissolved salt content of 23 to 25 per cent. Nothing lives in it and its shores are desolate. Nevertheless, the climate in the Bronze Age may have been better than it is now, and certainly the Bible speaks highly of the fertility of the region at that earlier period.

The cities of the plain were defeated by the raiders and sacked, and the Bible goes on to describe the manner in which Abraham rescued his nephew Lot, who had been captured by the raiders. The cities did not survive physically, for in the nineteenth chapter of Genesis, the tale is told of their destruction by fire from heaven. It is possible that an earthquake or volcanic eruption, or even a large meteorite, caused a slight subsidence of the land, so that the waters of the Dead Sea flooded southward. (The southernmost portion of the Dead Sea is shallow compared to the deep northern portion.) This, too, may have caused a worsening of the climate of the area.

The disasters that befell Canaan at this time — the raid from the east and the natural catastrophe, whatever it was — made it possible for Egypt to assert its supremacy in the area after the two-century interruption caused by the Amorite invasion. About 1850 B.C. the Middle Kingdom was at its height, and the Egyptian king, Sesostris III (see-sos′tris), was able to send an army into Canaan that reached as far north as Shechem.

THE CHARIOT

The Amorites had done their worst by this time, though, and civilization was recovering. Indeed, one of the Amorite rulers, Hammurabi (hahm″oo-rah′bee), had established his capital at the until-then undistinguished town of Babylon and built the most impressive empire that Asia had yet seen. The entire Tigris-Euphrates region came under his rule in 1700 B.C. and reached a new peak of culture with Babylon itself a world capital for the first time — a position it was to hold for fourteen centuries.

Trouble was brewing to the north, however, beyond the mountains that rimmed the Fertile Crescent in that direction. The barbaric tribes of central Asia had tamed the horse and by 1800 B.C. had developed a way of harnessing the animal to a light two-wheeled cart strong enough to hold a man. This was the horse and chariot.

Chariots could carry an army over ground far faster than that same army could march on foot. Furthermore, charging horses could usually break a line of foot soldiers. To their horror the men of the Fertile Crescent found themselves facing irresistible soldiers.

The first horsemen included a group of tribes known to us now as the Hurrians. They descended upon the northern arch of the Fertile Crescent from the foothills of the Caucasian mountain range north of the Tigris-Euphrates immediately after the death of Hammurabi. The horses and chariots thundered down the western prong of the Fertile Crescent, into and through Canaan. The Amorite rulers, dazed at the onslaught, could not resist. Some joined the raiders and accompanied them beyond Canaan and rode west across Sinai and into Egypt.

For the first time in Egypt's history she had to face an enemy from beyond Sinai. Egypt could not face the horses any more than Canaan had been able to. Egyptian forces could only break and run and the Hurrian-Amorite raiders occupied the northernmost portion of the Nile Valley, about 1680 B.C., and did so without a fight. The Middle Kingdom broke down and came to an end.

For a century these non-Egyptian raiders ruled over the Nile

Delta. Their religion and culture was not that of the native Egyptians and they were hated in consequence. The Egyptians called the invaders Hyksos ("foreign rulers"). The later Egyptian historians felt deeply humiliated at this episode of defeat in the nation and spoke as little as possible of it except to vilify the Hyksos as godless and cruel. For that reason we know almost nothing about the Hyksos period.

Apparently, though, in that century, there was a centralized kingdom stretching over northern Egypt and Canaan with its capital at Tanis (tay′nis) on the easternmost branch of the Nile. In the Bible the city is referred to as Zoan (zoh′an).

Although the capital was on the Nile Delta, so that the Hyksos rulers might be near the center of wealth and power, the heart of the dominion lay in Canaan, where the population could identify itself with the rulers, rather than in Egypt, where the population was violently hostile. It was the first time in history that a Canaan-centered realm ruled territory outside the western half of the Fertile Crescent.

One important Canaanite center in the time of the Hyksos was Hazor (hay′zor), about ninety miles north of Jerusalem. It had a large sloping rampart surrounding it on all sides, far outside the city proper — a method of fortification devised to hold back the charge of horsemen. Similar remains are found all the way to Carchemish (kahr′keh-mish) on the upper Euphrates, 400 miles north of Jerusalem.

Those later inhabitants of Canaan who considered themselves descendants of Abraham had legends concerning the entry of their ancestors into Egypt at the time of the Hyksos invasion. Abraham had a grandson Jacob, according to the tales preserved in the Bible, who had twelve sons. One of the sons, Joseph, won the favor of the Egyptian king (presumably one of the Hyksos rulers) and served as what we would today call the prime minister. Joseph then brought the rest of his family to Egypt and there they multiplied.

During the century in which the Hyksos kingdom flourished,

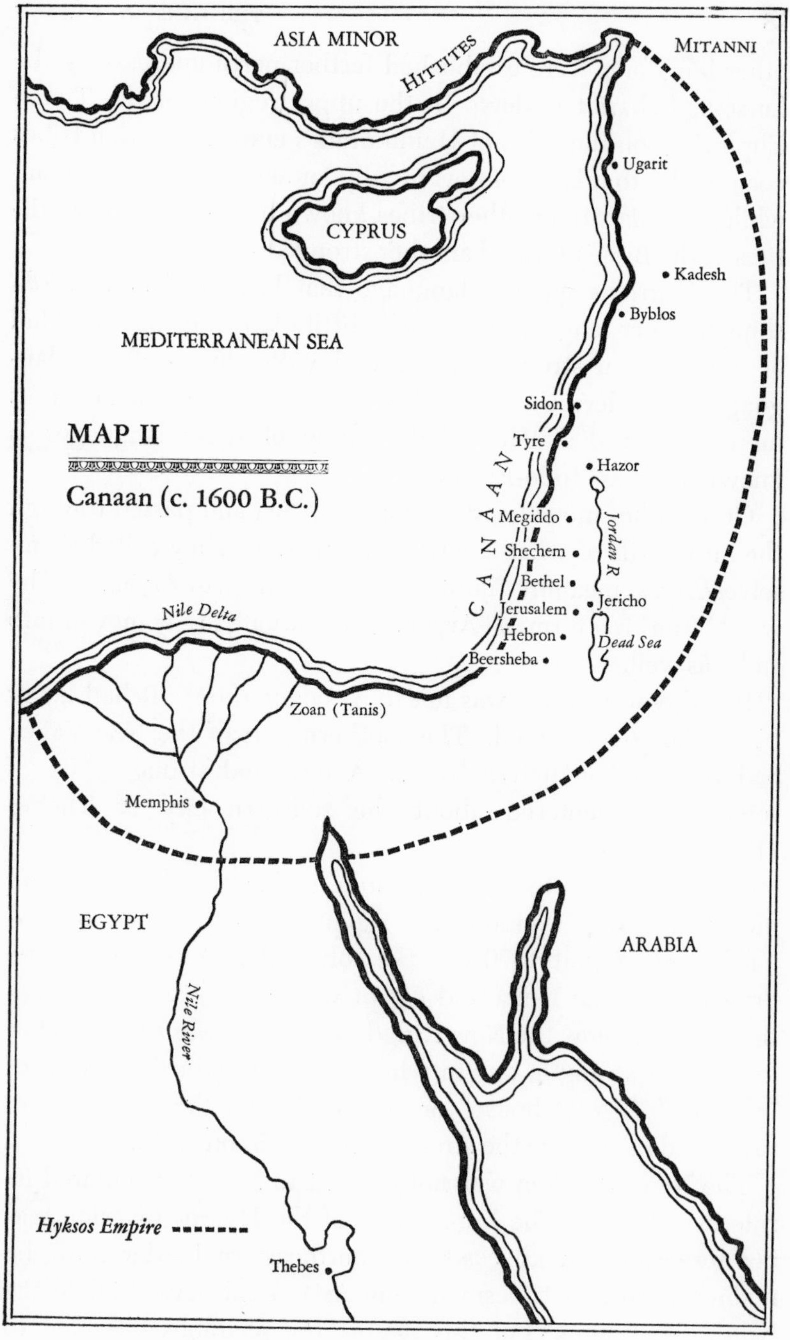
ASIA MINOR
HITTITES
MITANNI
Ugarit
CYPRUS
Kadesh
Byblos
MEDITERRANEAN SEA
Sidon
MAP II
Canaan (c. 1600 B.C.)
Tyre
Hazor
CANAAN
Megiddo
Jordan R
Shechem
Bethel
Nile Delta
Jerusalem
Jericho
Hebron
Dead Sea
Beersheba
Zoan (Tanis)
Memphis
EGYPT
ARABIA
Nile River
Hyksos Empire
Thebes

other kingdoms were established farther north and east by the horse-and-chariot raiders. In the upper regions of the Tigris-Euphrates, on the ruins of Hammurabi's empire, Hurrian tribes coalesced into a kingdom eventually known as Mitanni. Meanwhile, in Asia Minor other tribes known as the Hatti (or Hittites in the Bible) formed another strong kingdom.

The Hurrians spoke a language that has no clear relationships to other languages, but the Hittite language has the kind of grammatical structure associated with almost all the languages of modern Europe and of parts of modern Asia, even as far east as India. The whole family of these languages is known, now, as "Indo-European."

Other tribes moved east of the Black Sea and passed through the hilly lands of what is now modern Iran. They called themselves Aryas, meaning "noble," and we call them Aryans. (The word "Iran" is a form of "Aryan.") Eventually, they moved into India as well.

But Egypt, at least, was not to be counted out. It had never been wholly conquered. The southern part of the Nile Valley had remained in native hands. A new and strong group of rulers arose centered about the southern city of Thebes (theebz).

These had adopted the technique of horse and chariot and under their king, Ahmose, the Egyptians of the south pushed northward. About 1570 B.C. the softened Hyksos rulers were driven out of the Delta and Egypt was reestablished in its entirety. It was now the New Kingdom and this was the period of its greatest strength, one in which its kings gained the title of "pharaoh" ("great house" or "palace," from the place where they lived) and were the strongest monarchs on earth.

The New Kingdom was not content to have consolidated its rule over Egypt. The humiliation of the Hyksos invasion was not forgotten. At all costs, the northeastern border must be made safe so that tribesmen from Asia could never violate the Nile Valley again. For this reason, the pharaohs intended to occupy Canaan — not merely for their economic benefit but as a military outpost guarding the homeland, an outpost that was to be heavily garrisoned with troops.

On the other hand, this was exactly what the new powers north of Canaan did not want. Mitanni, which at this time was the strongest kingdom of the north, was intent on placing Canaan under its own influence in order to ward off the resurgent Egyptian power.

Between these two strong nations lay Canaan. The Hyksos defeat in Egypt had destroyed Canaan's unity and it was once more a congerie of city-states. It could by no means fight off both Egypt and Mitanni, or even either one separately, if left to itself. It had to choose one of them as a friend and ally, and on the whole the Canaanite cities chose Mitanni. First, Mitanni was closer in tradition and culture to themselves than Egypt was. Second, it was rather the weaker of the two and it is better to have a somewhat weaker ally than a stronger one. (A strong ally too easily swallows those its helps.)

The New Kingdom reached its height when Thutmose III (thoot-moh′suh), after a long minority, became sole ruler of Egypt in 1469 B.C. As virtually the first act for which he alone was responsible, he decided to settle matters in Canaan. Facing him was a league of Canaanite city-states under the leadership of Kadesh (kay′desh), about 325 miles north of Jerusalem. It represented perhaps the last remnant of Hyksos power and would therefore most fear the vengeance of Egypt. It was moreover close enough to Mitanni to rely on military help in case of emergency, in addition to the financial and material help which it undoubtedly received.

To reach Kadesh Thutmose III had to take the town of Megiddo, which lay 160 miles to the southwest. Megiddo was not a large town, or important in itself, but it was on an eminence that controlled the best pass between southern and northern Canaan. If Thutmose III could not force his army through that pass, Kadesh might remain safe for a long time.

Kadesh, realizing this well, had fortified Megiddo strongly. Now it could only wait.

Kadesh had to guess by which route Thutmose would approach Megiddo, for it lacked the force to guard all possible approaches. Kadesh guessed wrong and its chariots lay idly in wait while Thutmose bypassed them by another route. The battle opened near Megiddo in 1468 B.C. with the Canaanite chariotry absent. By the time they reached the scene it was too late, and Thutmose III had won a complete victory. Part of his army he then left behind to keep Megiddo under siege. After seven months it capitulated.

Year after year Thutmose III returned to his Canaanite campaigning, and by 1462 B.C. he reached Kadesh itself and destroyed it. He then crossed the Euphrates into Mitanni, for he rightly thought that the Canaanite league could never have withstood him so long were it not for Mitannian support, and that he could never keep Canaan securely while Mitanni remained to stir up revolt. He therefore ravaged the Mitannian countryside in an endeavor to teach it discretion.

He left no troops beyond the Euphrates, however, after the raid. That was too far from home to maintain an army successfully. Even so, he held all of Canaan from the Sinai Peninsula to the Euphrates River and this, together with the Nile Valley, made up the "Egyptian Empire." It was the peak of Egyptian strength.

THE ALPHABET

For a century Canaan remained under firm Egyptian control. Mitanni did what it could to stir unrest, but it dared not go too far and an occasional northward march of the Egyptian army sufficed to quell revolts and sent Mitanni into a hostile but definite retreat.

It was another time of prosperity for Canaan. It often happens that a foreign occupation, even if resented, brings peace over an area that would otherwise spend its time in internal squabbling. With peace and with increasing trade under the aegis of a protective power (unless that power is suicidally repressive, which Egypt was not) comes prosperity.

It was in this time that Canaan made another gigantic contribution to world culture — in addition to the invention of cities, pottery, and sea voyaging. This new contribution involved the matter of writing.

At first writing consisted of pictures of what it was that was being referred to. Eventually it became tedious to try to draw recognizable pictures and short-cut symbols were used. It was not necessary to draw an entire ox, if a triangular head with two horns (like an upside-down A) would do the trick. After a while the scrawls that came to be accepted as standing for a particular object had to be learned independently, for they became too schematic to be recognized by anyone who was not told what they were to begin with.

In the Tigris-Euphrates valley, where soft clay was the common substance on which to write, the symbols were made by punching into the clay with a stylus that left small "cuneiform" ("wedge-shaped") marks. In Egypt, with its papyrus, the signs might be written with a brush, and were much more graceful.

As time went on and writing grew more common, the things which needed to be written about grew more abstract and elaborate. In consequence the symbols became ever more intricate and hard to grasp. The symbol for a horse might also indicate "speed," that for "mouth" might also mean "hungry." Two symbols together might indicate something that had nothing to do with either symbol in reality but only in sound. In English, for instance, if we had a symbol for "under" and another for "stand," we might use the two together to mean "comprehend."

Naturally there were attempts to short-cut the process. Why not have symbols that stand for syllables, even if the syllables in themselves are meaningless. If, in English, you had a symbol for "ba" and another for "na," neither of which is a word in itself, a combination of "ba," "na," and "na" again would represent a yellow fruit. The advantage of this is that there are fewer different syllables than there are different words.

You might even let a symbol stand for the sound with which it starts. If you have a symbol for a pot, an arch, a rat, and a tent, you might let each stand for the initial sound only and have pot-arch-rat-tent symbolize "part." It may seem ridiculous to have four symbols do the work that only one might do, but the same symbols could be put together in all sorts of ways and in the end you could have two dozen symbols used for many thousands of words — and only have to memorize the two dozen in place of the many thousands.

The Egyptians thought of all this but never took the step of simplifying their writing system. They used syllables and initial sounds but merely added these to their original symbols for intact words and ideas. The reason for this may have been that the writing was in the hands of a priesthood which saw an advantage to itself in keeping writing complicated.

Complications made certain that writing would not become too common — that laymen would remain illiterate. That would leave the priesthood essential to the state as long as writing was essential and would naturally increase the priests' power. So associated were writing and the priesthood in Egypt that the Egyptian writing was later called "hieroglyphics" by the Greeks, the word meaning "sacred carvings."

Not so in Canaan, where the tradesmen found that intricate writing systems meant loss in revenue. It was necessary for them to understand something about both the complicated cuneiform writing and the complicated hieroglyphic writing, if they were to trade with both the Tigris-Euphrates and the Nile valleys. In addition, they had constantly to prepare lists, receipts, bills of sale, and all the other paraphernalia of merchandising, in one system or the other, or maybe both. They desperately needed some short cut.

Some Canaanite merchant — some utterly nameless genius — decided to use the notion of having symbols represent their initial sound, as the Egyptians sometimes did, *and to use it exclusively.*

Thus, the Canaanite word for "ox" was "′aleph," where the ′ represents a glottal stop or very soft grunt which isn't used in English. Why not let the symbol for "ox" stand for ′ wherever it occurs. In the same way, the symbols for "house," "camel," and "door," which in Canaanite were "beth," "gimel," and "daledh," could stand for the consonants we write as "b," "g," and "d," wherever they occur.

In the end, the Canaanites found that some twenty-two signs were sufficient to form all the words they could use. These twenty-two signs represented consonants only. To us, this seems strange since vowels are so important. How can you tell whether "ct" stands for "cat," "cot," "cut," "kit," "coat," "Kate," "kite," "cute," or "acute"?

As it happens, though, the Semitic languages are based on triple consonants. Each set of three consonants represents a basic idea and, by adding vowels, variations on this basic theme are struck. The three consonants by themselves tell you enough (if you speak a Semitic language) to get the idea, and you can then, from the sense of the sentence, fill in the vowels for yourself.

The earliest recorded examples of alphabetic writings have been located in the ruins of an ancient Canaanite city named Ugarit (oo″gah-reet′) on the coast, 100 miles north of Byblos. These inscriptions date back, perhaps, to 1400 B.C. (Ugarit was destroyed by an earthquake about 1350 B.C., which is why these very early inscriptions were preserved. They were not drowned in a flood of later artifacts.)

The alphabet is a much more unusual invention than that of writing itself (though not as fundamental, for it merely made the earlier invention simpler). Whereas the notion of writing occurred to various peoples independently, the notion of an alphabet seems to have occurred only *once* — in Canaan some time before 1400 B.C.

Once the notion appeared it spread. It spread to the Greeks, for instance. The Greeks who, in later times, were quite proud of their own culture and who were sure that all other people were culturally inferior, did not try to hide the fact that alphabetic writing was not their invention. In their legends they speak of one Cadmus, a prince of Canaan (and a brother of Europa, whose abduction by Zeus had begun civilization in Crete) who reached Greece and brought alphabetic writing with him.

The Greeks distorted the (to them) meaningless names of the letters into sounds that seemed more natural to them. Thus, "aleph," "beth," "gimmel," "daledh" became "alpha," "beta," "gamma," "delta." The new words had no meaning in Greek, but they were easier for people used to Greek words to say. And it is from the first two words of the distorted names that we get our word "alphabet."

The Greeks made an extremely important contribution of their own. Since they spoke an Indo-European language and not a Semitic one, the triple-consonant system did not apply to them. They could not get along without vowels. They therefore had some of the Canaanite symbols represent vowel sounds. Thus, the first letter which represented the glottal stop, they used to represent the vowel we call "a."

The alphabet spread farther, too, both symbols and names being further distorted at each adoption, with new letters being added or old ones altered to represent sounds present in the language of the adopters which were not present in other languages. In the end, every alphabet used on earth can be traced (it is thought) to the original alphabet of Canaan.

While writing existed for fifteen centuries before the alphabet, it was only with the alphabet that there arrived a decent chance of having ordinary people learn to read and write. It was the alphabet that made mass literacy possible, and with more and more people having access to learning, more and more people could make further contributions. The alphabet thus made a huge contribution to the development of culture and technology.*

The coastal cities of Canaan also developed still another important technique in these generally peaceful and prosperous times, a technique involving dyeing. Man has always found color, in tasteful arrangements, to be pleasing. Even the prehistoric cave dwellers of the Old Stone Age used colored earths in preparing their paintings. It is not surprising, therefore, that men should try to add color to their colorless textile clothing.

Colored substances, which could be used to stain the textiles, were generally unsatisfactory. They were dull in the first place, or would leach out when the clothes were washed, or would fade in the sunlight — or all three. Along the Canaanite shores, however, there lived a snail that could be so treated as to yield a colored substance that would dye cloth perfectly. It would form a rich bluish-red color that would neither wash out nor fade.

This dye was much in demand throughout ancient times and, as it sold for high prices, it contributed immensely to the prosperity of the coastal cities. Here was a case where the Canaanites were not merely buying from one and selling to another; they were producing something of value themselves. This was particularly important, for while other people might

* Even so there remained groups, both ancient and modern, that never accepted the notion of the alphabet despite all its advantages. Ancient Egypt, a most conservative culture, stubbornly insisted on keeping its own writing system to the end of its history. In modern times China is an example of another nation that maintains a writing system that is nonalphabetic and is every bit as complicated as that of ancient Egypt.

become merchants and compete with the Canaanites, only the coastal Canaanites could produce the dye — by a process they carefully kept a state secret.

About this time the Phoenicians also developed better techniques for making glass — a material which the Egyptians had been making for a thousand years.

The later Greeks called the coastal Canaanites Phoinike, which may have been simply their own version of the word for "merchant," which is what "Canaanite" might also mean. The usual etymology of the word, however, derives it from the Greek word for "blood red" and is supposed to signify the dye the coastal Canaanites sold.

It is this Greek word which becomes "Phoenician" to us, and generally we tend to forget who these people are. The word "Canaanite" is familiar to us chiefly from the Bible, where it refers to the men of the interior, while the word "Phoenician" is familiar to us chiefly from Greek history, where it refers to men of the coast. I will use "Canaanite" for men of the interior and "Phoenician" for men of the coast, because that is the common way of speaking. Still, one must remember that Phoenicians *are* Canaanites.

But the prosperity of the century following the victory of Thutmose III at the Battle of Kadesh did not last. Nothing does.

THE DESCENDANTS OF ABRAHAM

In 1379 B.C. Amenhotep IV (ah″men-hoh′tep) became pharaoh of Egypt. He was a religious reformer who worshiped the Sun as sole god, took the name of Ikhnaton (ikh-nah′tun) — "the Sun is satisfied" — and devoted himself to persuading all Egypt to accept his notions. He failed to move the stubbornly conservative Egyptians but, while making the attempt, he utterly neglected Canaan.

The Egyptian garrisons in the Canaanite city-states found themselves forced to defend their areas against onslaughts from the eastern desert area. Once more Arabia was stirring and its tribes were seeking haven in the delectable riches of the fertile regions.

From the outposts came a stream of reports to Ikhnaton concerning the activities of these "Apiru." This may represent the word which eventually came to be "Hebrew" in our language. This is, in turn, usually derived from a Semitic word meaning "one who is from across," that is, an outsider from beyond or across the Jordan River.

These Hebrew tribes were of similar origin to the Amorites but were far lower, at the moment, in the scale of civilization. They spoke a dialect of the language already spoken in Canaan (the one we now call Hebrew but which might, with better logic, be called Canaanite). They went on to adopt the Canaanite alphabet and many other aspects of Canaanite culture.

Despite Ikhnaton's neglect, Egypt was able to prevent the Hebrew tribes from remaining permanently west of the Jordan. They had to content themselves with establishing a series of small kingdoms east of the Jordan along the very rim of the Fertile Crescent. East of the Jordan River itself was Ammon (am′on). To the south of Ammon and east of the Dead Sea was Moab (moh′ab). Still farther south, beyond the southern end of the Dead Sea was Edom (ee′dum).

After Ikhnaton's death in 1362 B.C., the attempted religious reform faded away and Egypt was in near-anarchy. In 1319 B.C., however, a new strong pharaoh appeared, Seti I (seh′tee). By that time the Egyptian hold on Canaan was tenuous indeed, and the new pharaoh set out to correct the situation.

As it now appeared, Canaan was again a congerie of city-states with the Hebrew kingdoms on the eastern and southern rim, counting only as additional small items. The great danger lay to the north, where the Hittites of Asia Minor had become a major power.

About 1350 B.C., while Egypt was struggling with the chaos brought on by Ikhnaton's reformist fervor, the Hittites, under a strong king, had crushed the Mitanni, who then disappeared from history. In their place, the Hittite Empire now extended down into northern Canaan.

Seti I led his army into Canaan to reestablish Egyptian dominion but he could not duplicate the feat of Thutmose III and reach the Euphrates. Kadesh, which had withstood Thutmose III a century and a half before, was again anti-Egyptian and now represented the southern limit of the Hittite power.

The reign of Seti's successor, Rameses II (ram′uh-seez), who came to the throne in 1304 B.C., saw the climactic duel between the two powers. In 1298 B.C. Rameses II led his army against the Hittites. He approached Kadesh carelessly, having been led to believe by his intelligence reports that the Hittites were far away. They weren't. They were waiting in ambush and the vanguard of the Egyptian army, led by Rameses II himself, found themselves suddenly under attack while the rest of the army was still quite distant.

Rameses II found his division cut to pieces and he himself in imminent danger of death or capture. All that saved him was that the Hittites couldn't resist looting the Egyptian camp. That delayed them long enough to allow Egyptian reinforcements to arise. The Hittites were finally beaten off, but Rameses II was only too glad to retreat in safety after having suffered considerable casualties. Later on, in the records he had set up, the Battle of Kadesh was treated as a huge victory, with Rameses II himself mowing down hordes of enemies after he had been surrounded. This, however, was lying propaganda. The battle was an Egyptian defeat.

The war continued indecisively till 1283 B.C., at which time the Egyptians and Hittites signed a peace treaty in which Canaan was split into equal halves, the north for the Hittites, and the south for the Egyptians.

The long war thus seemed to end in a draw, but that meant both sides had lost, for both were terribly weakened in a bitter duel that had ended nowhere. Rameses II ruled for a total of sixty-seven years and in his senile old age allowed Egypt to decay. The Hittite kingdom was ruled by several weak kings during this period, and found itself hard-pressed by the Assyrian kingdom that had now succeeded Mitanni in the upper stretches of the Tigris-Euphrates.

In the last years of Rameses II's reign, new Hebrew tribes were battering at the Jordan River. A number of them entered into a league for the purposes of common military action against Canaan. They expressed this league in tribal fashion by identifying themselves as descended from various sons of the legendary ancestor Israel — who was identified with the legendary Jacob, grandson of Abraham. Thus, these allied Hebrew tribes came to call themselves "the children of Israel," and we know them best as Israelites.

A tradition was retained that they had come from Egypt where they had been enslaved. This may be a kind of dim memory of the time, over three centuries before, when the Hyksos were driven out of Egypt. Some of the Israelite tribes may have been among the Semitic elements who remained in Egypt after the departure of the Hyksos and who were enslaved by the vengeful Egyptians. It is difficult, however, to decide what lies behind the tradition, since there is no record of the Israelite stay in Egypt or their escape from that land, except for the Israelites' own traditions which have come down to us in the Bible.

The Israelites recognized their kinship to the Hebrew tribes who had preceded them in the attempt to take over Canaan in the time of Ikhnaton, a century and a half before. This was expressed tribally by supposing all the Hebrew tribes to have descended from the family of Abraham. (In one place in the Bible, in fact — Genesis 14:13 — Abraham is referred to as "the Hebrew.")

Thus, the Edomites were supposed to be descended from Edom, who was identified with Esau, a grandson of Abraham and, therefore, a brother of the Israelites' own ancestor, Jacob-Israel. The people of Ammon and Moab were supposed to be descended from Lot, a nephew of Abraham.

If the people of Edom, Ammon, and Moab recognized this common kinship, we cannot say. None of their historical traditions have come down to us. Concerning them we know only what the Israelites tell us in the Bible.

The Israelites intended to take over the Canaanite territories west of the Jordan, an area richer and more fertile than the Transjordanian regions exploited by the earlier invaders. The area west of the Jordan, with its springs and its strongly fortified and wealthy cities, seemed to the dwellers of the Arabian desert truly a "land of milk and honey." Ammon, Moab, and Edom barred the way, however.

THE ISRAELITE CONQUEST

The Israelite tribes might well have been stymied by the united opposition of the Hebrew kingdoms, but at just about this time, Moab was attacked by the Canaanite city of Heshbon (hesh′bon), just east of the lower reaches of the Jordan River. Its territory marked the northern limit of Moabite control, but now it revolted, and successfully. The Moabite forces were driven south of the Arnon River (ahr′non), which flows into the Dead Sea from the east.

No doubt Heshbon had been encouraged to revolt by the fact that the Moabite forces were concentrated on the east against the Israelite menace but, if so, it did not profit by its calculations. The Israelite tribes took rapid advantage of the fact that the land north of Arnon was in chaos. They attacked the momentarily victorious city of Heshbon and overwhelmed it, driving their way through to the Jordan River just north of the Dead Sea.

About 1240 B.C., in the last fading portion of the reign of Rameses II, the Israelites forced their way across the Jordan. According to their legends, they did so under the leadership of Joshua, the successor of the lawgiver, Moses, who had died just before the crossing could be made.

In the Biblical Book of Joshua, the circumstances of the crossing and the subsequent conquest of the land west of the Jordan are given in highly idealized form, as one uninterrupted succession of victories. According to the tale there told, the Israelites crossed the Jordan and established themselves first at Gilgal (gil′gal) about five miles west of the river and but a mile to the east of Jericho.

Jericho, despite its strong fortifications, was taken and sacked, with the undermining of its walls attributed in later legend to divine intervention. From there, the Israelites moved westward into the heart of Canaan.

Twelve miles northwest of Jericho was the city of Ai (ay′igh) and two miles further northwest, the important city of Bethel. The Israelites, overconfident at first, attacked frontally with too few numbers and were beaten off. Joshua then tried a more subtle strategy. He placed a contingent of men in ambush, then feinted an attack with another group. The feigning attackers pretended defeat and ran. The men of Ai and Bethel, overconfident in their turn, incautiously left their defenses to engage in hot pursuit. The Israelite contingent in ambush quickly marched into the undefended cities. At an appropriate moment the retreating contingent turned to fight and when the Canaanites attempted to return to their cities they found them occupied. Ai, at least, was destroyed and never rebuilt.

Five miles south of Ai was the city of Gibeon (gib′ee-on). The Gibeonites despaired of defeating the fierce Israelite tribesmen, made an alliance with them, and offered tribute in return for being left alone. The Canaanite cities of the south, under the leadership of the large towns of Jerusalem and Hebron, had by then formed a confederacy against the common foe and now marched against Gibeon in order to force it back into the Canaanite ranks.

Joshua hastened his Israelite army to the relief of Gibeon and, in a pitched battle, forced the Canaanites into a retreat that quickly became a rout. It was in the course of this battle that the Bible lyrically states the sun and the moon had stopped in their courses in order to lengthen the day and give the Israelites a chance to complete the destruction of the enemy army. Joshua then engaged in quick campaigns in the north and south, whereby all of Canaan was cleared by the Israelites.

So much for the later idealization of the conquest. What really happened? Actually, information is meager outside the Bible. The Book of Judges, which follows Joshua in the Bible, seems to include older traditions and probably more realistic ones, and it speaks of a Canaan in which the Israelites were most insecurely established and in which the Canaanites maintained themselves in many areas. We can assume that, despite the tale of Joshua, the conquest was neither rapid nor complete.

It may be that the legendary Joshua led the forces of only three tribes across the Jordan: those of Ephraim (ee′free-um), Manasseh (muh-nas′uh), and Benjamin. These are called the "Rachel tribes," for they were viewed in later legend as having been descended from Israel-Jacob and his wife Rachel.

This early thrust of the Rachel tribes did not take place without opposition. Rameses II of Egypt had finally died in 1237 B.C. at the age of ninety or more and was succeeded by a son, Merneptah (mur′nep-tah″). In 1232 B.C. Merneptah led his Egyptians into Canaan and apparently inflicted a defeat on the Israelites. At least in the record he left of the campaign, he said, with typical official exaggeration: "Israel is desolate; its seed is not."

Exaggeration or not, we might fairly suppose that, left to itself, Egypt would have taken care of the Israelite invasion and that the conquest would not have taken place. Egypt, however, was not left to itself, for at about this time the entire ancient world was sent into a convulsion.

It started in the region north of the Aegean Sea in Europe at about the time the first Israelite contingents had entered Canaan. A tribe of Greek-speaking peoples, the Dorians (daw′ree-unz), hacked their way southward, overthrowing the kingdoms set up by an earlier group of Greeks, the Achaeans (uh-kee′unz), who, in their turn, two centuries before, had overthrown the Cretan Empire. The Dorians made their way to the southernmost tip of Greece, then moved overseas to the islands of Crete and Rhodes. Meanwhile, another group of tribes called the Phrygians (frij′ee-anz) moved from north of the Aegean Sea into Asia Minor, where they overthrew the weakened and tottering Hittite kingdom, which now vanished from history.

Many of the groups who were overturned by the invaders saw no way out but to join those whom they could not defeat and go marauding against the next peoples in line. Bands of raiders, consisting of a mixture of Greeks and non-Greeks, crossed the Mediterranean from Crete and landed on the shore of Libya (the African coast west of Egypt). They joined with native Libyans in an attack on Egypt.

Merneptah, fresh from his victory in Canaan, found that he had to veer about and stand against the appalling attack of what the Egyptians called the Sea Peoples (because they had invaded by way of the sea). Merneptah managed to beat off the Sea Peoples but the effort effectively halted any further attempt on his part to reassert Egyptian supremacy in Canaan. The Israelites were left to conquer as they pleased — or as they could.

The menace of the Sea Peoples was not yet over, however. Beaten by the Egyptians, they nevertheless seem to have taken Cyprus. From Cyprus they eventually tried again. About 1185 B.C. the hordes invaded Canaan and approached Egypt from the direction taken by the Hyksos five centuries before.

Ruling Egypt at this time was Rameses III. Rallying Egyptian power, Rameses III, in a monumental effort, managed to turn back the raiders and drive them out of the land. It was, however, the last effort that Egyptians were to make as a great power for six centuries. Totally exhausted with its three-century effort to fight off the Mitanians, the Hittites, and the Sea Peoples, the nation sank back into a lethargy after the death of Rameses III in 1156 and took up a long-enduring policy of isolation.

Again the Sea Peoples were defeated by Egypt, but again they were not done. A group of them, called Peleset by the Egyptians, settled down on the coast just north of the Sinai Peninsula. To the Israelites they were "Pelishti" and, in English, this became "Philistines."

To the ancient Greeks it was the people of the coast who mattered, for it was those they encountered in their own sea trading. The area occupied by the Philistines, plus the entire hinterland which they did not occupy, was called by their name, the word coming down to us as "Palestine."

The Philistines effectively kept the Israelites from penetrating to the coast in the south. Further north the strong Phoenician cities did the same. The Israelites were confined to the central hill region of Canaan. Their strongest grip was taken along the western shore of the Jordan River, where the Rachel tribes established themselves, Manasseh in the north, Benjamin in the south, and Ephraim between.

They formed alliances with other invading tribes in the north whom they described as having been descended from Israel-Jacob by wives other than Rachel. These were Asher, Naphtali (naf′tuh-lee), Zebulon (zeb′yoo-lun), and Issachar (is′uh-kahr). Alliances were also formed with the tribe of Dan, which was struggling near the coast against the Philistines, and with those of Gad and Reuben on the eastern shore of the Jordan.

In the south were the invading tribes of Judah and Simeon (though only Judah counted, for it quickly absorbed the Simeonites). Judah was rather a special case. It occupied the southernmost portion of Canaan, the driest and least well-developed part of the land. The Judeans intermarried with the Canaanite families of the land, and although both Judah and Simeon are listed among the sons of Jacob in the Bible, those tribes never really formed part of the Israelite confederacy.

All in all, the later Israelites looked back at a confederacy of twelve tribes, including Judah and Simeon. It may not be accidental that the number was twelve, for twelve had certain mystical associations. It represented the number of cycles of the moon's phases that took place in one cycle of seasons. That is, the number of months in a year, and therefore the number of constellations in the zodiac. To nomads and hunters the moon was the logical method of time telling, but to agriculturalists the seasons were all-important. A method for reconciling the moon and the sun was therefore invested with all kinds of religious significance and the number twelve would naturally share in that.

In fact, the tribe of Levi (lee′vigh) was also part of the confederacy as a thirteenth member, but it was particularly small and it occupied a scattering of cities rather than a section of contiguous territory. It was not counted as a territorial tribe, therefore, and the number remained twelve. However, its descent was traced to Levi, a son of Israel, and to make it clear that Israel had only twelve sons, the tribes of Ephraim and Manasseh were considered to be descended from two grandsons of Israel. The two grandsons were sons of Joseph, the favorite son of Israel. (Ephraim and Manasseh are therefore sometimes lumped together as the "Joseph tribes.")

3

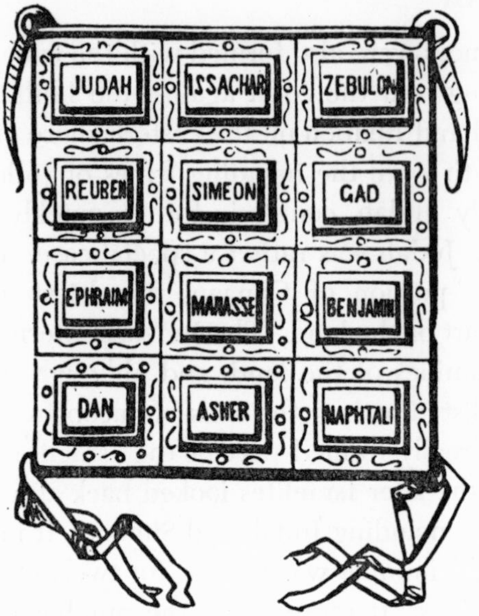

ISRAEL

THE TRIBES

The tribes of Israel formed a loose confederation which might be referred to simply as "Israel." The confederation was loose indeed, however, and the separate tribes, except in times of emergency, behaved almost as independent entities. Each had its own traditions and its own tribal leaders. Some of these leaders were vividly remembered in tradition for having been victorious over one enemy or another. These were called "judges," since one of the functions of a leader in a tribal society is to judge disputes and make some appropriate decision which would yield (it was to be hoped) maximum justice to all.

In Israel's later histories, these tribal traditions were interpreted as though they were part of the activities of a united nation. For that reason the various judges were supposed to rule over all the tribes, one judge ruling after another. Twelve judges were included because of the mystic value of the number, though some of these are dismissed in the Bible with no more than one or two verses.

As a result of this misinterpretation, calculations from the Book of Judges make it appear that the tribal period was over four hundred years long and that the Israelite conquest took place about 1450 B.C. Interpreting matters with (it would seem) greater realism, and assuming that the tribes were fairly independent and that different judges might rule concurrently, it would seem that the tribal period lasted less than a century and a half. This would be consistent with an Israelite conquest at about 1200 B.C.

In addition to the occasional necessity of defense against a common enemy, a strong factor holding the tribes together was religion. It is hard to tell what the religion of the Israelites was like at the time they crossed the Jordan, since the religious leaders of later times tended to read their own sophisticated beliefs back into primitive times. Probably the Israelite religion at the time of the conquest was not very different from that of the other nomadic tribes, and they worshiped a storm god not very different from other gods.*

The form of worship among the invading Israelites was primitive and lacked the color and elaborate ritual that had been developed in the long-civilized cities of Canaan. The austere desert tribesmen looked down upon the Canaanite practices as wicked. This is not surprising, for country folk have always disapproved of the sophisticated ways in the "wicked city" right down to the present time.

There grew to be two religious parties among the Israelites.

* The name of the Israelite god was written in four consonants as YHVH. The vowels were not expressed and since the later Israelites preferred not to use the name, for superstitious reasons, the nature of the vowels remains uncertain. The name Jehovah came to be used, but this is almost certainly wrong, and modern scholars prefer the name Yahveh.

Some adopted the various Canaanite rituals and occasionally even the Canaanite gods. Others clung to the older and simpler methods of worshiping Yahveh. These latter, whom we might call Yahvists, were not accustomed to the elaborate wooden or stone figures ("idols") that represented gods, and it was against "idolatry," the worship of idols, that they chiefly inveighed.

The Bible reflects the Yahvist view and probably makes the Yahvists seem more important than they really were. For some six centuries after the conquest, the Yahvists were a minority party and usually did not exert much influence over the Israelite leadership.

During the early tribal period, the strongest tribe was Ephraim and its most revered center of worship was at the town of Shiloh (shy′loh). Shiloh is located twenty miles north of Jerusalem. The reason for its selection as a holy site is not known. There is archaeological evidence that the site on which Shiloh stood was not occupied until after the Israelite conquest. Perhaps the Israelites deliberately chose such an unoccupied spot in order to erect a center of worship in a place not associated with Canaanite rule.

One way in which the other tribes indicated their adherence to the confederation was by making appropriate sacrifices at Shiloh, and at set times in the year men made the pilgrimage to the holy site from the different tribes.

Among the common enemies that held the tribes together were the Canaanites, of course, who were still strong in the north, even after central Canaan had been taken over by the Rachel tribes. The Canaanites of the north may well have had the support of the rich cities on the coast. These had suffered devastation as a result of the southward push of the Sea Peoples, but the city of Sidon (sy′don) had recovered first. Located forty miles south of Byblos, it now became the leading city of the area later called Phoenicia. In the Book of Judges, the coastal Canaanites are therefore referred to as Sidonians.

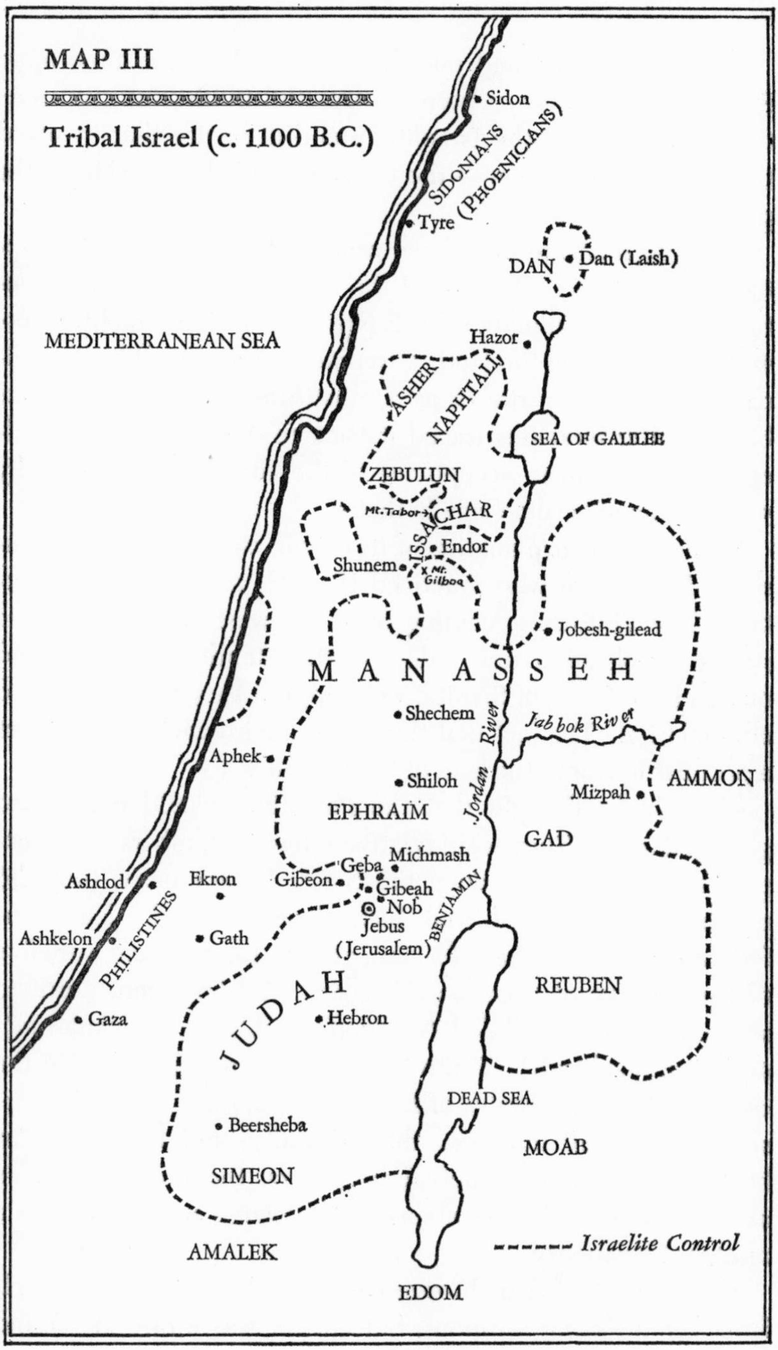

MAP III
Tribal Israel (c. 1100 B.C.)
Sidon
SIDONIANS
(PHOENICIANS)
Tyre
DAN
Dan (Laish)
MEDITERRANEAN SEA
Hazor
ASHER
NAPHTALI
SEA OF GALILEE
ZEBULUN
Mt. Tabor
ISSACHAR
Endor
Shunem
Mt. Gilboa
Jobesh-gilead
MANASSEH
Shechem
Jabbok River
Jordan River
Aphek
Shiloh
AMMON
Mizpah
EPHRAIM
GAD
Geba
Michmash
Ashdod
Ekron
Gibeon
Gibeah
Nob
Jebus
(Jerusalem)
BENJAMIN
Ashkelon
Gath
PHILISTINES
JUDAH
REUBEN
Gaza
Hebron
DEAD SEA
Beersheba
MOAB
SIMEON
Israelite Control
AMALEK
EDOM

A second enemy, and one that was at the same time more dangerous and more abhorred, were the Philistines. Between the Philistines and the Israelites stood a barrier that involved the rite of circumcision — the cutting off of the foreskin of the penis.

This rite seems to have been practiced by the ancient Egyptians first. It was adopted by the Canaanites during the centuries of their domination by Egypt and by the Israelites, too, when they entered the land. Circumcision may well have originated as a fertility rite or as a substitute for human sacrifice, but the later Israelites traced it back to Abraham and considered it as a form of acceptance of the covenant with God by which Canaan became legally theirs.

Whatever the explanation of its origin, circumcision was considered, by those who practiced the rite, as extremely important. The Philistines, coming from the west and possessing a strong Greek admixture, adopted the Hebrew language and many of the forms of Semitic worship, but they never accepted circumcision. The fact that they were uncircumcised lent them a peculiar horror in the eyes of the Israelites.

It might be thought that the Philistines would not be too great a danger. They were relatively few in numbers and occupied a restricted area along the coast. What's more, they did not even form a united front. Instead, they formed a loose confederacy made up, Greek fashion, of city-states. There were five of these, three of them on the coast. Reading from north to south, these were Ashdod (ash′dod), Ashkelon (ash′kuh-lon), and Gaza (gah′zuh). Ten miles inland from Ashdod were the two remaining city-states of Ekron (ek′ron) and Gath. Yet despite their small numbers, their disunity, and the particular hostility of their circumcised neighbors, the Philistines were actually able to take the offensive. To a large extent, this was a matter of weaponry.

For a thousand years bronze had been the material par excellence for tools and weapons, but copper was a rare metal and the tin required to make bronze out of the copper was even rarer. One metal at least was known to be better than even the best bronze, and that was iron — at least the iron alloy that was to be found in meteorites. Meteoric iron was much harder and tougher than bronze, but it was difficult to work and, worse still, it was even rarer than copper and tin.

But then it was discovered that just as copper could be obtained by heating certain minerals, so could iron. What's more, the minerals which would yield iron were much more common than those which would yield copper. The trouble was that to force minerals to yield iron, high temperatures were required and it wasn't easy to obtain that. What's more, the iron produced was all too often in a form that was hard but brittle, or else tough but soft. The kind of iron that would be useful for tools and weapons — we'd call it a kind of steel, now — had to be smelted just so.

The method for handling iron ore properly was developed in or near Hittite territory about 1400 B.C. and it slowly spread outward. The Dorian tribes who invaded Greece had iron weapons, and this was one reason why they so easily conquered the bronze-armored Achaeans. The Sea Peoples had iron, too, and when the Philistines took over the Canaanite coast, they had iron weapons with which to fight. Nor were they so foolish as to give out the secret of iron smelting. As long as they could keep the technique secret, the Israelites had to oppose them with inferior weapons.

Not only did the Philistines easily maintain themselves on the coast, thanks to iron, but they kept the tribes nearest to them — Dan, Judah, and Simeon — under tribute. Throughout the period immediately following the conquest, these tribes could play only a minor role.

The Bible does record the tale of a band of Danites, who, finding life intolerable under the Philistines, marched a hundred miles to the north, took the isolated Canaanite city of Laish (lay′ish), sacked it, and then settled there, renaming it

Dan. For some three centuries, Dan remained the northernmost city of the Israelite confederacy as Beersheba remained its southernmost. "From Dan to Beersheba" became a way of saying "All Israel."

THE JUDGES

The northern tribes, further removed from the Philistines and their iron weapons, had a chance to lead a less restricted life than did the tribes of the Dead Sea region. Over the northern tribes Ephraim maintained a definite military supremacy. This is shown in connection with a battle fought in the early decades after the conquest.

The tribes about the Sea of Galilee maintained themselves most precariously against the still-strong Canaanite cities of the region. Against the Israelites, Jabin (jay′bin), king of Hazor (hay′zawr), organized and headed a Canaanite league. The Canaanites, possibly with the help of their kinsmen in the Phoenician cities on the coast, were well equipped with chariots and iron weaponry. The Israelites of the far north could not match them in this.

The leader of the northern tribes was Barak (bar′ak), of the tribe of Naphtali. He gathered what men he could collect at Mount Tabor (tay′ber). This was about twenty-five miles southwest of Hazor, was centrally located, and was a strong defensive point. Even so, morale was low in the face of the superior armor of the Canaanite enemy and Barak knew he could not hold his men in line long. Before he dared fight, he had to negotiate with Ephraim, which was then (very unusually) under the leadership of a woman, Deborah. The help was promised but only under the condition (we may reasonably suppose) that the leadership in battle be granted the Ephraimites. The alliance was established, contingents arrived from the Rachel tribes, and only then were the Israelites ready for battle.

The Canaanites attacked but found their chariots could not negotiate the rocky terrain of Mount Tabor. The Israelites held out and then took advantage of a sudden rainstorm to counter-attack. The terrain turned to mud, the heavy iron chariots were mired, and the Canaanites were slaughtered. The Canaanite general, Sisera (sis′uh-ruh), had to abandon his own chariot and flee on foot. He was assassinated by a woman in whose tent he sought refuge. Hazor was destroyed and the Canaanite power in the north was weakened to the point where it was no longer a danger to Israel.

A paean of victory, apparently dating back to this time (possibly 1150 B.C.), is preserved in the fifth chapter of Judges, and is among the oldest passages in the Bible. The paean, called the Song of Deborah, lists the tribes who participated in the victory. First, naturally, is Ephraim, then the other Rachel tribes: *Out of Ephraim was there a root of them against Amalek;/After thee, Benjamin, among thy people;/Out of Machir [Manasseh] came down governors . . .*

Then the northern tribes who fought were mentioned: "*. . . the princes of Issachar were with Deborah*" and "*Zebulun and Naphtali were a people that jeoparded their lives unto the death.*"

Certain other tribes were, however, excoriated for not joining in the fight and retaining, instead, a neutral position. *For the divisions of Reuben/There were great thoughts of heart./Why abodest thou among the sheepfolds,/To hear the bleating of the flocks?/ . . . /Gilead [Gad] abode beyond Jordan:/And why did Dan remain in ships?/Asher continued on the seashore.*

There were perhaps extenuating circumstances. Asher was under the domination of the coastal Phoenicians and Dan under that of the coastal Philistines. Gad and Reuben, who were east of the Jordan, had to contend with Ammon and Moab respectively. Still, the looseness of the confederacy is plain. Ephraim had to be begged to rally the strong Rachel tribes to the support of the weak north. Four of the tribes did not take part at all.

Another interesting fact is that Judah and Simeon are not even mentioned in the Song of Deborah. Apparently at this time, these southern tribes were not considered part of the Israelite confederacy. In fact, during all the period of the Judges, their role seems to have been minimal. It is convenient, in some ways, to confine the term "Israel" to the ten tribes listed in the Song of Deborah and to speak of the southern peoples as "Judah."

The Ephraimite hegemony and the manner in which its leaders insisted upon maintaining it is made clearer in the tale of Gideon. The Rachel tribes, having nothing to fear from the broken power of the Canaanites in the north, were nevertheless victimized by raids across the Jordan by the Arab tribes (Midianites) of the desert. It was what the Rachel tribes had themselves done a century earlier and now they were cast in the defensive role in which the Canaanites had failed.

Bearing the brunt of the Midianite onslaught was the tribe of Manasseh, and the tribal leader, Gideon, took action against the Midianites. Angered, perhaps, at the sluggishness of the Ephraimite leadership, he rallied the northern tribes about him and set up the same coalition that had fought the Canaanites at Mount Tabor. He did not, however, appeal to Ephraim but seemed quite content to fight without that tribe.

The Midianite army was quite a different matter from that of the Canaanites. These nomads came on camels rather than horses and armored chariots. They were even more primitive in their equipment than the Israelites were and their only advantage was their mobility — their ability to strike and fade away. A full-fledged battle against them was useless; they would not stand still for it.

Gideon therefore organized a surprise raid against the Midianite encampment west of the Jordan. The Midianites, unsophisticated in the art of war, were unprepared for a night attack. Gideon led his small band by night to the heights overlooking the Midianite encampment and attacked suddenly with noise and lights rather than with arms. Roused, shaken, not knowing what was going on, convinced that a formidable host had surrounded them, the Midianites fled in panic east to the Jordan.

Gideon was ready for them there, too. With deliberate tardiness, he had informed Ephraim of his plans and directed the Ephraimite legions to the fords of the Jordan. There they were able to handle the fleeing Midianites and few of them escaped.

Nevertheless, the prestige of the victory lay entirely with Gideon and, therefore, with the tribe of Manasseh. The Ephraimites, whose role had been secondary, chafed and for a while it looked as though civil war would be inevitable. Gideon averted it only by a humble submission to Ephraim and an acknowledgment of Ephraimite supremacy.

Gideon's prestige was high enough even so for the tribe of Manasseh to wish to make his leadership hereditary; that is, to make him a king. And, indeed, after his death, one of his sons, Abimelech (uh-bim′uh-lek), seized the leadership by force, killing all his brothers (and there are usually many brothers in a society where the leaders are flamboyantly polygamous). The attempt lasted only three years and Abimelech was then killed while laying siege to a rebellious city.

It was a foretaste of what was to come and a sign of the growing sophistication of the Israelites. In the old nomadic existence before the conquest, the rough and ready democracy involved in choosing a new leader when the old one died did not cause too much trouble. But now property and wealth was accumulating, and the period of uncertainty and civil disorder between one leader and the next was becoming too expensive. Increasingly, thoughtful Israelites were beginning to favor a monarchy; that is, a system whereby father is automatically succeeded by son, thus increasing political and social stability. The first attempt, however, had failed, and still worse was to come.

The tribe of Gad, east of the Jordan, was harassed by the people of Ammon, the Hebrew tribe who had come to that section of Canaan before the Israelites had. As a result of the continuing struggle with Ammon, Gad had been in no position to join the tribes west of the Jordan in the struggle against either the Canaanites or the Midianites. (Gideon had sacked some of the Gadite cities in retaliation for the refusal of that tribe to aid him.)

But now a strong military leader had arisen in Gad, a man named Jephthah (jef′thuh). In a battle near Mizpah (miz′pah), just south of the Jabbok River (jab′ok) east of the Jordan, the Gadites won a complete victory over Ammon. In connection with this battle, Jephthah seems to have sacrificed his daughter. This was by no means an unheard-of event among the peoples of Canaan. The deities worshiped would be all the more pleased with so precious a sacrifice as the leader's own child (or sometimes even the leader himself). Undoubtedly the victory over the Ammonites was credited to the sacrifice and Jephthah was considered a great patriot. In later ages, though, those who edited the Biblical writings, and who were horrified at human sacrifice, softened the story (too well-known to omit) by having the sacrifice come as a consequence of a rash vow.

But Jephthah, like Gideon before him, had fought without due consideration for the jealously guarded leadership of Ephraim. This time the Ephraimites were not to be mollified; they crossed the Jordan intent on punishing the Gadites for their presumption in winning victories without them.

Jephthah coolly retreated before them and sent contingents to stand guard over the fords of the Jordan, for the Ephraimites, out of overconfidence, had not bothered to secure them. They did not expect to be retreating in panic.

But that was exactly what happened. In a sharp battle Jephthah defeated them and when the beaten Ephraimites fled, they found themselves trapped at the Jordan. Some, it would appear, pretended to be ordinary travelers, but Jephthah's tough fighters had instructions to demand that any doubtful wayfarer be asked to say "shibboleth" (meaning "stream"). The "sh" sound was lacking in the Ephraimite dialect, so anyone who said "sibboleth" was promptly killed. (This gave a word to the English language, for "shibboleth" now means any pet phrase or slogan of a political party.) This battle, perhaps about 1100 B.C., ended the Ephraimite hegemony that had endured for about a century, or since the time of Joshua.

THE PHILISTINES

This Israelite civil war and the weakening of Ephraim was catastrophic for Israel generally. Without the Ephraimite contingents about which to rally, the tribes were that much more helpless before their enemies. Indeed, all that held them together now was the sanctuary at Shiloh, for Ephraim's religious leadership survived its political and military decline. (This frequently happens. Thus, in our own culture, we have witnessed Rome remain a religious center many centuries after its political and military importance as the capital of a great empire had vanished.)

Worse still for the Israelite tribes, this period of disunity and weakness coincided with a period of growing unity and strength of the Philistines. It was at about this time that the five Philistine city-states had come under the domination of

Gath and were in a position to exert their influence more strongly than ever over the nearby tribes of Dan and Judah.

It was to this period, perhaps, that the tales of the Danite hero Samson belong. What really happened is obscured under the traditional trappings of the strong-man legend, the sort of thing that finds popularity in every culture (in our own Paul Bunyan, for instance). We may guess that Samson led a guerrilla fight against the Philistines but was in the end taken prisoner.

With the Philistines controlling all the area west of the Dead Sea, it was tempting to try to extend that control further. Immediately to the north of the Philistine line were the cities of Benjamin and Ephraim. Ephraim still bore the prestige of its one-time leadership and of its control over the central Israelite shrine at Shiloh. If Ephraim could be defeated — and it had never recovered from the disaster at the fords of the Jordan — then all the Israelite confederacy might fall into Philistine hands. The Philistines would then have the start for what might turn out to be a sizable empire.

The details of the gathering crisis are not known to us, but by about 1050 B.C. there came time for a crucial battle. The Philistines, well armored and well disciplined, had moved up the coast and were now inland at the city of Aphek (ay′fek.) This was thirty miles north of the Philistine capital at Gath and only twenty miles west of Shiloh.

The Ephraimites, with whatever contingents they could gather from the other members of the confederation, faced the enemy uncertainly. In a preliminary skirmish, the Ephraimites were badly beaten and it seemed to their leaders that the only hope for survival lay in some drastic measure to restore sagging morale.

At the sanctuary at Shiloh, there was the "ark of the covenant," a sacred box which had, according to tradition, been brought into Israel at the time of the conquest a century and a half before. It was the holiest object of the Israelite cult and was, in the absence of idols, the most concentrated expression of the Israelite god.

The ark was sent for and brought into the camp with all possible ceremony. The Ephraimites were expected to feel that their god was now personally in camp and would fight with them against the Philistines. The fact was not kept secret from the Philistines, of course, for it was important that the enemy expect to be facing the Israelite god and be correspondingly disheartened.

Such a maneuver might easily have been an effective bit of psychological warfare, since it was a common belief among the peoples of the time that each culture had its guardian god, so to speak. The Philistines were perfectly ready to believe in the existence and power of the Israelite god over Israel and simultaneously in the existence and power of their own gods over themselves. At the crucial moment, it was a matter of which set of deities was to be stronger. With the Israelite cult-object actually in camp and on the scene and with their own most powerful idols at home, the Philistines might be expected to feel nervous.

(The Israelite beliefs of the time were just as primitive. In later times, it would have seemed clear to them that their god did not have to be brought to the camp; that he existed everywhere and could bring his people victory regardless of where the ark was or even whether it existed at all — but this was for the future.)

In any case, the psychological maneuver missed fire. The Philistine leaders, anticipating the bad effect on morale of the coming of the ark, allowed no time for it to take effect. They ordered an attack at once and the Ephraimites could not withstand the iron-armored charge. They were slaughtered, the ark of the covenant was captured by the Philistines, and Shiloh itself was taken and sacked. It was utterly destroyed and disappeared from history.

The ark, however, did not. The Philistines had it, but treated it gingerly. It represented a god which, though defeated, might yet have magic power and which, therefore, deserved careful treatment. They did not want it in their own territory, since a god might be expected to resent being in exile and their own gods might resent the intruder. It was eventually left, therefore, at Kirjath-jearim (kir′ee-ath-jee′uh-rim), a small town in northern Judah.

A kind of Philistine empire now existed, and virtually the entire Israelite confederation was under Philistine domination. The only national resistance that remained was under a leader named Samuel. He maintained himself, guerrilla fashion, in the hill country of Ephraim and Benjamin.

Again, details are missing. The Philistine tide receded for a while; perhaps there was quarreling among their cities. At any rate, Samuel did maintain himself and the Israelite cause looked somewhat brighter. In Samuel's old age a younger man Saul, of the tribe of Benjamin, became prominent in the continuing resistance.

It seemed clear to many Israelites by now that the cause of their troubles lay in their disunion and in the disorganized character of their leadership. There would have to be a tighter union and a stronger leader. In short, there would have to be a king, and Saul seemed a logical candidate for the post. Samuel lent his own prestige to this and helped consecrate Saul as king of Israel.

The Biblical editors of later centuries, working at a time when the kingship had failed, introduced passages which made it appear that Samuel opposed the establishment of a king. And, indeed, Israel was to experience the difficulties that arose from differences between the political leaders and the religious leaders. (Nowadays we would say the friction between State and Church.)

On the side of Saul, or of any king, there would be the armed men, the guerrilla bands who were resisting the Philistines and who saw no salvation but in superior force. On the other side would be groups of men who devoted themselves to ecstatic devotions, who would play instruments, sing, dance, put themselves into wild trances, and fall down in frenzy. In these frenzies they were thought to be in close touch with the deity, and their incoherent mutterings and mouthings were taken as divine messages. These men and their followers would feel it would be safer to be guided by such messages first of all.

These ecstatic individuals who might be described by the modern word "dervishes" (taken from such people in the Mohammedan religion) were known in earlier times as "prophets," from a Greek word meaning "to speak forth" (with reference to their ecstatic statements). Since prophetic utterances were supposed to be informative concerning the future, the word has come to mean "someone who can foretell the future."

At the very beginning, then, Saul found the assumption of the kingship a difficult one. The other tribes were not overjoyed at the prospect of a Benjamite king, and the prophetic party was only lukewarm. What was needed was some spectacular feat that would raise Saul's prestige.

This came about through events east of the Jordan River. The Philistine hold was weak beyond the Jordan and the tribe of Gad retained a larger share of independence than did most of the Israelites west of the river. But that didn't mean a lack of ample trouble. Gad still had the kingdom of Ammon to contend with, as in the days of Jephthah nearly a century before.

The city of Jabesh-gilead (jay′besh-gil′ee-ad) was, at the time of Saul's emergence, under siege by the Ammonites. It was reduced to the point of surrender, but the Ammonites had offered the inhabitants their lives only on condition that the right eye of each man be put out. As a last resort, then, the men of Jabesh-gilead decided to hold out a bit longer and to send a plea for help to the tribes west of the Jordan.

Saul took instant action. Gathering what men he could and evading any Philistine forces in the way, he proceeded by forced marches to cover the fifty miles that separated Jabesh-gilead from his own base. By arriving sooner than expected, he achieved surprise. Falling on the unsuspecting Ammonites, he routed them and rescued the city.

It was a spectacular feat — the first military action the Israelites could really take pride in since the time of Jephthah. Saul's reputation skyrocketed and the drive to make him king was triumphant. Samuel proceeded to consecrate him with full religious ritual.

In those days kings had very much a priestly character of their own, and it was quite common for the same man to be both king and high priest of the nation. For that reason, the ritual that made Saul king was very much like that used for the consecration of a high priest. An important part of the ritual was an anointing with sacred oil. Oil was used for cleansing the body in those days and anointing with oil represented a cleansing away of sin. The ceremony of anointing was so essential that a king or high priest, or any individual who was both, was referred to as "the Anointed One." This is, in Hebrew, "masheeakh," and the word is usually written in English as "Messiah."

SAUL

Saul became king about 1020 B.C. and established his capital at Gibeah (gib′ee-uh), a town in Benjamin about four miles north of Jerusalem. Clearly, the mere act of calling himself king was a provocative affront to the Philistines and it meant war at once. Where the Philistines might be content to meet guerrilla bands in a series of smoldering engagements, the establishment of a monarchy called for a major effort.

Saul reacted with the speed and decision he had displayed in connection with Jabesh-gilead. His son Jonathan led a diversionary raid against Geba (gee′buh), only five miles from Saul's capital. It held a small Philistine garrison, the closest to the center of Israelite resistance, and Jonathan surprised it and wiped it out. Meanwhile, Saul had established himself at a strong defensive position at Michmash (mik-mash), two miles northeast of Geba.

The angered Philistines, moving against the main Israelite forces at Michmash, were again surprised by a quick raid by Jonathan's men. Not much damage was done physically, but the Philistines mistook Jonathan's small party for a much larger army and retired hastily. The event was not an entirely happy one for Saul, for it was clear that the lion's share of the credit for the victory over the Philistines belonged to Jonathan.

It is not uncommon in monarchies, right down into modern times, for rivalry and even hatred to exist between the king and the heir apparent. Saul must have felt that if Jonathan grew too popular he could easily overthrow his father and succeed to the throne. Consequently, Saul ordered the execution of Jonathan for some infraction of ritual, and it was only the violent clamor of the army that forced him to rescind the order. Nevertheless, it was just this sort of popularity with the army that was particularly dangerous and Saul grew more than ever suspicious of his son.

After the Battle of Michmash, the Philistines were forced to retire and the sudden brightening of Israel's fortunes seemed to inspire Judah to rebel. Judah had been dominated by the Philistines for almost all its history and now it gladly switched allegiance to Saul. A combined Israelite-Judean army defeated the Philistines at Shocoh (shoh′koh), a town about fifteen miles southwest of Jerusalem, and all of Judah passed under Israelite control.

Saul went further. With Judah cleared of the Philistines, he led his army still farther south and conducted a victorious campaign against the Amalekites, a nomad people who dwelt south of Judah and whose raids against the Judean population had been most galling. It was a most politic thing to do, for Saul in this way not only showed his power to the Judeans at close quarters but earned their gratitude for the destruction of a particular enemy.

Saul reigned for about twenty years — a hard reign occupied by continual war against the Philistines — and he had much to show for it. By 1005 B.C. his inland kingdom (nowhere did it touch the coast, which continued to be dominated by Philistines in the south and Phoenicians in the north) extended nearly 180 miles from north to south and was 70 miles wide at its widest. It was perhaps as large as the state of Massachusetts, and the Israelites were stronger than they had ever been before.

Yet there were dark spots in the reign, too. Saul had internal enemies and chief among them was Samuel, leader of the prophetic party. It seemed to Saul that since he was anointed king, he was automatically anointed high priest as well. Saul attempted to act in this priestly capacity and to conduct sacrifices. It was Samuel's view, however, that Saul's kingship was purely secular and that it was Samuel himself who retained the priestly function.

The quarrel came to a head after Saul's victorious Amalekite campaign. Saul had captured the Amalekite chieftain, Agag (ay′gag), together with much booty in the form of cattle and sheep. To Saul, with an eye for a good political maneuver, it may have seemed sensible to keep Agag alive and then free him in return for suitable concessions. It also seemed sensible to distribute the loot among the soldiers and insure their enthusiasm in future battles. To old Samuel, the religious leader, however, it seemed much better to kill Agag and slaughter all the animals as an offering to God in order to insure *His* enthusiasm in future battles.

Samuel had his way in this case; Saul was humiliated and not likely to forget that. Samuel prudently went into retirement, but from that moment on the prophetic party went into the opposition and Saul knew it. Saul knew that anyone who rose in rebellion against him would be able to count on Samuel's support and on the support of that portion of the population to whom the prophets seemed holy men or who resented the Benjamite supremacy.

It is not surprising, then, that Saul grew depressed and suspicious, and turned a baleful eye on any subject who, he felt, was growing too popular with the people. That meant Jonathan, in the first place, but it also meant someone else.

Once Judah became part of Saul's kingdom, Judeans flocked to the court and among them was David, a member of an important family of Bethlehem, a town about five miles south of Jerusalem. David had a keen intelligence, a sure political instinct, and was, besides, a skillful military leader. He could be of enormous help to Saul, if he could be trusted, but as time went on, the suspicious Saul became increasingly certain he could *not* be trusted.

For one thing, David was a Judean and was therefore not quite a member of the Israelite confederation. For another, he had a flamboyance about him that seemed to endear him to the people. (In later years, legends about his youth arose, including the tale of a single combat at the Battle of Shocoh with a Philistine giant, Goliath. This probably falls in the same category as George Washington and the cherry tree, but the point is that David was the kind of gallant, charismatic leader about whom such stories could be believed.) Finally, it became clear that David and Jonathan were hand in glove and Saul decided that the two must be in a conspiracy to derive him of his throne.

He made plans to have David executed, but David, who was shrewd enough to see that the wind was turning, was also warned by Jonathan. David therefore slipped out of Gibeah and managed to get away to Judah, where he was forced to live as a guerrilla chieftain, fighting against Saul. In this struggle David was supported by Samuel and the prophetic party; it was not so much, probably, that they were for David as that they were against Saul.

(In later years, one of the legends concerning David's youth was that he had been secretly anointed king by Samuel. This may not have been true. It may have been, rather, the kind of propaganda tale designed to lend legitimacy to what was, in the end, a usurpation. But again, David was the kind of man about whom such tales could be believed.)

Saul, irascible and furious, overreacted. In his rage against David, he slaughtered a band of priests at Nob, only two miles southeast of Gibeah, after hearing that one of them had helped the Judean fugitive. If that was an attempt to drive the prophetic party back into line by a display of the iron hand, it backfired. The prophetic party turned more than ever against Saul.

Saul's firm and persistent pursuit of David had its effect, however. Most of the Judean clans were browbeaten into refusing him support and in the end David was forced into the kind of treason that the later Biblical writers had great difficulty in smoothing over and explaining away. He actually accepted the protection of the Philistine king of Gath, agreeing to fight in the Philistine service.

And it was time for the Philistines to make a great move again. With Saul's kingdom riven by internal dissent, with king and crown prince at loggerheads, with the king's men and the prophets at cross-purposes, and with David in rebellion, surely a strong Philistine blow would be successful.

In 1000 B.C., therefore, the Philistine army was gathered once again and sent into Israel. From Aphek, their old battleground, they moved rapidly northward, intending to cut off the northern tribes and then crush the central Rachel tribes between themselves on the north and David's Judeans — assuming he could or would raise them in revolt — on the south.

This Saul was bound to try to prevent. He hastened northward, too, taking up a position on Mount Gilboa (gil-boh′uh), forty miles north of Gibea and ten miles southeast of Shunem (shoo′nem), where the Philistines lay encamped.

The battle, when it came, was an utter disaster for the Israelites. The heavily armed Philistines carried all before them. The Israelites were routed; Jonathan was killed (fighting for his father to the last); and at one stroke, the Philistine mastery of Israel was reestablished.

All of Saul's work had gone for nothing, all had been undone, and in the aftermath of the battle, with all in ruins about him, Saul killed himself.

4

ISRAEL-JUDAH

DAVID IN HEBRON

In 1000 B.C. the Philistines could look upon their corner of the world with satisfaction. To be sure, the battle of Gilboa had not entirely wiped out Israel. Saul's general, Abner, had managed to retreat with part of the army and had fled across the Jordan, taking with him Saul's one surviving son, Eshbaal (esh-bay′ul). Together they established themselves at Mahanaim (may″huh-nay′im), a city whose site is uncertain but which may have been located four miles east of Jabesh-gilead.

Though in this way Saul's dynasty survived, the kingdom of Eshbaal was weak indeed and was confined to the region east of the Jordan River where the Philistines could, for the time, ignore them. East of the Jordan were also located the kingdoms of Ammon and Moab, who could be counted to continue their hostility against Israel and neutralize any efforts it made to recover. Moab had already entirely absorbed the old Israelite tribe of Reuben, for instance.

As for David, he persuaded the elders of Judah to proclaim him king of Judah and he then proceeded to establish his capital in the strongly fortified town of Hebron, twenty miles southeast of the Philistine capital at Gath. This ought to have alarmed the Philistines, for it meant Judah was much stronger than it had been in the days before Saul, yet David's charm and smooth diplomacy apparently had the Philistines convinced he would continue a loyal puppet. Besides, the Philistines counted on eternal enmity between Israel and Judah — because of David's defection from Saul — and also on the help of the kingdom of Edom to the southeast of Judah. Edom was always hostile to Judah and would always remain so.

Nor did there seem any serious ground for Philistine unhappiness in the north. The Phoenician cities were there, rich and strong, but they were no danger. Their one interest was trade and if they had schemes for expansion it was always by sea. At no time in their history did they fight a nondefensive land war.

During the time of the Judges, the Phoenician leadership was moving away from Sidon. About twenty miles to the south of that city was the coastal city of Tyre. It may have been founded by colonists from Sidon about 1450 B.C. in the time of Thutmose III. Originally, it had been located on the mainland but its greatness came when it shifted to a rocky island offshore, making itself almost immune (as long as it retained its navy) from capture or even from starvation by siege. Its very name ("Zor" in Hebrew) means "rock."

By the time of Saul, Tyre had become the acknowledged leader among the Phoenician cities, and it was to retain that position as long as Phoenicia had an identity. The first important king of Tyre was Abibaal (a″bee-bay′ul), who came to the throne about 1020 B.C. at just about the time Saul became king of Israel. Under Abibaal Tyre began to extend its power, but seaward, always seaward — and never in any direction that might disturb Philistine designs on the interior.

To be sure, the Philistines might expect danger from the Arameans, another group of tribes of the sort endlessly spawned by the fecundity of the inhabitants of the dry Arabian peninsula. From 1100 B.C. they had been pressing against the Fertile Crescent, but the Assyrians, who now dominated the upper part of the Tigris-Euphrates, had strength enough to deal with them. Though the Arameans infiltrated both arches of the Fertile Crescent, the process was a slow one and not catastrophic. The Philistines did not have to be concerned. Yet in one place and one place only the Philistines misjudged, and that misjudgment was fatal. They paid insufficient attention to David.

David was thirty years old at the time of Saul's death, and he had ambitions. He knew what he wanted and he was absolutely ruthless about the means he would have to use. So far he had managed to make himself king of Judah and establish himself at a fortified capital while keeping the Philistines quiet. His next step was to become king of Israel as well and succeed to Saul's power in full, but that would not be easy to bring about.

Even if he could defeat the rump state of Israel under Eshbaal and the capable Abner in straightforward battle, such an ostentatious victory would surely arouse Philistine suspicions. No, David's goals had to be achieved peacefully, one step at a time, with no one step sufficient to disturb the Philistines — at least until David was strong enough to deal with them. Fortunately for David, Eshbaal quarreled with his general, Abner, over a woman, and Abner was sufficiently angered to decide upon treason, so he opened negotiations with David. (The Bible doesn't say, but one can't help but wonder if David's hand were not somehow behind that quarrel.)

But David had a little harem business of his own. In the days when he was in favor at Saul's court, he had received Saul's daughter Michal (my′kul) in marriage. She had been taken back after David had fled the court a fugitive and outlaw. Now, however, David was king of Judah and he would not treat with Abner unless the Israelite general somehow delivered Michal back to him. The reason for that is plain. As long as David had Michal as his wife, he was son-in-law to the dead King Saul, and as son-in-law he could make a legitimate claim to the Israelite throne.

Abner delivered Michal and then signed an alliance with David, bringing over, presumably, portions of the Israelite army with him to the immense weakening of Eshbaal. That done, David took care to make it impossible for Abner, who had proven a traitor to his king once, to try his hand at it a second time. David's own general and trouble-shooter, Joab (joh′ab), managed to slip a knife into Abner after approaching him in all apparent friendliness. To be sure, David expressed his contrition over the death loudly and publicly — for he did not wish to lose the services of Abner's soldiers or alienate the Israelites generally — but Joab remained in David's service.

It was clear that David's position was strengthening and if it came to war with Israel now, David would surely win (supposing the Philistines allowed it). But it didn't come to war. Things continued to break well for the Judean king, for two officers of Eshbaal's household assassinated the Israelite king and brought his head to David. We might wonder whether this was brought about by bribes and subtle temptations on the part of David's agents, but we will have to keep on wondering. David himself labored to nip such suspicions by once again expressing loud and public revulsion at an act of assassination. This time, moreover, he ordered the instant execution of the assassins. Not only would this please those Israelites who would resent the murder of their king, but it would also keep the assassins from making any inconvenient revelations.

The Israelites were now without a king. They needed a leader in these dark days and who could it be but this confident king of Judah for whom everything seemed to break right, who was, after all, the son-in-law of Saul, and who seemed to be able to handle the Philistines. He was the natural candidate for the job.

The Israelite elders could not have enjoyed having to approach a Judean, but they did. Humbly, they came to Hebron, where David, in full majesty, granted them audience. Humbly, they asked David to rule over them and David granted their request. In 991 B.C. he became king of Israel as well as of Judah.

DAVID IN JERUSALEM

The united kingdom over which David thus came to rule is called simply Israel in the Bible, but the kingdom was never truly united. Israel, the northern two-thirds, was always conscious of its greater sophistication, urbanization, size, and wealth, as compared with rustic Judah, and for it to be ruled by a Judean dynasty was a humiliation. Its every action in later years showed this to be so, and it might be best to express this imperfect amalgamation of the two parts of David's nation by calling it Israel-Judah.

David was aware of the difficulties of keeping the two nations together and he labored to devise methods of unification. It seemed to him he could scarcely keep his capital at Hebron, for the presence of the court in that Judean city would make it continually apparent to the Israelites that they were being ruled by a foreign king.

His eye therefore fell on the city of Jerusalem, which qualified as his capital for a number of reasons. For one thing, it was located squarely on the boundary of Israel and Judah, and belonged to neither. Ever since the entry of the Israelites into

Canaan two centuries before, Jerusalem had remained firmly in the hands of the Jebusites, a Canaanite tribe. They were still there and, on their nearly impregnable rock, they resisted capture by Israelites, Judeans, and Philistines with impartial ease. Precisely because it was such a strong position, it would make a good capital.

But how was one to take Jerusalem? The confident Jebusites were sure they could resist David as they had resisted enemies in the past. Yet David managed to take the city. Exactly how is uncertain, for on this point the Biblical verses seem garbled. He may have sent a contingent of men through a tunnel used for a water supply which the careless Jebusites had left unguarded.

In any case, Jerusalem fell and was at once made the capital of David's kingdom. It was to remain the capital of his descendants for centuries to come, and to be the very focal point of the Jewish people forever after. It is, indeed, a holy city today to three major religions.

Why the Philistines had held off this long is uncertain. The Bible doesn't tell us. Presumably, David, a past master at smooth diplomacy, kept them mollified through all the years in which he intrigued for possession of the Israelite throne. Even when he gained the rule over Israel-Judah, he must have managed to convince the Philistines that he was still their loyal ally.

Once he took Jerusalem, however, the pretense had to end. He had become a conqueror and, with the possession of the strongest position in all the Canaanitish interior, he was too strong to make his protestations of loyalty believable. No doubt the Philistines ordered him to give up Jerusalem as an earnest of his fidelity to them, and no doubt David, coming to the parting of the way at last, refused. That meant war.

For the Philistines, though, it was too late. They ought to have struck before David had Jerusalem. Now he was the head of a nation he had filled with pride. What's more, he had an army led by the daring skill of Joab and the other generals he had trained. In two separate battles south of Jerusalem, David defeated the Philistines. The erstwhile puppet had become a conqueror indeed and the Philistine dream of empire came to a sudden and permanent end. Beaten, they fell back on their cities, from which they were never again to emerge with any notions of conquest.

It was another mark of David's strategy that he never attempted more than he thought he could carry out. He did not try to take the Philistine cities themselves. That would undoubtedly have required a price out of proportion of the value of the prize. It was better to leave the Philistines in peace and with a certain amount of self-rule. They were then content to acknowledge David's sovereignty, to pay tribute, and even to furnish loyal contingents to the king's personal guard.

Now that David had his capital and had defeated the Philistines, he pondered on the next move to unite his double kingdom. There had to be centralized worship in the capital. Since the destruction of Shiloh by the Philistines a half-century before, the tribes had no central shrine. This was far from saying that they had no religion. Every community had its local spot, its sacred hill, or its sacred grove, where the necessary rituals designed to bring fertility to the lands and herds, and security to the people, were carried out. Such religious decentralization, however, was dangerous in the highest degree. It was impossible to rally the people to a do-or-die defense of the land, if they were chiefly concerned in protecting the local shrine.

As it happened, although Shiloh was destroyed, the ark of the covenant — the holiest of the holy — still existed. It was at Kirjath-jearim, where it had been brought after the disastrous Israelite defeat at Aphek. David might have earned Israelite gratitude if he had rebuilt Shiloh and restored the ark, but that was not his purpose. He wanted to drown Israelite and Judean self-awareness in their mutual acceptance of a higher nationalism. He therefore brought the ark to Jerusalem and housed it in a shrine built near the palace. He himself offered sacrifices and prayers and led the ritual dancing, thus taking up the post of priest-king.

To be sure, he appointed a high priest as the supreme religious figure of the nation who might spend full time at taking care of ritual, but he was careful to appoint one on whose loyalty and subservience he could count. This was Abiathar (uh-by'uh-thahr), who had been the sole survivor of the slaughter of the priests at Nob by Saul. Thereafter, Abiathar had been heart and soul with David.

With his nation knit together, politically and religiously, David felt able to embark on a program of naked imperialism. Not only would this serve to strength the kingdom but it would make Israelites and Judeans, together, a ruling people and give them a common feeling of victory. One after the other, he took the kingdoms at the rim of Canaan — Ammon, Moab, and Edom.

He turned northward, too. The Arameans had by now settled various areas north of Israel and had even established small kingdoms. These David conquered, extending his rule eventually as far as the upper Euphrates, at least in the sense that the northerners paid him tribute.

David did not attempt to try military conclusions with the Phoenician cities. Without a navy he would not have succeeded. Again he had the intelligence to gain his ends without trying his strength too far. It was enough to sign a treaty of alliance with the Phoenicians and to gain their friendship by offering them the opportunity for lucrative trade.

In the end, then, David, who had started as a fugitive and outlaw, was master of the entire western half of the Fertile Crescent. For the second time (the Hyksos Empire, five centuries before, had been the first time) all the western half was under unified native rule.

This Davidic Empire was quite respectable in size. At its peak it had an area of perhaps 45,000 square miles, six times that of Saul's kingdom and equal to the area of the state of New York. Its strength, however, was not to be compared with that of the Egyptian Empire at its height or the various empires of the Tigris-Euphrates at their height.

Indeed, that the Davidic Empire could exist at all was entirely due to the fortunate accident that in David's lifetime, the lands of the Nile Valley and of the Tigris-Euphrates happened both to be swamped in anarchy and weakness. This was a rare situation, indeed. Throughout the history of civilization it was almost always true, both before David's time and after, that when the Nile was weak the Tigris-Euphrates was strong and vice versa, and that whichever was strong dominated the western half of the Fertile Crescent.

It was David's fortune to be on the spot on the rare occasion of this double weakness. One can only wonder, though, what a man of David's ability might have performed if he had had behind him not the small base of Judea at the feeble end of the Crescent, but instead the Egyptian or the Assyrian Empire in its prime.

David's reign was sufficiently triumphant to make it seem a golden age to the men of later generations. Through all the disasters to come, the memory of David buoyed them up and gave them a persistent hope that such days would come again.

The boundaries of David's empire seemed to be the "natural limits" of the Israelite-Judean dominion, and when, in later centuries, the ancient traditions came to be written down, the land stated as having been promised by God to the descendants of Abraham was that of the Davidic Empire. The words of the promise are given as "Unto thy seed have I given this land, from the river of Egypt unto the great river, the river Euphrates" (Genesis 15:18) — but it was only in the time of David and of his son that this promise was really fulfilled.

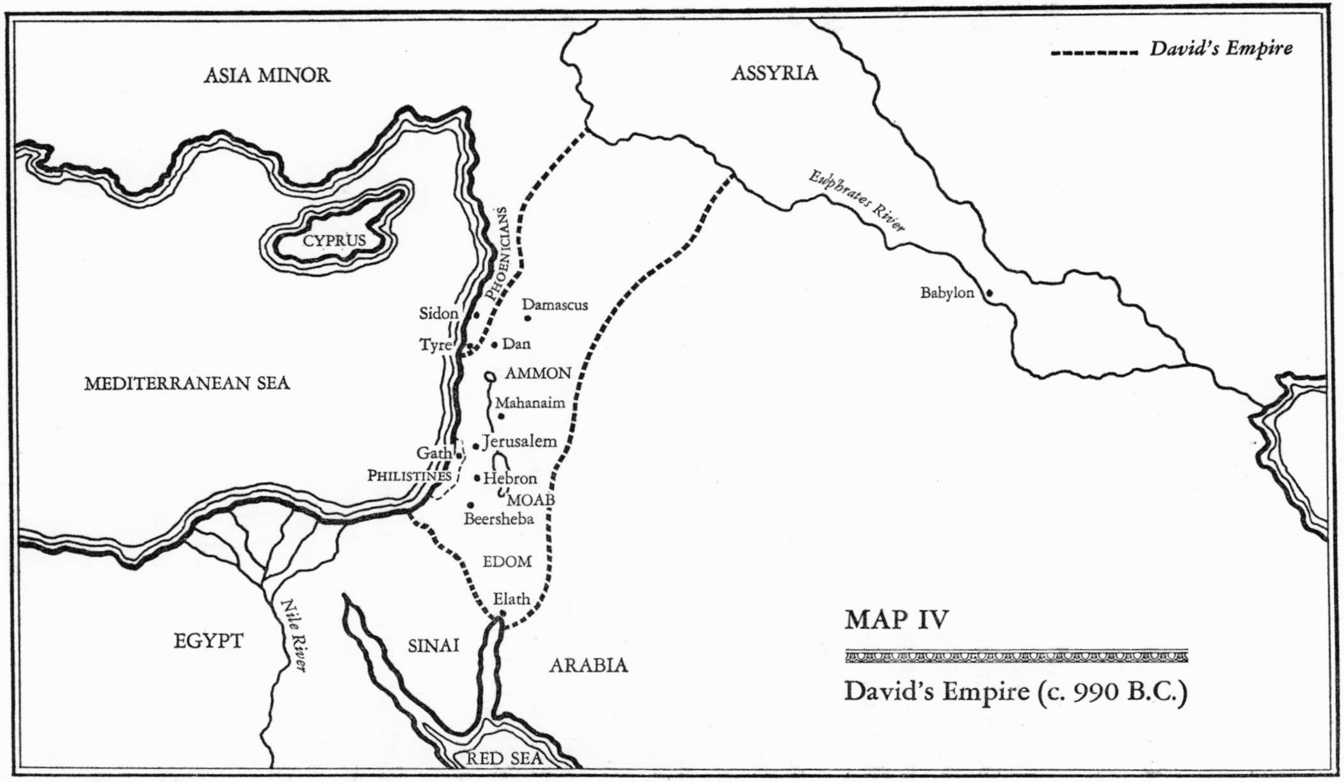
David's Empire
ASIA MINOR
ASSYRIA
CYPRUS
PHOENICIANS
Euphrates River
Babylon
Sidon
Damascus
Tyre
Dan
AMMON
MEDITERRANEAN SEA
Mahanaim
Jerusalem
Gath
PHILISTINES
Hebron
MOAB
Beersheba
EDOM
Elath
Nile River
EGYPT
SINAI
ARABIA
RED SEA
MAP IV
David's Empire (c. 990 B.C.)

DAVID'S SONS

Even after the empire was established, David was not free from care. The problem that most exercised him in his later years was that of the succession. In the first place, he naturally wanted it to remain among his own descendants, and that raised the question of the house of Saul, which still retained a lingering loyalty on the part of many Israelites.

David was prepared to be ruthless here. Those male descendants of Saul whom he could find he managed to execute on some pretext, and in the end he left only one alive. This was a crippled son of Jonathan, who could not succeed to the throne in view of his infirmity but whom David kept under virtual house arrest in Jerusalem. He found it more difficult to manage his own children, who were numerous.

It was a custom for Asian monarchs to accumulate a harem. This was not entirely a matter of lust (though few men would object to being in the position of having many women available). A harem helped give the impression of magnificence that kept the subjects of the king, and foreigners, too, in awe. Furthermore, an established way of honoring a family or a tribe or of sealing a treaty was to take a girl of the family, tribe, or foreign royal family into the harem. It was considered an honor.

The bad point of this was that different wives were out of sympathy with each other and each would naturally intrigue for the succession of her own son. This creates a kind of internal politics that often works to the disadvantage of the nation. What's more, as the king grows old in any monarchy where the harem system prevails, the tension among the sons increases. Once the king dies it is quite usual for the son who manages to secure the crown to kill the rest in order to prevent attempts at usurpation and rebellion. There is the strong temptation, then, to forestall matters by seizing the throne while the old man is still alive and while the other sons are still waiting — and are unprepared.

David's favorite son was Absalom (ab′suh-lom) and it was he who struck. Handsome and charming, he gradually built up a party favoring himself over his father (playing the role which Saul had feared Jonathan would play). When Absalom struck, David was caught entirely by surprise. To avoid being trapped in the capital and undergoing the humiliation of a siege that might continue for months, David scrambled out of the city with his household troops, including the loyal Philistine contingent. East of the Jordan he organized his men, rallied his loyal confederates, and then, with the lightning surety of old, he struck back across the Jordan. Absalom's hastily raised and poorly led levies were no match for David's experienced troops. Absalom was taken, and although David ordered him to be kept alive, the practical and pitiless Joab killed him.

David was careful to avoid retaliating harshly after the rebellion, yet this did not really help. The revolt of Absalom and the flight of David had raised hopes in the hearts of those Israelites who still viewed David as a foreign ruler and, particularly, in the men of Benjamin, the tribe of Saul.

Even though Absalom was defeated, it seemed that David's throne had been shaken and that a rebellion, striking in the immediate aftermath of the short civil war, might succeed. Under the leadership of Sheba, a Benjamite, Israel rose. But David struck at once, and almost as rapidly as the rebels sprang to action, they were crushed again. Still, the fact that there had been a rebellion at all demonstrated that despite all of David's far-sighted measures he had not succeeded in totally destroying the national consciousness of the Israelite tribes. That could not be done in a single generation by no matter how wise a ruler. If it were to be done, much would depend on the wisdom of David's successors — and, alas, they were to be found wanting.

In 961 B.C. David lay dying. He had ruled for forty years and his heroic life was coming to an end. His apparent successor was Adonijah (ad″oh-ny′jah), his eldest surviving son who, like his brother Absalom, was charming and popular. Moreover, Adonijah had the backing of Joab, the general of the armies, and Abiathar, the high priest. So certain was Adonijah of his position that he held what amounted to a victory feast, even while David was yet alive.

It was too soon, however. David had a favorite wife, Bathsheba (bath-shee′buh), and she managed to persuade the dying king to name her son Solomon as the successor. The king's voice prevailed and it was Solomon who was crowned. Adonijah and Joab were, in time, executed, and Abiathar was sent into obscurity. Taking Abiathar's place as high priest was Zadok (zay′dok). The high priesthood was to remain in his family for seven and a half centuries.

SOLOMON

Solomon, the son of David and the second king of Israel-Judah, has an unshakable reputation for wisdom, chiefly because the Bible says he was wise. Undoubtedly his reign was a time of peace and prosperity for the kingdom, since Solomon reaped the fruit for which David had labored a harrowing lifetime. Nevertheless, it can be argued that Solomon's wisdom was more in appearance than in reality, for the seeds of disaster were sown in his reign.

In one respect, Solomon *was* wise; he eschewed any thought of further conquest. He was satisfied with the size of the empire bequeathed him by his father. In this way he avoided the terrible and destructive strain that wars would have placed upon the land.

On the other hand, Solomon labored to raise his kingdom to a peak of magnificence, to make of it a world power on a par in civilization with the great cultures of the Nile and the Tigris-Euphrates. But this involved a strain almost as great as war would have been. The western portion of the Fertile Crescent simply lacked the base for munificence that the great river valleys offered, and though Solomon spared no pains, he brought his kingdom eventual ruin as the price for temporary splendor.

Solomon's attempt to make Israel-Judah into a full-fledged eastern monarchy included the establishment of a harem even larger than that of his father, since the power and glory of a king was measured, in part, by the size and elaborateness of his harem. The Bible is careful to mention the king's thousand wives and concubines. It is a sign of Israel-Judah's place in the world that included in the harem was a daughter of the Egyptian pharaoh.

And yet, perhaps, the relationship with Egypt was not as important as it sounded (though the Bible makes a point of it). If we think of Egypt's great days, then marrying into the exclusive pharaonic family would have been a rare honor indeed. Egypt had, however, drifted far downhill since the reign of Rameses III, two and a half centuries before. A long line of feeble do-nothings had been on the throne and in Solomon's time the land was in fragments. There was a king named Psusennes II (soo-sen′eez) who ruled over the Nile Delta only and commanded a kingdom smaller than that of Solomon. It was he who made an alliance with Solomon and handed over a daughter to seal his bargain. Undoubtedly, it was Psusennes II who sought and received Solomon's help, rather than vice versa, and the move worked, for the Egyptian kept his throne for well over thirty years, almost to the end of Solomon's reign.

Inside his kingdom Solomon undertook a vast building program. His father, David, had brought the ark of the covenant into Jerusalem and had established a central Yahvist shrine, one that honored the national god, Yahveh. To a certain extent, it served as a focal point that united all the tribes about a common worship, but Sheba's rebellion had proved it didn't work perfectly.

Solomon may well have felt that it would work better if the shrine were made more impressive. Besides, a capital city without a large and beautiful temple would have seemed a rustic and backward town indeed. Solomon therefore set to work at the very beginning of his reign to build a temple after the style common throughout Canaan, except that it was to have the ark as its central object of veneration, rather than the usual idol. For the purpose he made use of Canaanite architects obtained from the city of Tyre. The project took seven years and was finished and dedicated in 954 B.C. It was to serve as the center of Yahvist worship for nearly four centuries.

Solomon, having built a house for the Lord, also built a house for himself, and although the Bible spends a great deal of time describing the Temple, Solomon's palace was the more magnificent of the two buildings and took a much longer time to build.

Nor was the Temple the only house of worship that Solomon built. He recognized the fact that it would only serve the Yahvists among his subjects and that there were many subject peoples who were not Yahvists. The Moabites and Ammonites, for instance, had their own national gods. Solomon, who considered himself king of Moab and of Ammon as well as of Israel and of Judah, built temples in Jerusalem to the national gods of Moab and Ammon, too. He also let his foreign wives worship in their own fashion.

This was in accord with the customs of the time, when religious toleration was the norm. People generally assumed that everyone had the right to his own god; that all the gods existed, each for his own people. To be sure, the Yahvist Temple in Jerusalem was the largest and best and Yahvism took precedence over the other cults, but that was only right, since Israel and Judah, the lands peculiar to Yahveh, were the ruling part of the kingdom.

The later editors of the Biblical books, however, viewed the matter from the standpoint of their own period and at a different stage in the development of religion. They were shocked and embarrassed that Solomon had built temples to idols and denounced him for it. They traced the later troubles of the kingdom to this fact, though modern historians are apt to find more ordinary reasons.

While Israel-Judah was experiencing prosperity under Solomon, Phoenicia was going through a similar happy period. In 969 B.C. Abibaal of Tyre had died and was succeeded by his son Hiram. Hiram fortified and beautified the rock upon which the city was built. He maintained the alliance first with David, then with Solomon, and sent skilled architects to supervise the building of the Temple in Jerusalem.

Because he was completely secure on the landward side and because he had a sure customer in Solomon and his large kingdom, Hiram could concentrate on the sea. Under him Tyre and the Phoenicians generally began an extraordinary expansion of trade.

The Phoenicians had, of course, been a seagoing people for centuries and had sailed the sea as early as 2000 B.C. Their exploits as traders and pirates are mentioned in Egyptian romances written about 1100 B.C. and in Homer's poems written a couple of centuries later.

Still, their trading ventures in very early times had been rather limited. During the period of Egypt's greatness, when the Phoenician cities were young, the island of Crete, which had profited from Phoenician influence, had been the center of a great naval power that had dominated the eastern Mediterranean.

Crete collapsed in 1400 B.C. after a long, slow decline. The final blow seems to have been a tsunami, or huge wave, that battered its shores after the volcanic explosion of an Aegean island. The Mycenean Greeks took over and then there followed the turbulent period of the Sea Peoples.

In Hiram's time, however, the Mediterranean presented an unusual situation. The Egyptians had been in decline for three centuries and their role in the Mediterranean was nil. Crete and the Greek mainland were in the midst of a dark age following the Dorian invasion and Greek shipping had faded away. Indeed along the entire shore of the Mediterranean Sea, the *only* flourishing power was Israel-Judah, and that was entirely a land empire.

This was the great Phoenician opportunity. Their ships began to creep outward into the sea vacuum. They established bases on the nearby shores, notably on the east-Mediterranean island of Cyprus. They even had a base in Egypt, establishing a Phoenician quarter in the great city of Memphis from which they controlled the commerce of decaying Egypt.

More than that, they ventured westward into the dimly mysterious western regions of the Mediterranean. (It was at about this time that the Greek tales of the wanderings of the hero Odysseus were being composed and recited, and his adventures with giants and cannibals, preserved today in the *Odyssey*, take place in the mysterious west.)

It is possible that the Phoenicians were helped in their explorations by a notable advance in technology. The open sea lacks landmarks to guide the traveler for, as the word itself indicates, these are restricted to land. The stars in the sky might be landmarks if they did not steadily turn. They turn about a hub in the sky, however, and near that hub is the bright star Polaris, the one star that scarcely changes position at any time. It is possible that the Phoenicians were the first to learn to use Polaris as a "landmark" at sea and that it was this that opened the western Mediterranean to them.

According to tradition, the first city to be founded by Tyre in the western Mediterranean was Utica. This was founded on that portion of the African coast which is just southwest of the island of Sicily. The "wasp waist" of the Mediterranean Sea is located there, for a passage only ninety miles wide separates the western portion of the sea from the eastern.

Tradition places the founding of Utica very early, making it 1101 B.C. or even 1140 B.C. This, however, is almost certainly too early. (Ancient cities were only too apt to push back the date of their founding to give themselves the added prestige of age over their neighbors.) Very likely, Utica was founded during the reign of Hiram.

Tyre was driven on in its explorations by the fact that it was handling the trade of Solomon's kingdom. According to the Bible, it supplied two fleets for Solomon, one in the Mediterranean and one in the Red Sea. The Mediterranean fleet reached as far as Tharshish, a place whose location is mysterious, but which may have been in Spain.

Spain was at the extreme western end of the sea and the Tyrian sailors reached it soon after they penetrated past the wasp waist. Spain turned out to be a land rich in minerals, and by establishing smelters in the land and bringing back metals, Tyre further enriched itself.

The narrow Strait of Gibraltar marks the end of the Mediterranean, and the Phoenicians passed through into the Atlantic Ocean itself. There at the mouth of the Guadalquivir River, they founded the city of Tartessus (tahr-tes′us), which may possibly be the Biblical Tharshish. A few miles further south along the coast they founded Gadez (gay′deez), which still exists today under the scarcely changed name of Cadiz, one of the great seaports of Spain.

The second Phoenician fleet serving Solomon was based on Elath (ee′lath), on the northern tip of the Red Sea. This fleet traded with Ophir (oh′fer), a land described in the Bible as rich in gold, but whose location is unknown. Usually, it is suggested that Ophir was located at the southwestern corner of the

Arabian peninsula, where modern Yemen is to be found, though a few think the ships may have rounded Arabia and reached India. (Southern Arabia was prosperous in ancient times, and Solomon's trade with the region, and the arrival of trade missions in Jerusalem, probably gave rise to the legendary accounts of the visit of the Queen of Sheba.)

Solomon's trading policies enriched the land and Solomon used this wealth to build up still further the panoply of monarchy. He greatly increased the standing army and equipped it with chariots. He bought horses from Asia Minor to use with those chariots and established large stables to house them.

But once a policy of magnificence is embarked upon, it almost always exceeds the supply of ready money, however great that might be. Solomon found he had to increase the level of taxation and the efficiency with which those taxes would be gathered.

To improve the internal economy of the nation, Solomon centralized the government. He divided Israel into twelve districts which ignored the previous tribal boundaries and placed each under governors responsible to himself. This was a deliberate attempt to break down regionalism and tribal patriotism and it worked, for after Solomon's time we hear very little about the tribes of Israel. What's more, Solomon's administrative division made no distinctions between Israelites and Canaanites, and after his time we hear no more of the Canaanites in the interior. Only the Phoenicians on the coast remained.

This was useful as far as it went and undoubtedly increased the efficiency of government. Nothing, however, can make taxation or forced labor on building projects popular, and while Solomon managed to keep his kingdom reasonably intact, discontent rose to the boiling point.

There was guerrilla activity against the central government in Edom to the south of Judah, for instance. There Hadad (har′dad), a member of the old Edomite royal house, served as the center about which resistance rallied. In the north the

Aramean* city-states rumbled and a man named Rezon (ree′zon) came to power in the city of Damascus, 140 miles north of Jerusalem. There he made himself virtually independent.

Solomon's worst error lay in dividing only Israel for purposes of more efficient taxation and forced labor. He omitted Judah, which made it seem the imperial power, free of taxation, while Israel was as much subject to it as Moab and Ammon. Naturally, all Israel must have seethed with resentment.

The resentment had a religious basis as well. The establishment of a temple at Jerusalem with the ark of the covenant within must have horrified some of the conservatives in the north. The prophetic orders who had followed Samuel a century earlier must still have thought of Shiloh as the real center of Yahvism in Israel.

Matters came to a crisis in 930 B.C. At the head of the gangs of forced labor engaged in repair work and building activities was Jeroboam (jer″oh-boh′am), an Ephraimite. It is usually good policy to have labor gangs under the control of someone of their own group, but sometimes it backfires. Jeroboam fell under the influence of Ahijah (uh-hy′juh), a leader of the prophetic party that favored Shiloh as the center. Jeroboam therefore rose in revolt. As before, the Israelite revolt was put down, but it had received considerable popular support throughout Israel and Jeroboam's defeat had not removed the causes of discontent.

The situation took a turn for the worse in Egypt, too. There, Psusennes II, Solomon's father-in-law, had died in 935 and the Delta had been taken over by a Libyan general, Sheshonk I

* The later Greeks first encountered the Aramean tribes in the north, near Asia Minor. There they traded with a tribe that called itself Syri. As a result the Greeks called the Arameans Syrians, and the land they occupied — the northern two thirds of the western portion of the Fertile Crescent — Syria. I will do the same; so from now on when I say "Syria" I will mean the kingdom ruled from Damascus and, more generally, the region from Damascus northward to Asia Minor.

(shee′shonk). He felt it in his interest to promote any weakening of the power of the kingdom to his northeast. He offered refuge, therefore, for any rebel against Solomon. Jeroboam fled to Egypt and so did Hadad of Edom. There they could wait for the first good opportunity to return to Israel-Judah and promote its breakup.

Usually a good opportunity arises when an old king dies and a new one must establish his power during a period of uncertainty. In 922 B.C. Solomon died and succeeding to his throne was his son Rehoboam (ree″oh-boh′am).

5

ISRAEL AND JUDAH

THE TWO KINGDOMS

Rehoboam had no trouble whatever in going through the necessary ritual to become king of Judah. In order to be accepted as king of Israel as well, however, it was necessary for him to be crowned with the proper rites at Shechem, the onetime political center of Ephraim.

The Israelite leaders attempted to use the occasion to bargain for concessions, and demanded that the tax load be lightened. To this Rehoboam returned a contemptuous refusal and Israel burst into spontaneous flame. Undoubtedly this was encouraged by Sheshonk I of Egypt, who may have contributed financial help, and who certainly sped the exiled Jeroboam back to Israel.

This third attempt on the part of Israel to regain its independence by force succeeded. The ties between Israel and Judah, never strong at best, lasted only seventy years before snapping. When that took place, the outlying portions fell off almost at once. Where the united kingdom of Israel-Judah could control all the western half of the Fertile Crescent, Israel and Judah separately could hold very little. The Syrian kingdom with its capital at Damascus became fully independent and gradually brought a large area north of Israel under its sway. East of Israel, Ammon was independent again, and if Moab remained subject to Israel it was just barely. As for Judah, all it retained of David's conquests was Edom. The empire had ended. It was never really to return.

The two separate portions of what had been very nearly a great power soon learned the penalty of weakness. Sheshonk I (called Shishak in the Bible) invaded both Judah and Israel. He was the ruler of a feeble kingdom confined to the Nile Delta and would not have dared attack either David or Solomon. Now, however, with insulting ease, he sent his armies through both parts of the divided land. He even took Jerusalem and looted the Temple of the wealth accumulated there by Solomon.

Despite the disasters of the civil war, the empire's disruption, and Sheshonk's raid, the southern kingdom of Judah had certain advantages which were to stand it in good stead. It had the tradition of the glorious reigns of David and Solomon to fall back on — a memory that never faded — and its king was actually a grandson of David. What's more, Jerusalem remained the capital of Judah (together with the territory of what had once made up the small tribe of Benjamin just to the north of the capital) and in that city was the great Temple that Solomon had built.

The northern kingdom, however — Israel — had no immediate glories in its past. It had the memory of the disastrous reign of Saul and seventy years of subjection to the smaller and weaker Judah. It had no natural center, for Shiloh was destroyed and what had once been Saul's capital was now actually part of Judah.

Israel chose Jeroboam as its king and he established his capital at Shechem. This was natural, for he was an Ephraimite and Shechem was the old Ephraimite capital. However, the days of Ephraim's glory were too long past and it was not long before he moved to Tirzah (tur′zuh), eight miles to the north, which was more centrally located. Then, too, just as David had striven for a capital that would not make Judean domination too obvious, Jeroboam had to avoid the appearance of Ephraimite domination.

It was also necessary for Jeroboam to establish a religious center for the new kingdom. The natural step might have been to rebuild Shiloh and restore it to what it had been. Again Jeroboam avoided the appearance of Ephraimite domination and did not do this. In fact, he may have been concerned to weaken the prophetic party which had helped bring him to power and to avoid, therefore, any centralized worship. He founded two cult centers, one at the extreme south of the kingdom, at Bethel, only ten miles north of Jerusalem, the other at the extreme north of the kingdom, at Dan. Within each cult center he placed the figure of a young bull (a common fertility symbol and one particularly associated with the tribe of Ephraim).

The prophetic party was horrified by these innovations and moved into the opposition. For most of the existence of Israel there persisted the hostility between the crown and the prophetic party that now began, and this was a persistent source of weakness.

During the next couple of centuries the priesthood, both in Israel and Judah, collected the traditions of earlier times and put them into writing. The tales of the northern kingdom used "Elohim" as the name of the deity and these tales made up what is now called the E Document. The tales of the southern kingdom used "Yahveh" (or "Jahweh" in the German spelling) for the name and is called the J Document. The two initials are more convenient than they seem at first, since they also stand for Ephraim and Judah, which may be viewed as the geographical sources. In essence both deal with the same traditions—traditions which received their main form, no doubt, in the time of the empire of Israel-Judah, when David and Solomon labored to establish a common traditional history.

There were vague legends of man's creation and of his early history; of a huge flood and what followed—legends common throughout the Near East and based on Sumerian chronicles. There followed the tales of the patriarchs, Abraham, Isaac, and Jacob; of their very early stay in Canaan and of their title to the land as received from God himself. There was the story of Jacob's twelve sons—representing the ten tribes of the Israelite confederacy plus Judah and its subsidiary sister tribe of Simeon; of the sale of one of those sons, Joseph—the father of Ephraim and Manasseh—into Egypt; of slavery in Egypt and rescue by the lawgiver Moses; of wanderings through the desert and the final conquest of Canaan under Joshua.

The E and J documents differed in details and in style, but we don't possess either in the original. What makes up the first six books of the Bible is a combined and edited version of the two to which still other material has been added.

This common heritage—admitted to by both nations—and, to a certain extent, common religion—though the northern rites were more affected by Canaanite ways and the southern rites remained more primitive and simpler—did not prevent war from being the normal state of affairs between the two kingdoms. The war between Israel and Judah smoldered onward indefinitely and was a source of weakness for each.

Rehoboam of Judah died in 915 B.C., having reigned only seven years, and was succeeded by his son Abijah (uh-by'jah), who, after a two-year, thoroughly undistinguished reign, was succeeded in 913 B.C. by his son Asa (ay'suh). Asa was probably quite young when he was crowned and was to reign forty years.

The kingdom of Judah thus remained under the Davidic dynasty and indeed, with Asa (the fifth king), son had succeeded father for the fourth time. This record was to continue for over three centuries more and it is part of the success of David and of the strong hold his feats held on the imagination of the Judeans that through all the history of the kingdom there was never a popular rising against the dynasty.

Indeed, the constancy of the dynasty, the gradually growing feeling that it was an eternal fact of life, was the great strength of the small kingdom of Judah, the rock around which it held together. Even after the kingdom was destroyed, the memory of the dynasty was the central fact for the survivors — that, and the memory of Jerusalem and its Temple.

SAMARIA

Israel had no such fortune. Though stronger and richer than Judah, it somehow remained rootless. It never even developed a royal house about which it could truly rally.

When Jeroboam died in 901 B.C., his son Nadab (nay′dab) succeeded, but succumbed almost at once to an army coup. An Israelite general, Baasha (bay′uh-shuh), rose in revolt, seized Nadab, and had him and the remaining members of the house of Jeroboam slaughtered. This was in 900 B.C., so that Israel's first dynasty after its revolt from Judah had endured a bare twenty-two years.

Baasha now had the problem of establishing himself on the throne he had seized, and he chose the method of facing his people with an external war and asking them, so to speak, to rally around the flag. He reactivated the war with Judah, which had never quite ended but which was at a slow simmer about then.

Asa of Judah, finding himself under strong attack, looked for help abroad. When two neighboring nations are enemies, the natural ally of either is the nation on the other side of the enemy. Judah, to the south of Israel, naturally sought for help in the kingdom of Syria to the north of Israel. Benhadad I (ben″hay′dad) was now king of Damascus, and under him what had begun as a bare city-state in the last years of Solomon had become a nation as large as Israel. It was to Benhadad that Asa now sent gifts with a plea that he attack Israel.

Benhadad I was glad to oblige, and thus began a century and a half of chronic conflict between the two nations. In 878 B.C. as the first campaign of that conflict, the Syrian army drove southward, reaching the Sea of Galilee and annexing its eastern shores. One of the incidents of this invasion was the sacking and the destruction of the city of Dan. That city was apparently destroyed permanently, for it is mentioned no further in the Bible or in any other chronicle.

Baasha of Israel, in danger in the north, was forced to make peace with Judah. It was undoubtedly due to the continuing strength of Syria on Israel's northern flank that Judah to the south was able to retain its national identity.

The only other notable incident of Asa's reign in Judah was the repulse of an Egyptian raid. The son of Sheshonk, Osorkon I (oh-sawr′kon), was now in control of the Nile Delta and he sent an armed detachment under a Nubian (Ethiopian) officer against Judah. The memory of the repulse of this raid was magnified, five centuries later, by the writer of the Book of Chronicles in the Bible, as a major defeat of a million men, no less.

Since Baasha's war was a failure, the hoped-for result of establishing his dynasty on the rock of a glorious military conquest (as David had) went glimmering. While he was alive, he held on to the throne of Israel, but he died in 877 B.C. In 876 B.C. there was civil war and Baasha's son Elah was deposed and executed. Baasha's dynasty was ended after twenty-four years.

A short period of chaos followed, but before the year was out the capable general Omri (om′righ) was on the throne to establish Israel's third dynasty. Omri was a strong king who managed to hold off the Syrians and to strengthen his own grip on Moab. He recognized that one important weakness of Israel was its lack of an easily defensible capital. An invasion by an outer force, however strong, could not really succeed if the defenders had some stronghold into which they could retreat for an indefinite period. Judah had that in Jerusalem, but Israel had nothing comparable. Tirzah was inadequate and had, besides, been fouled by the occurrence of two successful army coups in the space of a quarter-century.

Omri's keen eye noted a hill eight miles west of Tirzah. It had a strategic position, being centrally located halfway between the Jordan and the Mediterranean, and it was excellently suited for defense. It was owned by the family of Shemer, but Omri bought it and on it built fortifications that developed into his capital and the largest city in Israel. He named it Shomron, from the name of the original owners, but to the later Greeks and, therefore, to us, it was known as Samaria.

The move was a complete success. Samaria remained the capital of Israel for the remainder of that nation's existence and Omri's deeds so caught the imagination of surrounding nations that Israel was called "the land of Omri" in the Assyrian chronicles, even after Omri's dynasty ceased to rule over the land. (We hear little about him in the Bible, however, because the Biblical historians were interested in religious rather than secular developments.)

To strengthen his kingdom Omri needed more than an efficient army and a strong capital. He needed a state cult of some sort. Judah had one, for instance. The primitive Yahvism of the days of the Judges had been developed under David and Solomon into a colorful religion centered about the elaborate Temple of Solomon in Jerusalem. The Yahvism thus elaborated held the emotions of the people and thus it effectively supported the king. There were few army coups in Judah, where

Asa and, later, his son Jehoshaphat (jee-hosh′uh-fat) together reigned for sixty-four years. They, in turn, strongly supported Yahvism.

To Omri, however, Yahvism did not seem proper. In Israel there was nothing like the Temple at Jerusalem. Besides, the traditions developed by David and Solomon — a dynasty foreign to the Israelites — could be little regarded. To be sure, Jeroboam had made use of some of the language of Yahvism in setting up the cult centers at Bethel and Dan, but it was the earlier Yahvism antedating David, and its influence was not powerful.

There were Yahvists in Israel, of course. The prophetic party that traced its traditions back to Shiloh and Samuel were Yahvistic, but they represented a minority of the population and almost never dominated the government. The kings of Israel distrusted Yahvism because, perhaps, they felt that through it, Judean domination might be reinstated. They sought avidly for some state religion that would unite the nation and give it a sense of self.

It is not easy. One cannot simply invent a religion and have it vital. It is easier and more effective to adopt or adapt some religion which is already popular with the people, if one can be found. Yahvism was out, as it was the religion of Israel's enemy Judah. The Syrian cults were out for similar reasons. That left Phoenicia. The Phoenician cities had a tradition of friendship with Israel that dated back to David's time over a century earlier. It had even survived the end of Hiram's dynasty.

After the death of Hiram of Tyre in 936, while Solomon was still on the throne, there succeeded a number of shadowy rulers concerning whom we know next to nothing. In 887 B.C., while Baasha was on the throne of Israel, the last of Hiram's line was assassinated by a conspiracy headed by Ithobaal (ih″thoh-bay′ul), who was, apparently, the high priest of the land.

Ithobaal succeeded as ruler of Tyre and was still on the throne when Omri became king of Israel. Both rulers were usurpers who lacked the security of legitimacy. That, perhaps, helped draw them together. Then, too, Omri may have shrewdly felt the advantages of the Tyrian national cult. Tyre worshiped the goddess Astarte (as-tahr′tee), with fertility rites that had a strong emotional appeal and with the kind of elaborate mummery that seemed to please women in particular. It was already popular in Israel and it was the religion of a friend, not of an enemy.

Ithobaal, now king of Tyre but once high priest of Astarte, would be interested in the spread of the cult, so both kings were easily agreed. Omri's son Ahab (ay′hab) was therefore married to Ithobaal's daughter, Jezebel (jez′uh-bel). In addition to everything else, it seems to have been a love match. When Omri died in 869 B.C., Ahab succeeded peacefully to the throne and, together with his queen, Jezebel, continued his father's policy of trying to make the Tyrian cult the state religion of Israel.

There was opposition, of course. The Yahvists of the prophetic party set their faces against the cult of Astarte and of her male consort, called simply Baal (bay′ul), meaning "lord." To the Yahvists, with a cult that had strong masculine traditions dating back to the desert days and who had strongly moralistic views concerning sex, the Tyrian cult of a fertility goddess seemed sinful to the final degree. They fought it desperately.

The Yahvist leader in Israel was Elijah (ee-ly′juh) and in later centuries, legends and wonder tales arose concerning him which were eventually enshrined in the Bible. Because the Biblical history was written from the religious view of Yahvism, Ahab is denounced as an evil king and Jezebel as a monster of wickedness. In actual history, however, Ahab seems to have been a most capable king and Jezebel a devoted wife. They held off the Syrians and fought down the turbulent Yahvists resolutely. Under them the kingdom of Israel reached its high-water mark in some ways.

Ahab's alliance with Tyre, made stronger by the religious

unity he tried to establish, was important economically and probably brought him the necessary wealth to fortify his northern cities against Syria and to beautify the capital city of Samaria. He was able to dominate Judah, forming an alliance with the Judean king, Jehoshaphat, in which the latter accepted Israelite leadership in foreign affairs, though he remained in charge of his domestic affairs.

Thus, what had once been David's empire was now, in Ahab's time, effectively split in two by a diagonal line running from northwest to southeast through the Sea of Galilee. Damascus controlled the territory north of the line; Samaria, south of the line.

Naturally, there was war between the two nations and, by and large, it was stalemated. About 856 B.C. Syrian forces invaded Israel and placed Samaria under siege. Now Omri's foresight paid off, for Samaria proved impregnable. The Syrian army, during the siege, was weakened by boredom and probably by sickness, which was common to any besieging army prior to modern understanding of hygiene. A skillfully led sortie by Israelite forces then drove the Syrians away and sent them on a rapid retreat back to Damascus.

In the following year, Israel was able to fight farther from home. The armies met at Aphek — not the same city as that of the disastrous defeat of Israel by the Philistines two centuries before — on the eastern shore of the Sea of Galilee. This had been Israelite territory till Baasha's reign and now Ahab, winning a second time, was able to retrieve part of the losses twenty years before.

THE DYNASTY OF OMRI

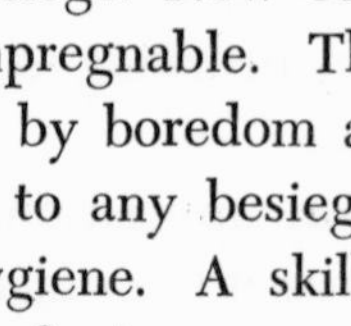

At this point, however, both Syria and Israel had to turn eastward. A new danger had arisen, and a dreadful portent of things to come. In the northwestern end of the Tigris-Euphrates valley was the land of Ashur (or "Assyria" to the Greeks, and to ourselves). Its capital was at Calah, some 450 miles northeast of Samaria in a straight line but farther if one follows the line of the Fertile Crescent, which is what armies would have to follow. This was a long distance in those days and unless Assyria were under a great conquering king it represented no threat to the lands bordering on the Mediterranean.

As it happened, Assyria was indeed occasionally under dynamic monarchs who made use of its large territory, its warlike people, and its trade-raised wealth to expand. About 1220 B.C., for instance, not long before the Israelites were crossing the Jordan and the Philistines were taking over the Canaanite sea coast, Assyria was in control of the entire Tigris-Euphrates, and was the strongest power in the western world.

Assyria then entered a period of decline, but in 1100 B.C., when Ephraim headed the Israelite confederation, the eastern power again expanded over the entire Tigris-Euphrates and even drove westward to reach the Mediterranean Sea. On this occasion, however, as in the former, the southern part of the Mediterranean coast, where the Israelite tribes were concentrated, was not touched and remained beyond the horizon of Assyrian power.

After that Assyria went through another period of declines — a period in which David and Solomon were able to rule over their empire undisturbed. In 935 B.C., toward the end of Solomon's reign, Assyria began to revive for the third time, and by the time Ahab was on the throne of Israel, the might of the eastern power was again edging toward the Mediterranean.

In 859 B.C. Shalmaneser III (shal″muh-nee′zer) became king of Assyria and set forth to enlarge his kingdom. His father had been content to accept tribute from the city-states west of the Euphrates, but Shalmaneser intended outright annexation.

In 854 B.C. he had reached the Mediterranean far north of Israel and took the city of Karkar (kahr′kahr), 230 miles north of Samaria. Here, however, he met a coalition of the powers of the Mediterranean coast under the combined leadership of Benhadad II of Syria and Ahab of Israel. These two inveterate enemies had actually managed to unite against the common foe. Syria seems to have supplied the largest contingent of infantry, but Israel supplied more chariots than any other ally.

We have only an Assyrian account of the battle that followed, for the Bible never mentions it. The Assyrian account describes the Battle of Karkar as an Assyrian victory, but it describes no annexation of territory and no further advances. From this we can deduce that the battle was no better than a draw for Assyria and possibly even a defeat.

In any case, the Assyrian menace was lifted, and though Assyria remained strong through the remainder of Shalmaneser's thirty-four years on the throne, the Mediterranean coast was left to itself, except for occasional forays. Indeed, so clearly was it left to itself that Israel and Syria could return to fighting each other.

Ahab's attempt to regain the territory lost under Baasha continued. The forces of Israel and Judah, in alliance, attacked Syrian positions at Ramoth-gilead, about thirty miles southeast of Aphek. The battle might have gone to the Israelites but a chance arrow struck Ahab and wounded him fatally. The battle was broken off and much of the land east of the Sea of Galilee remained Syrian.

The death of Ahab was the signal for revolt (as is often true of the death of any strong king). Moab promptly rose in rebellion. Moab, east of the Dead Sea, had been conquered by David and had remained in Israelite hands after the division of the kingdom in Rehoboam's time. Moab had nearly regained its freedom in the disastrous reign of Baasha, but Omri had subdued it again. Toward the end of Ahab's reign, Mesha (mee′shuh) was the Moabite leader. He had already led an unsuccessful revolt against Israel and once Ahab died, he tried again.

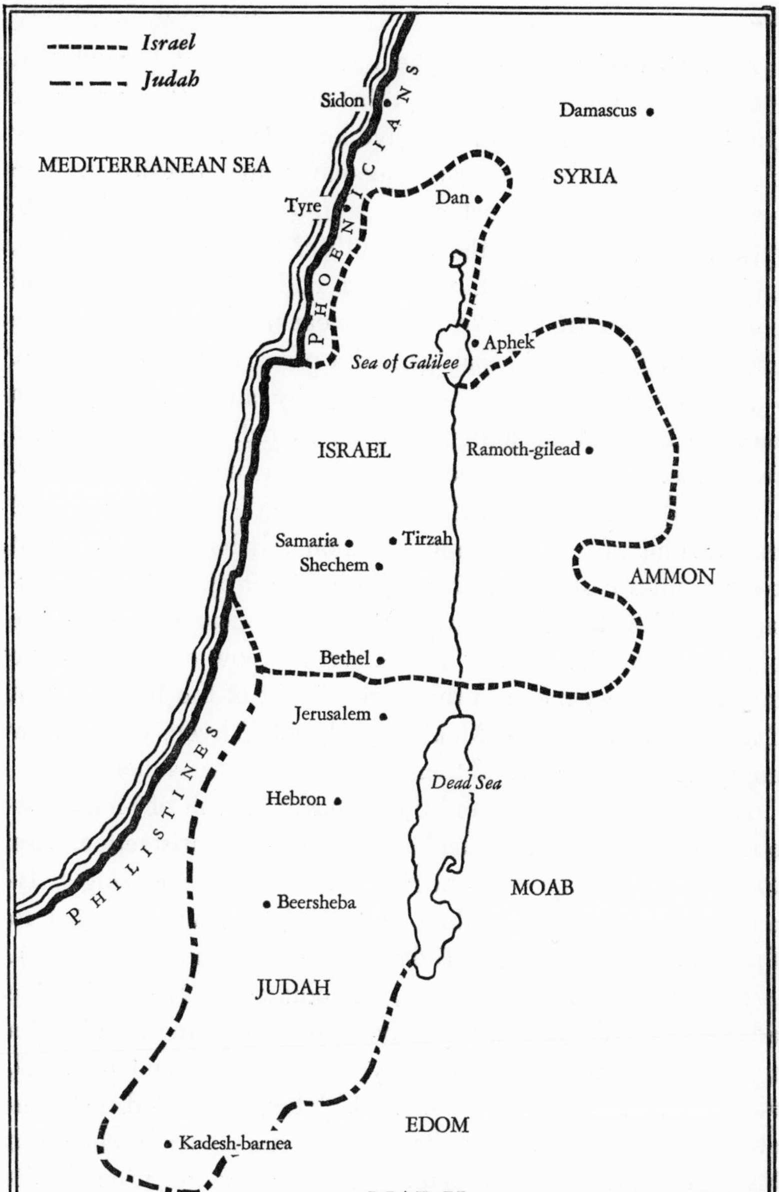

MAP V

Israel and Judah (c. 850 B.C.)

Ahaziah (ay″huh-zy′uh), the son of Ahab and Jezebel, had succeeded to the throne as the third member of the dynasty of Omri, but he was ill and didn't live long. He was succeeded by his younger brother Jehoram (jee-haw′rum) in 849 B.C. The new king immediately set about trying to crush the Moabite revolt. In alliance with the still faithful Jehoshaphat of Judah, he led his army around the southern end of the Dead Sea and northward into Moab. We are not clear on the details, but the expedition failed and Moab gained a precarious independence.

Mesha commemorated his victory by an inscription on a piece of black basalt about three and a half feet tall and two feet wide. The importance of this lies in the fact that it survived and is known as "the Moabite Stone." It was discovered in the ruins of Mesha's capital, Dibon (dy′bon), a city about twelve miles east of the Dead Sea, in 1869 by a German missionary, F. A. Klein. The inscription is in ancient Hebrew, the oldest lengthy inscription in that writing now extant, and the language is very much in the spirit of that of the Bible, except that it is Chemosh, the Moabite god, not Yahveh, who is now angry with his people and then repents and rescues them.

Despite Ahab's death and the successful revolt of Moab, Jezebel, now queen mother, had some reason for satisfaction. Her son Jehoram, completely under her domination, was king of Israel. Her daughter Athaliah (ath″uh-ly′uh) was married to the son of Jehoshaphat of Judah (a son also named Jehoram).

Jehoshaphat died in 849 B.C., immediately after the abortive advance into Moab, and so Jezebel had a son ruling Israel and a son-in-law ruling Judah. The Tyrian cult, dominant in Israel, was now penetrating Judah as well. Jehoram resisted that penetration, but in 842 B.C. he died and his son Ahaziah reigned in his place. He was completely under the domination of his mother, Athaliah, so that Jezebel had a son over Israel and a grandson over Judah, Tyrian cultists both.

Yahvism was now at the point of its greatest danger. The Israelite leader of the Yahvistic prophetic party, Elijah, had died, but his place was taken by Elisha (ee-ly′shuh), another strong personality concerning whom wonder tales are told. Elisha took the path of conspiracy. It was only necessary to find the proper tool. It would have to be a general with troops under his control — and in Israel's short history, generals had twice overthrown the government. Naturally, though, it would have to be a general with Yahvist sympathies.

In 842 B.C. the war with Syria was continuing and Ramoth-gilead, where Ahab had died, was still the bone of contention. In the course of the fighting there, Jehoram of Israel was wounded and he left the front lines to recuperate at the royal city of Jezreel, twenty miles to the west and twelve miles north of Samaria. There he was visited by his royal nephew, Ahaziah of Judah, come to pay his respects as a kinsman and ally.

The Israelite army was left with a general, Jehu (jee′hyoo), at its head, and that was Elisha's chance. Jehu was either a Yahvist by conviction or was willing to become one for the sake of the throne. With the king disabled and the army completely under his control, Jehu made a deal with the prophetic party.

Jehu had himself proclaimed king by the army and then led it on a rapid march westward to Jezreel. He achieved total surprise, took the city, and wiped out all the male members of the house of Omri. Not only did he kill Jehoram of Israel but Ahaziah of Judah as well. When that was done, he ordered the queen mother, Jezebel, killed also.

Thus, in utter disaster, came an end to Israel's third dynasty. It had included four kings, of whom two, Omri and Ahab, were strong and capable, and had endured for thirty-four years. With Jehu, began Israel's fourth dynasty.

In Judah, however, beyond Jehu's reach, there remained Athaliah, daughter of Jezebel. When news of Jehu's coup reached her, she realized that the Yahvists in Judah, relatively stronger than in Israel, would surely strike. She therefore moved first, and bloodily.

In a whirlwind of action, she ordered all the male members of the Davidic dynasty slaughtered, including, apparently, her own grandsons. She may have intended to marry someone else and found a new dynasty but, in point of fact, she did not. For a period of six years, from 842 to 836 B.C., she ruled alone, and this was the only period in the entire existence of the kingdom of Judah that the dynasty of David was not enthroned. Athaliah's reign was precarious, however. Yahvism in Judah had something that Yahvism in Israel had not — the Temple. Athaliah dared not touch it, or the high priest, for she knew full well that would unite the army and the people against her.

She could only hold on desperately waiting for events and possibly hoping only to end her life on the throne, with no concern for what might happen afterward. As it was, the period of her rule was disastrous. Edom, under Judean rule since the time of David two and a half centuries before, now revolted and gained its independence. The Philistine city-states on the coast were so far from being subdued that they actually raided Judah. Indeed, all that remained under the domination of Jerusalem was the old territory of the tribe of Judah itself, a region no larger than the state of Connecticut.

High priest at the time was Jehoiada (jeh-hoi′uh-duh). Throughout Athaliah's reign he must have felt harried indeed, for he could never have known when Athaliah might decide to move against the Temple after all. Somehow he had to rally the army and the people against her. There seemed only one way, and that was to use the dynasty of David — the descendants of the glorious David and Solomon, whose reigns, though they had come to an end a century before, were as alive as ever in the minds of all Judeans and, of whose line, six members had ruled Judah since Solomon's death.

To be sure, the dynasty had been wiped out by Athaliah, but could anyone be sure of that? In 836 B.C. Jehoiada organized a secret meeting of Judean army leaders and produced before them a seven-year-old boy along with a dramatic story. Six years before, he said, when Athaliah had killed off the descendants of David, a baby had been saved, a one-year-old son of Ahaziah. The high priest's wife (a sister of Ahaziah) had snatched her baby nephew from the inferno and had brought him to the Temple. In the Temple, he had been carefully hidden and had been guarded ever since.

Was this really so? Or was the boy an imposter produced as a rallying point? How can we tell? How can anyone tell? The Bible reports Jehoiada's version of the story and so it is generally accepted. The Judean generals also accepted the story and proclaimed the boy, Jehoash (jee-hoh′ash), king. The people also accepted the story. There was wild jubilation at the reinstatement of the Davidic dynasty, and Athaliah was taken and killed.

The Phoenician influence was thus at an end in Judah as in Israel. The dynasty of Omri had been eradicated everywhere. Yahvism with the Temple was dominant for the moment in Judah; Yahvism without the Temple, in Israel. As far as could be seen, Elisha and the prophetic party had won the victory.

THE DYNASTY OF JEHU

Balancing Yahvism's triumph within, however, there was trouble without. In Syria, in 842 B.C., the year of Jehu's coup, there was also a coup. Benhadad II was assassinated by a court official, Hazael (haz′ay-el). Apparently, Elisha had a finger in this as well, for a royal assassination seemed to him to be an efficient way of bringing about at least a temporary chaos. Unfortunately for him and for Israel it didn't work out that way. Hazael seized the crown and proved a more capable king than the man he had supplanted.

What's more, the year of confusion in all three kingdoms — Syria, Israel, and Judah — proved a temptation for Assyria. A dozen years had passed since the eastern power had burned its fingers at Karkar, but Shalmaneser III was still on the Assyrian throne and now he moved in for vengeance.

His armies raided Syria and northern Israel and laid siege to Damascus. It might have meant utter destruction for the kingdoms, but Damascus held out desperately and there were troubles on Assyria's other borders. Shalmaneser had to be satisfied with extorting a sizable tribute, and then left. He raised a monument to his victory, however, a black obelisk that recorded the kings defeated and the tribute paid. In it he lists Jehu among the defeated kings, referring to him as the "son of Omri," the usual title of the Israelite kings among the Assyrians, even though Jehu had just wiped out all the descendants of Omri that he could reach.

As for Phoenicia, though she had lost her chance of attaining religious ascendancy over Israel and Judah, and perhaps even Syria as well, that must have meant little to her. The Phoenician cities could not very well have established a land empire anyway, not one that would have been made to stick in the face of the creeping Assyrian menace. As it was, Phoenicia had helped in the Battle of Karkar, but had then had to pay tribute when Shalmaneser returned more successfully in that year of confusion of 842 B.C.

No, the future of Phoenicia lay at sea, and there matters went better than ever. Throughout the ninth century B.C. Phoenicia was still the only sizable naval power in the Mediterranean and its trade remained her monopoly. In 814 B.C. (the accepted date) the city of Tyre actually gave birth to one greater than herself.

In that year a party of Tyrian colonists, under the guidance, according to tradition, of Dido (dy′doh), the sister of the Tyrian king, established a city just a few miles south of Utica on the African shore west of Sicily, a city almost on the site of modern Tunis. The Phoenician colonists named it Karthadasht ("new town"), presumably because Utica was the "old town."

To the Romans in later centuries the name became "Carthago," and to us it is "Carthage" (kar′thij). The Romans called the Carthaginians "Poeni," their version of the Greek word for Phoenician, so that the adjective "Punic" is equivalent to "Carthaginian."

But what about Yahvism during all this? How did it hold up in Israel and Judah?

Assyria was dangerous, but for a while it continued to be involved with its other borders and, in fact, after the death of Shalmaneser in 825 B.C., its power declined again. The Phoenician cities were rich but they were intent on the sea, and they made no effort to retrieve their cultist position in Israel and Judah. It was Syria that was still the chief enemy and for the moment that was danger enough.

Though Syria had had a coup in 842 B.C., this was followed by no internal religious upheaval. It recovered from the Assyrian incursion much more rapidly than did Israel, where Jehu was uprooting the Tyrian cult and attempting to establish Yahvism in its place.

Hazael, the usurping king of Syria, reorganized his army and sent it southward against the feeble Yahvistic kingdoms. He had little trouble. In one campaign he took all the Transjordanian territory from Jehu. Land that had been Israelite since the days of the Judges was now under the rule of Damascus. Another prong of the Syrian army pushed down the coast and established its dominance over the Philistine cities.

By the time Jehu's reign was ended by his death in 814 B.C., the year of the founding of Carthage, Israel and Judah were penned between the Jordan River and the Dead Sea on the east and the coastal plain on the west. Their rule, even over the hill country, was left to them at the price of tribute to Syria.

When Jehoahaz (jee-hoh′uh-haz), the son of Jehu, succeeded to the throne in 814 B.C., it looked as though Israel might be utterly wiped off the map. Hazael in his last years could more than once have taken Samaria itself.

Judah also suffered in this period. Under Jehoash, the boy king who was supposed to have represented the all-but-miraculously-preserved Davidic dynasty, there was only continued defeat. Hazael of Syria threatened even Jerusalem itself and withdrew only at the price of heavy tribute.

Internally things were no better. It is to be expected that in his early years the young king would be utterly dominated by the high priest who had saved and preserved his life, or had, perhaps, selected him to play the role of survivor of the Davidic dynasty. In adulthood, having worn the mantle of royalty for decades, he grew impatient. When Jehoiada died and his son became high priest, Jehoash asserted his independence and maneuvered to have the new high priest stoned to death.

This lost him the support of the priesthood. The fact that he was defeated by Hazael and had to pay tribute — which meant a raid on the Temple treasury — was a further blow to his popularity. In 797 B.C. he was murdered by an army coup. The fate he had supposedly escaped in 842 B.C., according to Jehoiada, overtook him nearly half a century later.

What could Elisha's thoughts have been? The coups he had organized in 842 B.C. had backfired in the sense that it was Hazael the non-Yahvist who had profited most. Nevertheless, Yahvism was back in power in Israel and Judah, however diminished they might be, and this perhaps satisfied the leader of the prophetic party.

He also lived to see the tide begin to turn again. In 806 B.C. Hazael died after having briefly brought almost the entire western part of the Fertile Crescent under his domination. Assyria was then in its period of decline, but even so a flick of its tail was sufficient to disrupt the west. Only months after Hazael's death, an Assyrian army besieged and took Damascus, enforced heavy tribute, and left the land shaken and prostrate. Syria held on to its independence but its decade of imperial greatness was over and was never to return.

When Jehoahaz of Israel was succeeded by his son Jehoash

in 798 B.C., the new king found the situation quite changed. It was Syria that was in disarray and in the renewal of the war between them, Israel had the upper hand. Her armies defeated Benhadad III, the son of Hazael, in three successive battles. Israel was restored to the position she had held under Ahab, and Elisha, who died about 790 B.C., lived long enough to see that.

The Davidic dynasty, or what was accepted as that, also recovered in the aftermath of Hazael's death. The assassination of Jehoash of Judah was followed by the accession of his son Amaziah (am″uh-zy′uh). Amaziah was able to win victories over Edom and to restore Judean domination over that land, which had held on to its independence for only half a century.

About 786 B.C., then, the two Yahvistic lands of Israel and Judah were each ruled by a king with a record of conquest and of restoration of earlier power. It was almost inevitable that they should try their strength against each other, and this for the first time since the reign of Baasha, a century and a quarter before. It was Amaziah of Judah who was, apparently, the aggressor in the struggle.

Judah was the weaker just the same, as it quickly found out. In a battle at Beth-Shemesh (beth-shee′mesh), fifteen miles west of Jerusalem, Israel won a decisive victory. Amaziah was taken prisoner and was forced to agree to the temporary occupation of Jerusalem. Some of the city's fortifications were destroyed and the Temple treasury was looted. Although Judah retained its own king and a certain amount of self-rule, it became a tributary of Israel, very much as it had been in the days of Omri and Ahab.

Jehoash of Israel died in 783 B.C. and his son Jeroboam succeeded. Because a Jeroboam had been the first to rule over Israel after the death of Solomon a century and a half before, the new king is usually known in the histories as Jeroboam II. He completed his father's conquests, reducing all of Syria to the role of tributary and making Samaria dominant over the western half of the Fertile Crescent, as a quarter-century before, Damascus under Hazael had been dominant.

A new religious change was beginning to take place in the reign of Jeroboam II. After Elisha's death the prophetic party lost its vigor, but a new kind of religious leader began to arise. These weren't interested so much in the mere acceptance of a particular group of rites, or in whether this set of priests or that controlled the chief temples. Instead, they took up the cause of social reform, giving it a religious cast. They were still called "prophets" but with them the word no longer came to mean an ecstatic dervish, but a stern proponent of reform calling on the people to repent of their evil-doing and warning of divine punishment if they did not.

The first of the new breed was Amos, a Judean shepherd who ventured into the Israelite shrine at Bethel about 760 B.C. to denounce worship there as an idolatrous version of Yahvism. What's more, he denounced the kind of religion that emphasized ritual rather than the decent life. He quoted God as saying:

I hate, I despise your feast days, and I will not smell in your solemn assemblies./Though ye offer me burnt offering and your meat offerings, I will not accept them;/neither will I regard the peace offerings of your fat beasts./Take thou away from me the noise of thy songs; for I will not hear the melody of thy viols./ But let judgment run down as waters, and righteousness as a mighty stream.

Amos did not accomplish much. The priest in charge of the Bethel sanctuary warned him to get back to Judah and stay there and, apparently, Amos did so. Nor did the Israelite version of Yahvism change. Amos's speeches, nevertheless, were preserved (though we can never be sure how far they were altered by later editors) and exist today in the Biblical Book of Amos, the oldest of the Biblical books to have been written down in its present form.

Not long after the time of Amos's activity, an Israelite, Hosea (hoh-zee′uh), also preached a message of concern over ethical values rather than of ritual. His preachings came in the last years of the reign of Jeroboam II and are to be found in the Book of Hosea. He is the only Israelite whose utterances are preserved in the various prophetic books of the Old Testament. The rest, including Amos, are all Judeans.

During the reign of Jeroboam II of Israel, Judah's defeated king, Amaziah, fell prey to an army coup, as his father had, and in 769 B.C. was assassinated. His son Azariah (az″uh-ry′uh), better known by another version of the name, Uzziah (uh-zy′uh), succeeded to the throne.

Uzziah ruled over a Judah that remained a puppet of Israel, but there was no attempt to alter that situation and, indeed, Judah flourished while in this condition. Uzziah rebuilt the fortifications of Jerusalem that had been broken down in his father's time. He seized control of some of the Philistine city-states and rebuilt the seaport of Elath on the Red Sea, which had been important in Solomon's time. The revival of trade helped bring prosperity to Judah.

There was, however, an internal problem in Judah in the rivalry of king and high priest. In Israel there was no such problem; the king was supreme. In Judah, however, the Temple had a unique influence, and the high priest was always a power to reckon with.

To be sure, David and Solomon had taken no nonsense from the high priest, had made and unmade them at will, and had supervised the solemn sacrifices when they wished to. The interregnum under Athaliah, however, had to a certain extent destroyed that precedent. While Athaliah reigned, the high priest was the only leader of the Yahvists of Judah. When the boy Jehoash was placed on the throne, the high priest remained the chief power. For the half-century since, there had been a struggle on the part of the Judean kings to regain their power and on the part of the high priests to keep them from doing so.

Jehoash and Amaziah had both been assassinated, and it seems possible that priestly influence lay behind both coups.

Uzziah also attempted to assert the royal prerogative with respect to priestly functions, all the more so since the successes of his reign, both military and economic, had probably made him popular. He even attempted to supervise the sacrifices in the Temple and thus emphasize his authority over the high priest.

The attempt failed. We don't have the details. Apparently, toward the end of his thirty-four-year-long reign, he was incapacitated and had to live in isolation. From 749 B.C. his son Jotham (joh′tham) served as regent. The legend rose (and was preserved by the editors of the Biblical books who were, of course, heart and soul on the side of the high priest and against the royal pretensions) that Uzziah was stricken with leprosy, a condition that disqualified him from even entering the Temple. What's more, the leprosy struck him (it was said) the instant he tried to supervise Temple worship.

This represented the final victory of the high priest over the king. From the time of Uzziah's reign on, the high priest was supreme over Yahvism and the king, if he was to have any independence at all, would have to turn away from Yahvism. Many did.

(The victory of the high priest, as described in the Bible, was to have an important effect on future history when, in the Middle Ages, there were continual struggles between Church and State among the Christians.)

6

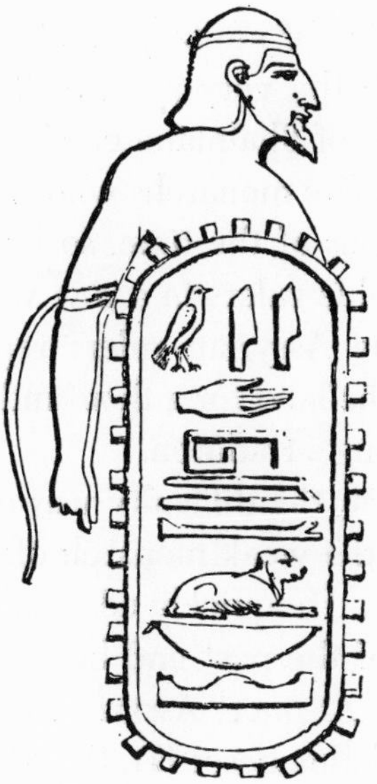

JUDAH

THE FALL OF ISRAEL

In 748 B.C. Jeroboam II died. His thirty-five-year-long reign had been uniformly successful and he died with his kingdom intact. His son Zechariah (zek″uh-ry′uh) came to the throne. He was the fifth member of the dynasty of Jehu. Four times in succession the throne had passed from father to son, a record for Israel. But that ended it. Within six months, a palace coup brought death to Zechariah and the dynasty of Jehu came to an end after ninety-four years.

For a few weeks, there was wild confusion in Samaria, but then an army officer named Menahem (men′uh-hem) was accepted as king. The position, however, no longer had the glory it had held when Jeroboam II was on the throne. It never would again, for in the east, Assyria was stirring once more.

For the fourth (and last) time in its history, Assyria was

about to enter a period of military greatness, one in which, indeed, it was to reach the very peak of its power. For eighty years, since the death of Shalmaneser III, Assyria had suffered under a succession of five monarchs who were weak and incompetent. In most nations of the time, so long a period of weakness and so many feeble rulers in a row would have invited an insurrection. But the Assyrian rulers represented a dynasty that had ruled over the land for a thousand years, and it is difficult to put away so long a tradition.

In 745 B.C., however, the difficulty was overcome. An Assyrian general deposed the weak monarch of the moment and set himself on the throne. He quickly adopted the name of a great Assyrian conqueror of the past and became Tiglath-pileser III (tig′lath-py-lee′zer). At once, Assyria was on the move again.

As in the days of Shalmaneser III, the nations of the Mediterranean coast tried to combine in order to resist the giant of the east. Uzziah of Judah was the leader of this anti-Assyrian coalition (as we learn from the Assyrian records, for it is not mentioned in the Bible).

The coalition failed. In 738 B.C. it went down to defeat before the Assyrian army and Tiglath-pileser III levied tribute on all the coastal nations. Both Menahem of Israel and Uzziah of Judah bent to the yoke in order to retain what fragments of self-rule Assyria would allow them. Certainly all hopes of empire were gone. Syria was completely free of Israelite domination once more and a king now ruled in Damascus who was the equal of the king in Samaria — or at any rate equally subservient to Assyria.

Menahem died in that same year and his son Pekahiah (pek″uh-hy′uh) ascended the throne. Pekahiah did his best to remain at peace with Assyria and continue the payment of tribute as the only way of avoiding utter destruction. However, the tribute entailed a back-breaking load of taxation, which the people resented. This, together with the all-too-common hatred of foreigners and a lack of popular appreciation of Assyria's strength, gave rise to an increasing level of anti-Assyrian feeling.

In 736 B.C. an army coup under an officer named Pekah (pee′kuh) brought death to Pekahiah and the end of Israel's fifth dynasty after only twelve years. Pekah at once threw himself into the organization of a new anti-Assyrian coalition. With him in this project was Rezin (ree′zin) of Syria, son of Behadad III.

Essential to success in the eyes of the Israelite-Syrian allies was Judah's adherence to the alliance. While the northern states were still building their coalition, however, Uzziah of Judah died in 734 B.C. and was soon followed by his son Jotham. The son of Jotham, Ahaz (ay′haz), succeeded. Uzziah and Jotham, having taken to heart the lesson of Assyrian strength, did not wish to join the coalition. Nor did Ahaz. In this decision, the new king of Judah was supported by Isaiah (igh-zay′uh).

Isaiah was one of the new breed of prophets that had come on the scene with Amos a quarter-century before. Isaiah entered public life in the year of Uzziah's death, emphasizing ethics and social concern rather than ritual as his view of religion. Apparently of an aristocratic Judean family, Isaiah had ready access to the king and to the priestly leaders.

In the crisis that faced Judah now, Isaiah suggested strict neutrality. Judah must not join any league against Assyria. When Israel and Syria threatened Judah with war if the latter did not join the anti-Assyrian league, Isaiah discounted the danger. Israel and Syria could not win such a war, since clearly Assyria would not allow the strengthening of its enemies. All Judah had to do was stand firm.

Isaiah told Ahaz this in strong terms and his statement is preserved in the collection of sayings attributed to him and making up the Book of Isaiah. In the New English Bible, which translates the Hebrew into modern English, Isaiah's statement reads: . . . *the Lord himself shall give you a sign: A young woman is with child, and she will bear a son, and will call him Immanuel. By the time that he has learnt to reject evil and choose good, he will be eating curds and honey; before that child has learnt to reject evil and choose good, desolation will come upon the land before whose two kings you cower now.* The language, as reported, is not completely clear, but what it seems to be saying is that in the time it takes for a child now about to be born to reach the age of weaning, both Israel and Syria would be destroyed — presumably by Assyria.

As it happened, the combined forces of Syria and Israel did invade Judah and quickly overran the country. Seizing the opportunity, the Edomites and the Philistines broke free of Judah and soon Ahaz found himself ruling over little more than Jerusalem and its environs. Here Ahaz' courage failed him. Though Isaiah counseled patience, Ahaz could not wait for Assyria to come of its own accord and appealed for help, thus accepting its own role as Assyria's puppet all the more firmly.

Tiglath-pileser answered the Judean appeal. The Assyrian armies came marching resistlessly westward. In 732 B.C., Syria was smashed and Damascus taken. Syria lost its independence forever and its history as a political unit came to an end only two centuries after it came into existence in the final years of Solomon's reign and only seventy years after Hazael had temporarily placed it in control of almost all that had once been David's empire.

The Syrians (or Arameans, to use once again the name by which they called themselves) did not disappear, however. Earlier Assyrian monarchs had attempted to discourage rebellion in conquered provinces by a program of stark terror, killing and mutilating wholesale. Tiglath-pileser III made use of a subtler method which, on the whole, worked better. He carried out wholesale deportations. He moved much of the aristocracy of one province out of their homes and settled them in strange territory, bringing in strangers to take the emptied place.

As a result, national consciousness was weakened and sure

hostility was introduced between those old inhabitants who remained and the newcomers who were brought in. This internal hostility consumed those energies that might otherwise have been turned against Assyria.

The Syrians were thus scattered over the empire, carrying their language with them. The Aramaic language was much simpler (with its Phoenician alphabet) than the intricate cuneiform Assyrian language. Beginning with the eighth century B.C., Aramaic became a kind of international language of western Asia and was to remain so for thirteen centuries. Through its language, then, Syria exerted more influence on world culture for long centuries after its political death than ever it had before.

As for Israel, it survived the destruction of Syria, but just barely. Assyria wrested the northern two thirds of its territory out of its control and converted them into captive provinces. Pekah remained king but his rule was confined over the area about Samaria.

Pekah did not remain king, however. He could not survive the humiliation of the defeat for long and was assassinated in still another palace coup, Israel's last. The leader of the coup, Hoshea (hoh-shee′uh), had himself declared king in 732 B.C. Apparently, he was recognized by Assyria on the condition of utter subservience in the form of a large tribute.

In 728 B.C. the situation changed again, or seemed to. Tiglath-pileser III died, and there seemed a gambler's chance that Assyria would once again settle into a decline for a longer or shorter period as had so often happened before at the death of a strong king.

Even against an enfeebled Assyria, the rump kingdom of Israel could not stand without foreign help, however. The only sizable power within reach of Israel that might be willing to oppose Assyria was Egypt. What's more, it was to Egypt's interest to offer such opposition, for if the western half of the Fertile Crescent came utterly under Assyrian domination, that mighty power would then be on the Egyptian border and this Egypt could not want to happen.

In 736 B.C. Egypt had come under Shabaka (shab′uh-kuh), the first of a line of kings from a region of the upper Nile called Nubia (or Ethiopia). It was to Shabaka that Hoshea of Israel turned.

Thus began a century and a half during which Egypt consistently encouraged rebellions in the western half of the Fertile Crescent against the dominant powers of the eastern half. Unfortunately for those she encouraged, Egypt had little power of her own. She might subsidize and bribe, but she could not effectively support militarily. Those nations which listened to Egyptian blandishments and accepted Egyptian gold invariably found that at the crucial moment, when it was a matter of spear against spear, Egyptian help was nowhere to be found or was, at best, inadequate. And so it proved for Israel.

Shalmaneser V, the son and successor of Tiglath-pileser, was determined to continue his father's strong foreign policy. He reacted to Hoshea's refusal of tribute at once, marched against Israel, laid it waste, captured and deposed Hoshea, and then, in 725 B.C., laid siege to Samaria.

With the courage of despair Samaria, isolated and hopeless, managed to continue its resistance for three years. Perhaps this resistance exasperated the Assyrians generally and Shalmaneser was made the scapegoat. In any case, Shalmaneser died in 722 B.C., possibly through assassination, since a usurper (perhaps the head of the conspiracy) came to the throne and served as the first monarch of Assyria's last and most spectacular dynasty.

The usurper, Sargon II (sahr′gon), completed Shalmaneser's work and brought the siege of Samaria to a quick and successful conclusion. Thus in 722 B.C. there came a permanent end to the kingdom of Israel, which had existed exactly 200 years since the successful rebellion led by Jeroboam I.

Sargon followed the tactics of Tiglath-pileser III and attempted to end the possibility of revolt in Israel — now made an Assyrian province — by deporting some 27,000 of the ruling classes of the nation, the landowners and administrators. The deportees were settled in the region of the Khabur River, near the apex of the Fertile Crescent, some 450 miles northeast of Samaria. There they intermarried with the native peoples and gradually lost their sense of national identity. The deportees are renowned in legend as the "Ten Lost Tribes," and for many centuries they were thought to exist intact and to make up a powerful nation somewhere in the interior of Asia. This was sheer nonsense.

To replace the depopulated areas that had been Israel, Sargon brought in deportees from other restless, conquered provinces. These newcomers to Israel intermarried with the Israelite peasants who had been left behind and this population made up of immigrants and natives, centered about the city of Samaria, became known as Samaritans in later generations.

The Samaritans continued to worship somewhat in the fashion of the earlier Israelites and were Yahvists in religion. They considered themselves descendants of the Israelites and minimized the effect of the Israelite deportations and the influx of immigrants. They maintained that their form of Yahvism was the pure and original.

The inhabitants of Judah to the south, however, who insisted on the validity of their own form of Yahvism, maintained the Samaritans to be a mongrel breed and held that their Israelite predecessors had been driven out of the land en masse while the Samaritan form of Yahvism was a worthless and wicked heresy. It is the Judean version which appears in the Bible.

HEZEKIAH

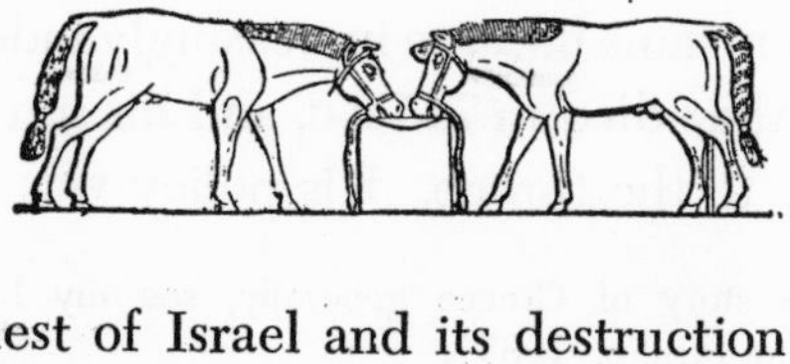

After the conquest of Israel and its destruction as an independent state, Sargon made no attempt to annex the lands to the south. The petty kingdoms beyond Israel quickly made their profound obeisance to the mighty king of Assyria and paid tribute. The Phoenicians and Philistines on the coast, Judah, Ammon, Moab, and Edom in the interior — all retained native rulers and remained masters of their internal affairs. In all that counted, however, they were Assyrian puppets and they paid heavily to retain even that puppetry.

Of the remnants of old Canaan still existing, the Phoenicians were in the best position. Their navies made them capable of resisting Assyria but even so, they had come to the end of the greatest period in their history. After Sargon's time, the Phoenician cities would never again be completely independent.

What's more, for the first time in five centuries their control of the sea was being challenged. Greece was emerging from the dark age into which it had been plunged at the time of the upheaval of the Sea Peoples. Its expanding population sought release by colonization abroad. As new Greek cities began to dot the coasts of Asia Minor and the shores of the Black Sea, Greek shipping and trade grew more extensive. In the eighth century B.C., even while the Phoenician cities found themselves occupied with Assyria, Greek ships brought Greek colonists to the shores of Sicily and southern Italy.

The eastern Mediterranean came to be dominated by the Greeks and was to remain dominated by them for six centuries.* The western Mediterranean remained, however, under Phoenician influence largely through the successful rise of the Tyrian colony-city Carthage. The distance of the western colonies from the Phoenician motherland, plus the Greek-dominated stretch of sea between, began a process whereby the western Phoenicians became increasingly independent.

In Judah Ahaz died in 715 B.C. and his son Hezekiah (hez′ih-ky′uh) came to the throne. His policy was both tortuous and

* For the story of Greece generally, see my book *The Greeks* (Houghton Mifflin, 1965).

difficult, for he paid tribute to Assyria but seized every opportunity to resist Assyrian domination.

One avenue of resistance involved religious reform. In those days, political domination involved religious domination as well. The cult of the victors was expected to be received with respect by the conquered, for when one nation defeated another nation in the prosaic battles on earth, the gods of the victor were considered to have defeated the gods of the vanquished. This meant that the gods of the Tigris-Euphrates had to receive ritualistic respect in Judah.

Hezekiah, however, did his best to prepare the nation for eventual revolt by strengthening and centralizing Yahvism. He did his best to destroy subsidiary places of worship and to suppress local rites, concentrating everything at the Temple at Jerusalem. He added new elaborations to the agricultural festival of the Passover, adding political overtones to it by strengthening its aspect as a celebration of the legendary escape from Egypt, thus spurring on the population to dream of equal escape from the Assyrians.

In Hezekiah's time, too, the legends of the early times of the Patriarchs and the Judges, as presented by the now-conquered Israelites, were combined with similar legends evolved in Judah. Some of the material we now have in the early books of the Bible began to take their present shape.

Nor did Hezekiah neglect purely military measures. He fortified and provisioned various cities and built a special water conduit to lead water into the Jerusalem fortifications. (With ample water and with generous stores of grain, a well-fortified city could hold out for a long time against the siegecraft of the day, and could wait for boredom and sickness to wear out the besiegers.)

Hezekiah also attempted to establish close relations with the Yahvists of what had once been Israel, to extend his power over the Philistines and the Edomites, and to obtain the financial help of Egypt. It remained only to find a good opportunity for a rebellion that would snap the Assyrian hold. In all of this, of course, Hezekiah had the wholehearted support of the Yahvist priesthood and of independent prophets such as Isaiah.

And then in 705 B.C. Sargon II died and his son Sennacherib (seh-nak′uh-rib) succeeded. Again the death of a strong king was the signal for revolt. The Chaldean tribes who dominated the lower tracts of the Tigris-Euphrates were in a state of chronic hostility to the Assyrian masters. Sargon II had been so preoccupied with them that he had been able to pay only small attention to the west — which was what had allowed Hezekiah to make his preparations. Now with Sargon's death, the Chaldeans broke into open revolt.

With a new and untried king over the Assyrians, and with that king utterly tied up with the Chaldeans, Hezekiah felt his time had come. In alliance with Phoenicia, Philistia, and Egypt he refused tribute to Assyria, a deed equivalent to a declaration of independence.

By 701 B.C. Sennacherib had extricated himself sufficiently from his Chaldean involvements to send a sizable army down the Mediterranean coast. The rebellious allies felt the full weight of Assyrian punishment at once. The Phoenician cities were swept up and the king of Tyre was forced to flee the city and take refuge in the Phoenician colonies on Cyprus.

In Philistine territory the Egyptian army was encountered, easily defeated, and sent tumbling backward. Thereafter, with scarcely a pause, Sennacherib marched his men into the Judean interior, devastating the land, and taking the fortified cities one after the other. Before the year was out, Hezekiah was penned up in Jerusalem like a rat in a cage.

Sennacherib settled down to a siege. By now Hezekiah had had enough, of course, and was willing to pay an enormous tribute, merely in order to return to puppetry with his promise of future loyalty. The angry Assyrian king, however, was reluctant to give in that far. Perhaps he planned to do what his father had done to Samaria and Israel: take the city and end the kingdom.

But well-provisioned, well-defended Jerusalem would withstand a long siege and, what was worse, the Egyptians attacked again. Sennacherib detached a portion of the besieging army and defeated them easily, but it meant further losses. This, combined with news of troubles elsewhere in Assyria's broad dominions, suddenly convinced Sennacherib of the folly of spending too much time before a small and relatively unimportant city. He decided to accept Hezekiah's humble offer of an enormous tribute, and left.

Sennacherib was willing to allow Judah to retain a limited freedom and to allow the dynasty of David to occupy the throne. The land, however, was prostrate, and it might well have learned its lesson this time. It would undoubtedly wait long before daring to provoke Assyria again. If this was in Sennacherib's mind, he was correct. Judah never rebelled against Assyria again.

Nevertheless, the fact that Sennacherib had retired without actually taking Jerusalem proved of the greatest importance — not only to Judah, but to the world. Twenty years before, Samaria, under similar circumstances, had been taken, and Israel brought to an end. Now Jerusalem had not been taken and Judah stood.

Why the difference?

Jerusalem had the Temple. Legends arose that Sennacherib had been turned back by a plague sent by God that had destroyed his army; that the Temple was invulnerable; that Yahveh could not be defeated and that he was stronger than the Assyrian gods no matter how powerful Assyria might seem on earth. There came the beginnings of a new view of religion and of God, one that was not tied down to the prosaic facts of victory or defeat on earth.

JOSIAH

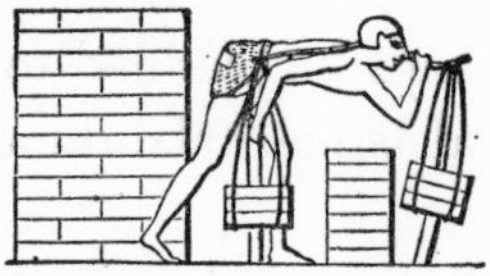

But whatever the mystique that arose in the aftermath of the events of 701 B.C., the immediate situation was plain. Judah had been devastated and had suffered the worst defeat of its history.

Hezekiah, tired and disgraced, willingly accepted his oldest son, Manasseh, as co-ruler in 697 B.C. When Hezekiah died in 687 B.C., Manasseh succeeded as sole ruler and continued so to his death in 642 B.C. The total reign of fifty-five years makes Manasseh's rule the longest in the history of Judah. Moreover, that period of fifty-five years was one of profound peace for the land.

Manasseh completely reversed the policy of his father which had obviously brought nothing but disaster to Judah. It was clear that the price of puppetry was far lower than the price of rebellion, so through all his long reign he paid tribute punctually and bowed his head patiently to the Assyrian king. What's more, he accepted and encouraged the Assyrian cult and did his best to discourage Yahvism, which continued to preach the spirit of resistance that Hezekiah had roused.*

During Manasseh's reign Assyria reached the very peak of its power. In 681 B.C. Sennacherib was assassinated by two of his sons, but a third, Esarhaddon (ee″sahr-had′un), promptly seized the throne. Curbing all disorders with a firm hand, Esarhaddon invaded Egypt in 671 B.C. and took the lower regions of the Nile Delta. For the first time in history, the Nile

* The Bible, written entirely from the religious standpoint of Yahvism, goes into great detail concerning Hezekiah's reign, praising him to the skies and picturing his catastrophic anti-Assyrian policy as resulting in the triumphant salvation of Jerusalem. It then goes on to skip over Manasseh's long, peaceful, and prosperous reign, denouncing him as an idolator and persecutor.

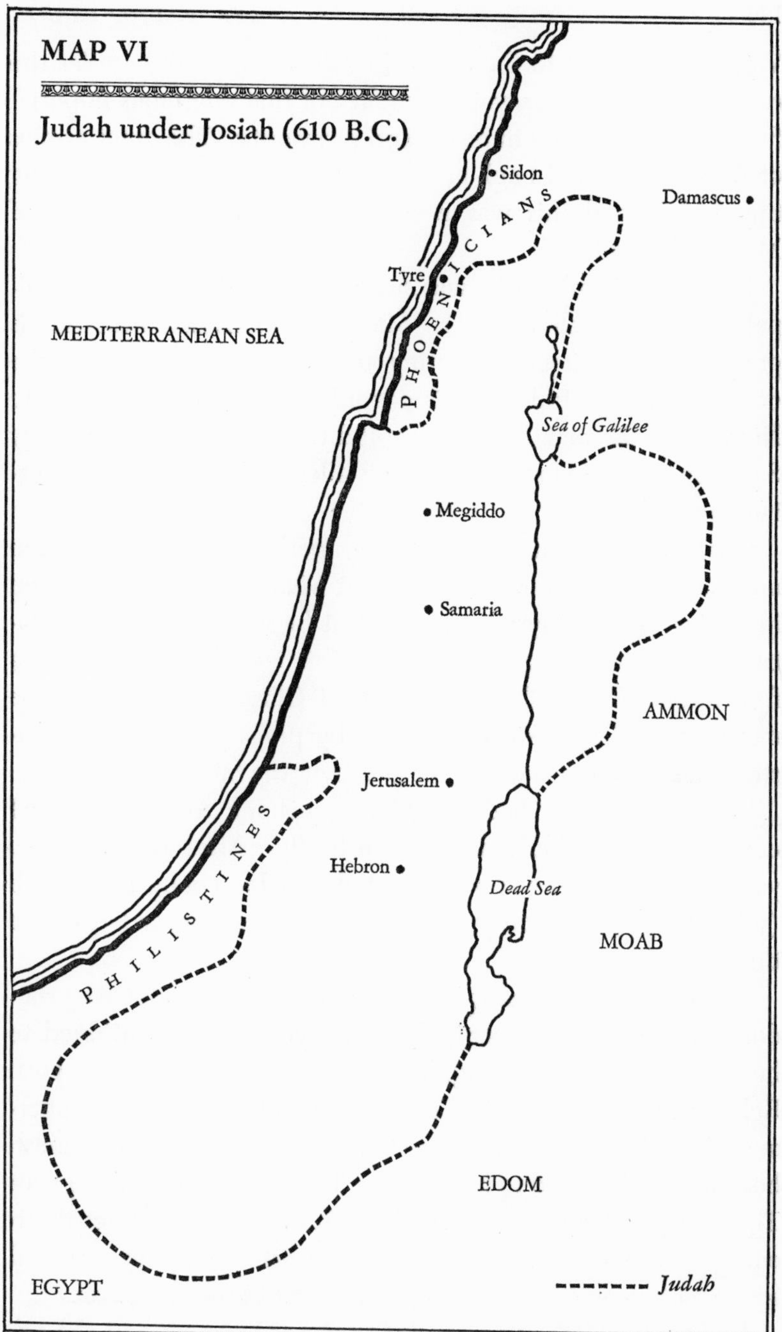
MAP VI
Judah under Josiah (610 B.C.)
Sidon
Damascus
PHOENICIANS
Tyre
MEDITERRANEAN SEA
Sea of Galilee
Megiddo
Samaria
AMMON
Jerusalem
PHILISTINES
Hebron
Dead Sea
MOAB
EDOM
EGYPT
Judah

Valley in addition to the entire Fertile Crescent was under the rule of a single power, yet in the face of that enormous imperial fact, Judah remained in peace and prosperity. The great armies of Assyria marched back and forth to Egypt without touching tiny Judah, and this was a tribute to the practical value of Manasseh's policy.

In 669 B.C. Esarhaddon was succeeded by his son, Ashurbanipal (ah″shoor-bah′nee-pal). Manasseh remained firm in his pro-Assyrian policy, attempting to take no advantage of the death of a king. Indeed, it is possible he may have traveled to Nineveh — the new Assyrian capital that had been founded by Sennacherib — in order to offer his allegiance to the new Assyrian monarch.

Centuries later a legend arose, perhaps out of the dim memory of this trip to Nineveh, that Manasseh had been taken in chains to the Assyrian capital, that he repented of his idolatries and became a good Yahvist. This legend, enshrined in a few verses of the Biblical Book of II Chronicles, seems to be merely an edifying story invented by pious priests to demonstrate the power of the true religion over the false.

When Manasseh died in 642 B.C., his son Amon (ay′mon) continued his father's policies faithfully. After reigning two years, however, he was assassinated and his young son Josiah (joh-sy′uh), only eight years old at the time, succeeded to the throne in 640 B.C.

But now a great change was coming over the vast Assyrian domain. Under Ashurbanipal, the Assyrian army continued to be strong and domineering, but at a constantly increasing cost. Rebellions were becoming more numerous and more dangerous. Egypt, which had been Assyria's most recent conquest, became the first land to break free. The Chaldeans of the lower Tigris-Euphrates were almost free. Judah felt a distinct lightening of the load, and shrewd observers of the scene could foresee a time when Assyria's empire would surely collapse.

As Assyria slowly weakened, therefore, Yahvism and the nationalism it represented grew stronger. We don't know for sure what the cause of Amon's assassination had been, but it is at least possible that it was engineered by the Yahvist priesthood, who were anxious for the succession of a child-king who might, conceivably, be molded in their image in the good times to come if the Assyrian Empire crumbled. Sure enough, by 632 B.C. when Josiah was sixteen, he had become distinctly Yahvist and the official Assyrian cults were pushed into the background.

In 627 B.C., Ashurbanipal died. He was the last great Assyrian king and with his death, there were instant rebellions among the subject peoples. Almost from the moment of the king's death, Assyria entered a precipitous, and final, decline.

Judah was among the subject kingdoms that took full advantage of the situation. The forces of Judah moved quickly northward into what had once been Israel, occupying the land nearly to Damascus and taking Transjordania as well. For the first time since the death of Solomon three centuries before, the territories of Israel and Judah were united under the Davidic dynasty ruling from Jerusalem.

In 622 B.C. Josiah ordered a complete renovation of the Temple, which had deteriorated greatly during the long period that had elapsed since the death of the last Yahvist king, sixty-five years before. The Yahvist priesthood, which had urged this, was ready. In a hidden recess of the stonework the high priest, Hilkiah (hil-ky′uh), announced the discovery of an old copy of a "Book of the Law." Cynics might suppose that this copy had been freshly prepared by the priesthood but the story that was put out, and accepted, was otherwise. The Book of the Law, which established Yahvism as the only permitted religion and which greatly enhanced the power of the priests and the prestige of the Temple, was dated back six centuries to the days of the legendary Moses, who was supposed to have received the Law in final and unchangeable form from God Himself on Mount Sinai.

The exact contents of the Book of the Law cannot be known for certain. It hasn't survived. Most Biblical scholars, however, are quite certain that it was very close to what we now call the Book of Deuteronomy, which contains a series of addresses supposedly given by Moses to the Israelite people shortly before he died and they crossed the Jordan.

Josiah accepted the book as an authentic relic of Mosaic Law and launched immediately into a complete and thoroughgoing religious reform. All traces of non-Yahvist worship were eradicated from the land. All local sanctuaries, Yahvist or not, were closed down, and all local worship was forbidden. The Temple was made the only shrine and Josiah presided over a grand Passover which seemed to see Judah reenter the golden age of David and Solomon.

The Phoenician cities also seemed to expand in the freedom that came with the rapid decline of Assyria. Although the rising Greeks continued to control the eastern Mediterranean, the Phoenicians penetrated all the further into the west, to a distance that was not to be exceeded for two thousand years.

During this period they established bases in what is now Algeria, occupied the Balearic Islands, extended their ancient occupation of the Spanish coast. They had ventured beyond the Strait of Gibraltar in the past for short distances, but now they burst forth massively. For the first time in history, the ships of a civilized power sailed the Atlantic Ocean, and they were ships manned by Canaanites.

North and south went the Phoenician sailors. Those that turned northward found new sources of the metal tin, so important in the manufacture of bronze — still an important material even in the growing age of iron. This tin, a new source of wealth for Tyre and its sister cities, was found in what they called the Tin Isles. Where these were we cannot be completely certain, but the common guess is that they were the Scilly Isles, a group of islets off Cornwall on the southwestern tip of England. Cornwall itself may have served as a tin source (and it still produces a little tin to this day).

Southward the Phoenician navigators made even more remarkable voyages. In the pay of an Egyptian king, they explored the African shores and made a complete circumnavigation of that giant continent. The only notice we have of that is in the works of the Greek historian Herodotus (hee-rod′oh-tus), who wrote two centuries later.

Herodotus didn't believe the tale told by the Phoenicians because they claimed that at the southern tip of Africa, the noonday sun appeared in the northern region of the sky. Since the noonday sun was always toward the south when viewed from Greece or, indeed, from any Mediterranean land, Herodotus felt that this was an invariable law of nature and that the Phoenicians were lying and, therefore, making up the whole story.

The southern tip of Africa is in the South Temperate Zone from where the noonday sun is indeed always to the north. The mere fact that the Phoenicians should describe this apparently impossible fact tells us that they really were that far south and probably did circumnavigate Africa.

But the golden age of Judah under Josiah did not last long. To be sure, Assyria tumbled and crashed. The Chaldeans, with their capital at Babylon, allied themselves with the Medes, a nomadic people to the northeast of the Tigris, and in 612 B.C. they took the Assyrian capital of Nineveh. The subject peoples howled with delight (as typified in the short Biblical Book of Nahum). By 610 B.C. one last Assyrian army was fighting hopelessly along the upper Euphrates River.

But now Egypt stirred. A new pharaoh was on the Egyptian throne. He was Necho II (nee′koh) and he aspired to have Egypt play a new and almost forgotten role. For the first time in six centuries, for the first time since Rameses III, Egypt aspired to an imperial role in Asia. After all, Egypt had suffered Assyrian occupation when that power had dominated the entire

Fertile Crescent, and it was to Egypt's interest to see to it that no new power should take over the total domination. The Chaldeans held the Tigris-Euphrates and that was enough.

The thing to do, Necho decided, was to advance to the Euphrates, support the last Assyrian army, and keep the western half of the Crescent free of the giant power to the east. While doing so, he might also pick up as much territory in the west as he could. This would serve as a further buffer between Egypt and the Chaldeans. With all that in mind, Necho II hurried his armies northward in 609 B.C.

In his way, however, stood Josiah of Judah. Josiah had extended the boundaries of Manasseh's small principality and had reestablished a major part of David's kingdom. He felt himself to be the head of an important power. What's more, he had reestablished the true religion and firmly believed that God was on his side — and the priesthood undoubtedly confirmed this belief.

Josiah was ready, therefore, to bar the way to any invading army. He gathered his forces and met the Egyptians at Megiddo, fifty-five miles north of Jerusalem, where over six centuries before Thutmose III had fought and won a great battle against the Canaanites. The verdict was the same this time. Again the Egyptians won, and Josiah was killed. The new golden age of Judah came to an abrupt end.

THE FALL OF JUDAH

Even a victory was a fatal blow to Necho's grand design, however. It delayed him, and the delay ruined everything. By the time he reached the Euphrates, the last Assyrian army was gone forever. The Chaldeans were in control, and were more formidable than ever. Necho flinched from a direct confrontation, but did take over all the territory south of the Euphrates. For a time, it almost seemed that the great days of Thutmose III had returned and that there was an Egyptian Empire once more.

Yet even so, the line of David did not come to an end. Judah remained and Jerusalem was unconquered. The people of Judah placed Jehoahaz (jee-hoh′uh-haz), a younger son of Josiah, on the throne. He kept the throne for only a few months, since he was unsatisfactory to Necho, who considered him insufficiently subservient to Egypt. Necho ordered him taken off to Egypt for life imprisonment and had an older son of Josiah, Jehoiakim (jee-hoy′uh-kim), take his place.

Judah was in no position to resist. It was not the great power Josiah had thought it to be. It was, after all, still the small kingdom that had to bend before the storm as in Manasseh's day. Jehoiakim swore allegiance to Egypt and paid tribute faithfully.

But there was still the Euphrates border, where Egyptian forces on the west glowered at Chaldeans on the east. The Chaldeans had consolidated their hold over the Tigris-Euphrates and felt it was time to put the Egyptians in their place.

The Chaldean king sent his son Nebuchadrezzar (neb′yoo-kad-rez′er) to take care of the matter. In 605 B.C. Nebuchadrezzar was on the frontier, organizing an offensive against the Egyptians. Before the inevitable battle was fought, the Chaldean king died and Nebuchadrezzar succeeded to the throne. Almost immediately thereafter the two armies fought at Carchemish, and the Chaldeans won a smashing victory. Necho's short-lived dream of glory (even briefer than that of Judah under Josiah) was shattered. What was left of the Egyptian forces tumbled southward.

Nebuchadrezzar and his Chaldeans now took over the Mediterranean shore, while the petty kingdoms of the region fell all over themselves in their haste to shift allegiance from Egypt to

Chaldea. Jehoiakim was one of these, but he was restless about it. He may have felt that his record as a loyal Egyptian puppet made him an object of suspicion to Nebuchadrezzar, who would therefore seize the first opportunity to replace him. Whether for that reason or for another, he kept an eye open for the first opportunity to rebel.

Egypt, which now found the Chaldean Empire to be only the Assyrian Empire under a new name, fell back on the old policy of encouraging and financing revolt. Jehoiakim who, in this period of national danger, nevertheless initiated a great building program, needed money, and it was to Egypt that he could turn for that.

At least one important spokesman in Judah warned against the policy of adventurism on which Jehoiakim embarked. This was Jeremiah (jer″uh-my′uh), who gloomily maintained that Nebuchadrezzar was too strong to be withstood, and that hope for aid from Egypt was a delusion. He recognized the element of psychological danger that existed in the ever-repeated story of the escape of Jerusalem from Assyrian siege under Sennacherib a century before, and the folly that lay in the growing trust (since Josiah's reform) in the Temple as the invincible guardian of the city.

Jeremiah insisted that one could not trust blindly in the Temple. In the Book of Jeremiah, he is recorded as saying, "Trust ye not in lying words, saying, The temple of the Lord, The temple of the Lord, The temple of the Lord . . ." (Jeremiah 7:4). He pointed out that it was not ritualistic worship that would save Judah, but ethical reform, and quotes God as saying: "Will ye steal, murder, and commit adultery, and swear falsely . . . And come and stand before me in this house . . . and say, We are delivered . . ." (Jeremiah 7:9–10). He also recalled that an earlier sanctuary at Shiloh, in the days of the Judges, had been destroyed. Jeremiah, however, spoke in vain.

In 601 B.C. Chaldeans again faced Egyptians but this time at the border of Egypt itself. The Egyptians, fighting desperately, threw the Chaldeans back and preserved their independence. That was enough for Jehoiakim. He refused tribute to Nebuchadrezzar. It took some time for Nebuchadrezzar to react. There were other matters in his far-flung empire that had to be tended to first. By 597 B.C., however, Jehoiakim's turn had come. The Chaldean army encircled Jerusalem and settled down to a siege.

In the course of the siege Jehoiakim died. He may even have been assassinated. His teen-age son Jehoiachin (jee-hoy′uh-kin) succeeded, but it was to a position that was completely unenviable, for it was apparent to anyone without blind faith in divine intervention that Jerusalem could not hold out much longer.

Three months after Jehoiachin's succession, Jerusalem fell and the Chaldean army marched in. Nebuchadrezzar, considering that Judah was utterly at his feet, was merciful. What he did was to take Jehoiachin and some thousands of the ruling classes off to exile in Chaldea. In this way, he hoped to break Judean national consciousness as Tiglath-pileser had done by similar treatment to Israel a century and a quarter before.

Nevertheless, Judah itself was kept alive, with Jerusalem and the Temple intact. It even retained a king, for Nebuchadrezzar allowed the enthronement of Zedekiah, the uncle of Jehoiachin and the third son of Josiah, to sit on the throne in Jerusalem.

Judah was now so weak as to be utterly insignificant and yet it still listened to the blandishments of Egypt. Despite all that Jeremiah could do, Zedekiah, pushed on by a priesthood still infatuated with the mystical protection of the Temple, waited for a chance to rebel yet again.

In 589 B.C. he decided the time was propitious. Egypt had managed to persuade all the petty kingdoms of the area — Moab, Ammon, Edom, Tyre — to stand against Nebuchadrezzar. She herself promised to fight as well. So Zedekiah refused tribute, and when Nebuchadrezzar came thundering southward in 587 B.C., all the other nations, including Egypt, discovered they had other things to do and Judah was left to face the music by itself. Jerusalem was taken for the second time and now Nebuchadrezzar decided he would put an end to it. He sacked Jerusalem and destroyed the Temple, razing it to the ground 367 years after it had been dedicated by Solomon. What's more, when the fleeing Zedekiah was captured by the Chaldean forces, he had him blinded and his sons executed. Zedekiah had been the twenty-first king of the Davidic dynasty to sit on the throne in Jerusalem and he was the last. The Davidic dynasty came to an end 427 years after the accession of David.

Another large group of Judeans were then carried off into exile, while those who yet remained were placed under Gedaliah (ged″uh-ly′uh), a Judean of good family who now ruled as governor over a Chaldean province.

Gedaliah remained as governor for only three months and was then assassinated. In the Bible, the assassination is said to have been at the instigation of the Ammonite king, but it seems more likely, surely, that he was killed by Judean nationalists who considered him a Chaldean puppet. Certainly, the Judeans still in Judah felt that Nebuchadrezzar would interpret the event as yet another recrudescence of Judean nationalism and react accordingly. There was panic in Judah and a number of Judeans fled to Egypt, taking Jeremiah (against his will) with them.

Thus, Judah, like Israel before it, was depopulated. Its ruling classes, its landowners and administrators were scattered over the valleys of the Tigris-Euphrates and of the Nile. Left behind on the land were only the unlettered and unsophisticated, who remained Yahvists on a rather primitive level. The last remnant of the work of David seemed to have been undone.

7

JUDAISM

EXILE

It might have been reasonable to suppose that Yahvism would now die out or, at best, linger on as an insignificant cult for some centuries. Had this taken place, as men at the time would have every reason to think it would, the entire history of the world would have been changed and would have moved in unknown directions.

It did not happen. The movement that had begun with Hezekiah's reforms, the feeling that had arisen out of Sennacherib's failure to destroy Jerusalem, the conviction that Yahveh and his Temple were supreme even over powers that seemed much greater in the battles of the earth, the exaltation that came with the continuing reforms of Josiah — all seemed to linger and to uplift the men of Judah even in exile and in utter defeat.

Instead of feeling that their religion could be practiced only on their native ground and the home territory of their god, they carried him about in their hearts and their faith, as once they had carried him about in the ark of the covenant.

In Egypt, for instance, a party of Judeans had been employed on the island of Elephantine on the Nile River, at just about the southern border of modern Egypt. There they could serve as hard-fighting mercenaries guarding the southern border of the land against the Nubians. And on that island, some 700 miles south of Jerusalem, they established a temple to Yahveh.

It was in Babylon and its environs, however, that the Judeans really accomplished a miracle.

That they did so was made possible by several factors. In the first place, Nebuchadrezzar was an enlightened monarch. He did not mistreat and persecute the exiled people of Judah. Having made sure they would no longer rebel and trouble his empire, he was satisfied. In the lower reaches of the Tigris-Euphrates valley, where they settled in a "Babylonian Exile," they were treated with complete toleration. They were even allowed to worship Yahveh freely.

It may have been Nebuchadrezzar's hope that they would assimilate themselves to Babylonian customs and prove a worthwhile addition to the prosperity and industry of the land. In this hope, he may have been justified in part. Certainly, the Judeans fit themselves into the economy and many of them became quite well-to-do. It is quite likely that a number of them (perhaps even a majority) became Babylonian.

Just the same, a sizable number of the exiles remained stubbornly Yahvist. That they could do so in exile and even with the Temple destroyed was owing, in part, to the fact that they now had copies of the Book of the Law that had been brought to public notice in Josiah's time, as well as the historical traditions that had been put into writing in Hezekiah's time, plus the scrolls attributed to such prophets as Isaiah and Jeremiah.

Those of the exiles who clung to Yahvism could therefore

gather freely in groups, read the Law, interpret it, ponder over it, and so on. Such an assembly met to study the law is a "congregation," from Latin words meaning "to gather together." The equivalent expression drawn from Greek words is "synagogue." Yahvism, deprived of its Temple, lived on in its synagogues.

The writings and traditions were not in final form, however. As they were copied and recopied, it was impossible to keep the sophistication of Babylon from entering the cruder records of the Judeans. Incorporated into the revered writings was the Babylonian legend of the creation of the earth, freed, of course, of its pagan elements. The story of Adam and Eve, the list of the long-lived descendants of that couple, the story of the great Flood that visited mankind, the tale of the Tower of Babel—all stem from Babylonian legend.

The Babylonians had the custom of dividing the years into seven-day periods because their complex astronomical science attached a great deal of importance to the seven planets. The exiled Judeans accepted this, and gave to the seventh day the religious significance that burgeoned into the Sabbath.

The great ancestor Abraham, from whom the Judeans and the Israelites traced their descent, had lived in Haran (hah-rahn′) prior to his arrival in Canaan, according to the records. Haran was a city at the top of the arch of the Fertile Crescent, sixty miles east of Carchemish. The Judeans now traced his tale further back and recorded him to have been born in Ur, an ancient city in Sumeria. In this way, the Judeans tied in their ancestry with that of the Babylonians themselves.

Despite all this assimilationism, however, there remained ardent Yahvists who did not give up their national longings. According to their view, Judah had been justly punished by Yahveh for its sins, but, after repentance, the exiles would be restored and a new Jerusalem would arise much better than the old, under a new king of the house of David, and a new nation would be established that would rule the earth and last forever.

The words of the prophets of earlier times were ransacked for passages that could be interpreted to fit the present longings. And it is not beyond the bounds of possibility that appropriate passages were added to the older writings in order that these might uphold the national spirit.

Thus, there is a passage in the writings of Isaiah, which goes: "*And there shall come forth a rod out of the stem of Jesse* [*the father of David*], *and a Branch shall grow out of his roots:/And the spirit of the Lord shall rest upon him . . .*" (Isaiah 11:1–2).

If this passage is authentic Isaiah, it may possibly have been part of a poem originally meant to celebrate the coronation of a new king of Judah, perhaps Hezekiah. Or else it celebrated the birth of an heir to the throne.

It was, nevertheless, easy to reinterpret such a passage and make it become a divinely inspired promise that a descendant of the house of David would yet sit on the throne in Jerusalem. The ideal kingdom that would result, once the men of Judah were free of all sin and were determined to follow the Law, was also found to be described in the writings of Isaiah. It was written there: ". . . *it shall come to pass in the last days, that the mountain of the Lord's house shall be established in the top of the mountains, and shall be exalted above the hills; and all nations shall flow into it. And many people shall go and say, Come ye, and let us go up to the mountain of the Lord, to the house of the God of Jacob; and he will teach us of his ways, and we will walk in his paths: for out of Zion shall go forth the law, and the word of the Lord from Jerusalem. And he shall judge among the nations, and shall rebuke many people: and they shall beat their swords into plowshares, and their spears into pruning hooks: nation shall not lift up sword against nation, neither shall they learn war any more*" (Isaiah 2:2–4).

This, which may have been no more than a mystical vision of an ideal society, might well be applied by the exiles to the triumphant Judah that awaited them on their return after their sins were forgiven. Naturally, it was difficult to talk openly about a return and about the reestablishment of the monarchy under a king of the old line, since this could be interpreted as sedition. Nebuchadrezzar was a tolerant monarch, but there are limits.

Consequently, the exiles were forced to speak with a certain cautious obscurity. They spoke of "the Anointed One" or "Messiah" in speaking of the king of the house of David who would rule over them on their return to Judah. This mystical looking forward to the establishment of an ideal Judah under an ideal king of the line of David is therefore called "messianism." From the Babylonian Exile onward, messianism persisted, growing stronger in times of trouble.

The most important spiritual guide of the exiles in Babylonia was Ezekiel (ee-zeek′yul). He seems to have been a member of the house of Zadok, which had supplied the succession of the high priesthood ever since the time of Solomon. He had been carried off into exile along with Jehoiachin in 597 B.C. after the first siege and capture of Jerusalem. A fiery Yahvist, Ezekiel believed in the restoration of the kingdom and carefully described the structure of the Temple and the nature of its ritual after the restoration.

The modified Yahvism worked out among the exiles in Babylon was never put into practice completely, but it served as a model on which later beliefs were based. The new Yahvism is what we would today call Judaism and Ezekiel is sometimes called "the father of Judaism."

From this point on, then, I will speak of "Judaism" as the dominant Yahvistic belief, reserving the older term "Yahvism" for those who, like the Samaritans, worshiped Yahveh in forms dating back to before the Babylonian Exile.

Those who practiced Judaism we can now call Jews, distinguishing them from the other inhabitants of the old land of

Canaan, and even from the men of Judah and their descendants who had been left behind in the old land when the wealthier and more learned classes had been dragged off into exile.

TYRE AND CARTHAGE

If the Jews in exile in the east were not too badly off and could indulge in the study of the Law and in messianic longings, Nebuchadrezzar in the west found that his troubles were by no means over with the fall and destruction of Jerusalem.

The Phoenicians still remained and their subservience was limited. It is a tribute to their strength of will and to the efficacy of sea power that they had been independent before the Israelites had stormed their way into Canaan and they still had a measure of independence after the Judeans had been driven out. A king had ruled in Tyre all through the period when the Davidic Empire had been at its height. Tyre had retained a king of its own through the entire period of the great Assyrian Empire and it retained its king even when Nebuchadrezzar was humbling the Mediterranean shore.

At the time of the fall of Jerusalem, Ithobaal III (ih-thoh-bay′ul) was king of Tyre. He had listened to the siren song of Egypt and had joined with Zedekiah of Judah in plotting rebellion. When the crunch had come, Tyre had cautiously refrained from action, but Nebuchadrezzar was not satisfied to let Tyre wait for a better opportunity. Immediately after the fall of Jerusalem, he demanded the surrender of Tyre; when that was refused, he laid siege to it.

Here, however, Nebuchadrezzar found matters more difficult than he expected. Jerusalem, an inland city, could be surrounded on all sides and, with reasonable persistence, could be starved into submission. Tyre, however, could not be starved as long as the sea was open and its ships were in commission.

Nebuchadrezzar, however, was prepared to be unreasonably persistent. For *thirteen years* he maintained the siege until Tyre, though impregnable, grew weary to death of the destruction of its industries, the attrition of its men, and its own imprisonment upon the small island. In 574 B.C. they offered Nebuchadrezzar a compromise peace and the Chaldean monarch, equally weary of the endless expense of the siege and of the drain on his manpower by disease and desertion, accepted the compromise. Tyre was spared occupation and sack. Its self-rule was not destroyed. Ithobaal III was removed as king but Baal I took his place, after having promised to remain a loyal subordinate to the Chaldeans.

The long siege, while leaving Tyre alive and intact, had weakened her to the point where any remaining influence it held over the Phoenician colonies in the western Mediterranean vanished. From this point on the colonies were completely independent, although an emotional tie undoubtedly persisted.

The colonies were independent of Tyre, that is, but yet not totally free. Carthage, the strongest of the Phoenician cities in the west, formed and headed a league of those cities which it dominated more and more. Carthage established its own colonies and outposts along the western Mediterranean shore both in Africa and Europe right out to the straits of Gibraltar. It became stronger and richer than any Canaanite city in history. It was to retain that position for four centuries.

The Carthaginians did not have everything all their own way by any means. The Greeks, having filled the coasts of the eastern Mediterranean, were coming west. They settled the coasts of southern Italy and of eastern Sicily.

In Sicily the Greeks were particularly dangerous to Carthage. If they succeeded in rimming the coast of the island with settlements, they would, at the western end of the island, approach to within ninety miles of Carthage itself. Carthage preempted that possibility by settling the western corner of the island itself. (The native peoples of Sicily were caught between the Greeks and Carthaginians, but though they sometimes fought with one against the other, they were never able to extricate themselves from the competing forces that were to fight each other over their heads for the next three centuries and more.) In Italy, the Greeks in the south were face to face with a people known as Etruscans,* who controlled the western shore of Italy farther north.

Both Carthaginians and Etruscans were reluctant to start a war. If the Greeks had stayed in the east of Sicily and in the south of Italy and had made no effort to expand farther, the situation might have remained tolerable for the western powers. About 550 B.C., however, Greek settlers pushed on beyond Italy. They founded a city on the northern shore of the Mediterranean which they called Massalia (and which survives to this day as Marseilles). They also landed on the islands of Corsica and Sardinia, just north of the Carthaginian shore of Africa and just west of the Etruscan shore of Italy.

The Carthaginians and the Etruscans formed an alliance, therefore, and about 540 B.C. fought a naval battle with the Greeks. The Greeks were defeated and this marked the end of the period of Greek colonization. Massalia remained in existence, but the Greeks were driven off the islands. Carthage took over Sardinia and the Etruscans took Corsica, each having the island nearer its base.

THE RETURN

The Jews continued their relatively comfortable life in Babylon. After Nebuchadrezzar died in 561 B.C., the lot of the Jews

* The Etruscans were of unknown antecedents but, like the Carthaginians, were thought to have arrived from the east — from Asia Minor, perhaps.

improved still further. The new king, Amel-Marduk (ah′mel-mahr′dook), who is called Evil-Merodach in the Bible, freed Jehoiachin, the exiled king of Judah who had been in not-too-onerous imprisonment for thirty-six years.

The Jews might have hoped that this would be a forerunner of the reestablishment of Judah, but, if Amel-Marduk intended such a thing or could be persuaded into it, we will never know. He was assassinated within two years and after that there was a period of anarchy until 555 B.C., when Nabonidus (nab″oh-ny′dus), who was a priest and not of the family of Nebuchadrezzar, became king. Nabonidus was a scholar and an antiquarian and left the main business of rule to his son Belshazzar (bel-shaz′er).

From the death of Nebuchadrezzar on, however, the Chaldean Empire was decaying rapidly, and a new conqueror was on the horizon. This was Cyrus, ruler of a group of tribes known as the Persians. In 559 B.C. he had made himself ruler of the vast territories north and east of Chaldea, founding the Persian Empire. In 546 B.C. he extended his rule westward over Asia Minor and it seemed clear that he had his eye on the Tigris-Euphrates valley itself — the richest, most advanced, longest-civilized region on earth. What's more, there seemed nothing to stop him, for the Chaldean Empire was in disarray.

The Jews in exile, or at least those among them who had the messianic dream, were in a state of ecstatic excitement. Possibly the quick vanishing of the glimmer of hope under Amel-Marduk had embittered them against Chaldea. Or perhaps there was merely the realistic calculation that if they embarked on a pro-Persian policy, they would be backing a winner, and Cyrus, out of gratitude, might restore them to Judah.

At any rate, they were pro-Persian, and this attitude found an expression in a prophet who was an extraordinary poet, but who is nameless forever. His writings were attributed to the prophet Isaiah, who had lived nearly two centuries before, in order to give them greater credence, and they appear in the

Book of Isaiah, from the fortieth chapter onward. Whereas the earlier chapters deal with the time of Sennacherib, the later ones suddenly involved Cyrus. The prophet who appeared in the latter years of the exile is therefore known only as "the Second Isaiah."

The Second Isaiah hailed the coming of Cyrus and in so doing, he put forth a new view of Yahveh. Yahveh was now no longer merely the god of the Jews and the only one they were permitted to worship. He was not even merely the greatest god in the universe; he was the *only* god in the universe and the only one *anyone* could usefully worship. Yahveh was the god of Jew and non-Jew alike.

All history, according to this view, was part of the design of God. If Jerusalem and the Temple were destroyed that was God's doing and Nebuchadrezzar was his tool. When the time came that Jerusalem and the Temple were to be restored, that, too, was God's doing and Cyrus was to be his tool.

The Second Isaiah describes God as having "raised up the righteous man [Cyrus] from the east, called him to his foot, gave the nations before him, and made him rule over kings" (II Isaiah 41:2). The Second Isaiah does not even hesitate to give Cyrus a messianic title, for he says, "Thus saith the Lord to his anointed, to Cyrus, whose right hand I have holden, to subdue nations before him . . ." (II Isaiah 45:1).

It is with the Second Isaiah that true monotheism came to be, the belief of a particular divine being as the one and only god of the universe. True monotheism thus becomes another of the great innovations presented the world by the peoples of the western portion of the Fertile Crescent.

The calculations of the exiles proved correct. In 538 B.C. Cyrus and his Persians invaded Chaldea, which collapsed nearly at once. (To what extent, the exiles served as a fifth column — or if they did — is not known.) In any case, Cyrus paid his debts. He granted permission for those Jews who wished to do so to return to Judah and rebuild their Temple. It was, however, a purely religious return he granted them. Nothing was said about restoring the kingdom of Judah.

At once a band of Jews began the journey to the spot where Jerusalem had once been. They by no means represented all the Jews in the Tigris-Euphrates. Many, probably most, remained behind, unminded to give up their settled and prosperous life for the adventure of rebuilding a ruined land. Many made contributions of money and goods to those who were returning, but they stayed where they were. Indeed, they and their descendants preserved a flourishing Jewish community in the Tigris-Euphrates valley for fifteen centuries.

The first band of Jews returning to Jerusalem was under the leadership of someone named in the Bible as Sheshbazzar (shesh-baz′er) and described as the "prince of Judah." Some identify him as a son of Jehoiachin. Jehoiachin was deposed as king and carried off into exile in 597 B.C., but at that time he may have been only eighteen years old. He died about 560 B.C. It was quite possible that a son of Jehoiachin would be alive in 538 B.C., but if so he would probably be in late middle age at best.

Sheshbazzar apparently presided over the laying of the foundation of the new Temple to be built on the site of the old one and then he disappears from the tale. Perhaps he died. His place was taken by Zerubbabel (zeh-rub′uh-bel), usually considered a nephew of Sheshbazzar and a grandson of Jehoiachin — and therefore the descendant, in the twentieth generation, of David.

With Zerubbabel was Jeshua (jesh′oo-uh), the son of the high priest who had officiated in Jerusalem at the time of the destruction of the Temple. Together they built an altar on the site of the old Temple, an altar at which sacrifices might be performed. Thus, there was continuity. Zerubbabel represented the house of David, the secular authority stretching back in an unbroken line to David himself. Jeshua was the priestly authority stretching back in an unbroken line to Zadok, high priest under Solomon, when the Temple was first built.

There was, however, trouble, as one might expect. The rebuilding of the Temple could not proceed in a vacuum. In the imaginations of the Jews in Babylonian Exile, it might have seemed as though Judah lay empty and desolate, but it was, of course, no such thing. There remained the common people who had never been deported, most of whom were Yahvists.

When the exiles returned, these Yahvists eagerly asked permission to share in the rebuilding. There had been a separation of half a century, however, and neither side understood the other. The returning exiles now had a Yahvism tinged with Babylonian notions and the teachings of Ezekiel — Judaism, in short. To the returning Jews, the Yahvists who remained on the land, and whom the Jews called Samaritans, were merely heretics practicing a debased form of the true religion. When the Samaritans offered to help with the Temple, the Jews were horrified and would have nothing to do with them.

The Samaritans were bitterly offended and, before long, came to realize that from their own point of view, the returning Jews had added all sorts of foreign accretions to their Yahvism, and it was the returnees who were heretics. Jews and Samaritans became bitter foes as a result and remained foes for centuries afterward. They were never reconciled. Nor was it the Samaritans only. The neighbors of Judah to east, south, and west still existed and had never forgotten the ancient enmity that had existed since David had placed them all under subjection.

Ammon and Moab existed east of the Jordan River and the Dead Sea and found in the projected restoration of the Temple only a recrudescence of Jewish imperialism. On the west the Philistine cities, who were enjoying a period of prosperity, were also hostile. They now controlled the entire coast south of Joppa and were united, with the city of Ashdod as their capital.

Then, too, during the time of the Chaldean Empire, an Arabic tribe called the Nabateans had pressed northward out of the arid peninsula into what had once been Edom. They established their capital at Petra (pee′truh), sixty miles south of the Red Sea, and attained prosperity there because it was an important crossing point for various trade routes.

The Edomites, driven back by Nabatean pressure, moved northward in their turn, into Judah, which, after the destruction of Jerusalem and the removal of the propertied classes, could not resist. A new Edom had been formed therefore in southern Judah; and this new Edom is perhaps best known by the name it later got from the Greeks — Idumea (id″oo-mee′uh).

There began a round of intrigue only dimly visible from this distance, for the Biblical tale is by no means clear. The direct use of force was impossible, of course, since all the lands were alike under Persian control. All that could be done was to attempt to influence the Persian governor on the spot or to go over his head to the Persian king. For quite a while, the enemies of the Jews had the better of it, and for this the Jews might have had only their own overenthusiasm to blame.

Two prophets of the time were involved: Haggai (hag′ay-igh) and Zechariah. Both were intent on pushing forward the work on the Temple and hailed Zerubbabel as the Messiah — that is, as the king of the house of David who would rule over the restored Judah.

But this amounted to rebellion. The Persians were willing to tolerate a religion but not to see an independent kingdom set up. Presumably, the enemies of the Jews reported the messianic pretension to the Persians and Zerubbabel disappeared. At least, he is no further mentioned in the Bible. Presumably, the Persians removed him and, possibly, executed him. It was both the first and the last attempt to restore the Davidic dynasty to the throne. That dynasty appears no more in actual history, though it continues to figure in messianic longings.

With Zerubbabel gone, however, the Jewish case grew stronger again. A new king had succeeded to the Persian Empire in

521 B.C., Darius I (duh-ry′us). He made the final decision that allowed the work on the Temple to proceed, and in 516 B.C., twenty-two years after Cyrus' initial permission and just seventy years after the Temple had been destroyed by Nebuchadrezzar, a new structure, usually called the Second Temple, arose in its place.

EZRA AND NEHEMIAH

The Second Temple must have been a poor piece of work, both in comparison with the mighty structures of Babylon, and with the no-doubt exaggerated memories of the first Temple. The restored land must have been an even greater disappointment. It could scarcely be called Judah, for it had nothing in common with the preexilic kingdom. It had no king, no independence, no power of even the smallest. Even the religion had changed in certain important ways. Rather than call it Judah, therefore, let us from this point on use the version of the name that stems from the Greeks, who were later to arrive on the scene, and call it Judea (joo-dee′uh).

At the foundation of the Second Temple, Judea was small indeed, perhaps 400 square miles in area, less than half the size of the state of Rhode Island. On all sides were bitter enemies: Samaritans to the north, Ammonites to the east, Idumeans to the south, and Philistines to the west.

Was this then the ideal kingdom that was to spring up on the occasion of the return from exile? The messianic dreams that had buoyed up the Jews through the decades of exile had turned out to be ashes, and enthusiasm withered. That the whole project did not collapse may have been due to one zealot, a man named Ezra.

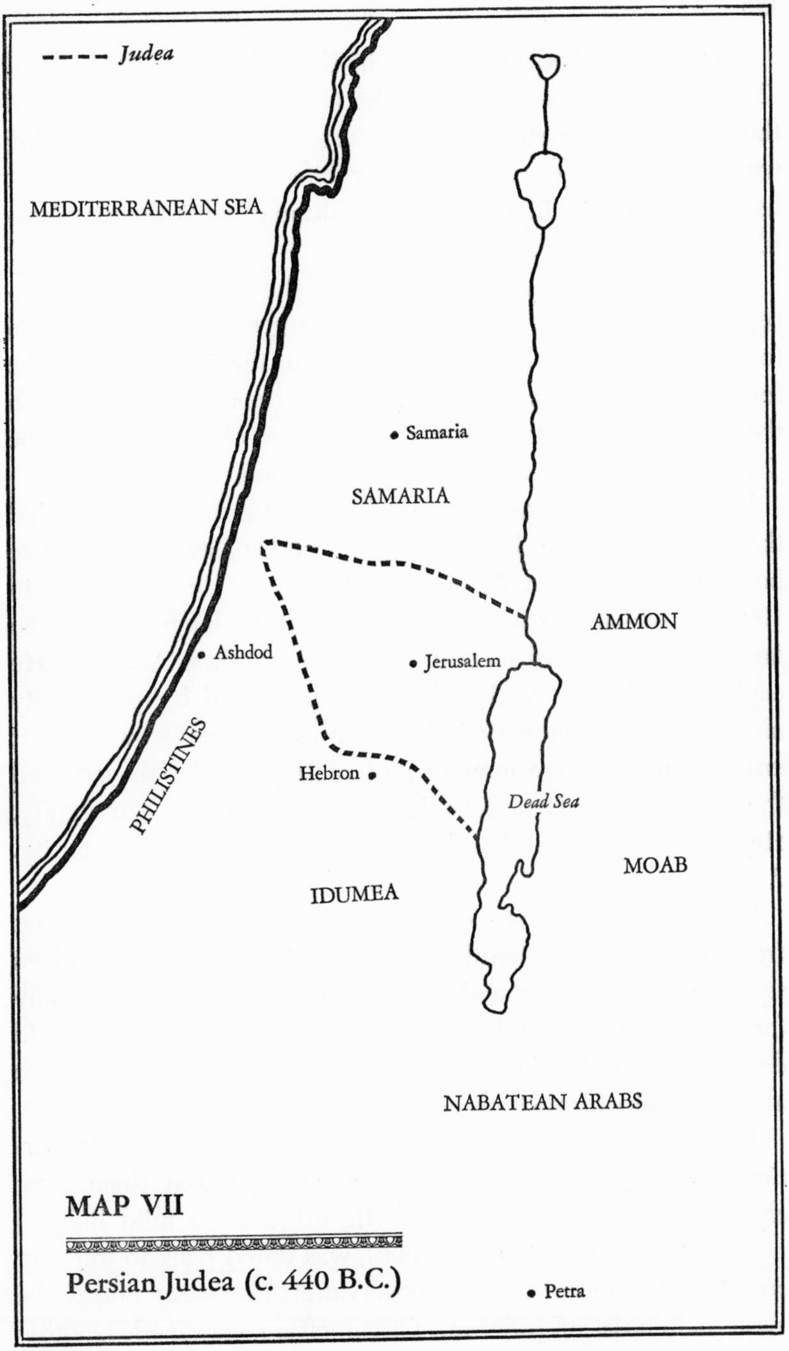

MAP VII

Persian Judea (c. 440 B.C.)

Ezra is described as a scribe in the Biblical Book of Ezra. That means that he was one of the group of Jews who devoted themselves to the study and analysis of the writings dealing with the ritual law of Judaism. While in Babylonia he must have worked out a highly idealistic notion of what the new Jewish state ought to be.

He came to Jerusalem in 458 B.C. (the most commonly accepted date, though not the only one suggested) and of course found the reality to be far removed from the ideal. In fact, he found the restoration dying. The Jews were intermarrying with the people of the land and the religious observances at the Temple were becoming increasingly slipshod.

Ezra began what would today be called a revival. He called the Jews together and read the books of the Law (the first five books of our present Bible) to assemblies. He read them in Hebrew, which was now becoming a sacred language, for the language of the Jews generally since the exile was Aramaic. He explained what he read as he went along and his personality must have been magnetic indeed, for he was greeted with great enthusiasm. A large enough part of the population accepted the Law to give Ezra considerable power in the community. He went on to demand and enforce a program of racial purity. All Jews were to put away non-Jewish wives and children.

This began a history of self-conscious separation of Jews from non-Jews (or Gentiles). Caught in a seemingly endless sea of enemies, so few and weak as to be helpless, without any form of political self-rule, it seemed to the Jews that they could defend their national consciousness only by keeping themselves absolutely aloof from their neighbors.

Rigid adherence to the Law was one way of doing this, particularly such portions of the Law as separated them most clearly. The notion of the Sabbath, originally a mild Babylonian custom of marking the weeks, was dated back to the very creation of the earth, and its observation was made one of the great hallmarks of Judaism. Circumcision was made another hallmark separating Jew from Gentile. One could not become a Jew without submitting to the operation.

Then, too, there were the writings considered particularly holy. To the books of the Law were added the early historical writings contained now in the books of Joshua, Judges, the two parts of Samuel, and the two parts of Kings. The writings of the great prophets of the days through the erection of the Second Temple were also included. A rewriting of the history of the kingdom of Judah (and ignoring that of Israel) designed to stress religious rather than secular matters was included also. This makes up the two parts of Chronicles, and, according to tradition, it was Ezra himself who wrote it.

Eventually other books of particular religious or literary merit were included, especially when they could be attributed to some eminent man of the past. There were included a collection of religious songs — Psalms — attributed to David, a collection of wise sayings — Proverbs — and an erotic poem — Song of Songs — attributed to Solomon, who was also supposed to have written the philosophic essay we call Ecclesiastes. There was a poem of lamentation — Lamentations — attributed to Jeremiah, and so on. In short, the Jews found themselves with the Bible and this, too, helped separate them from the Gentiles.

Undoubtedly not all Jews favored this program of separatism. It was about the time of the restoration that the small books of Ruth and Jonah were written, in each case showing sympathy for non-Jews. In Ruth the tale is told of a beautiful and virtuous Moabite girl who became the ancestress of the great king David. In Jonah the prophet's desire for the destruction of the capital of the Assyrian kingdom is rebuked by God. Considering that both Moab and Assyria were among the bitterest enemies of Judah in past days, these are remarkable pleas for tolerance — and were done well enough to insure the inclusion of both books in the Biblical anthology.

However, it was separatism that won out. From the time of

Ezra onward, Jews were different from the surrounding peoples and deliberately cultivated the difference. This resulted in the growth of religious intolerance, something the world had seen little of until then. The Jews could not make that intolerance effective, of course, since they were so few in numbers. The view was, however, inherited by Christianity and Islam, and intolerance then became a world tragedy, with the Jews themselves among the worst and most prolonged sufferers.

Even the religious revival under Ezra might not have endured long without some source of national self-respect. The minimum necessary for that was supplied by Nehemiah nee″uh-my′uh). Nehemiah was a Jew who held the post of cupbearer to the Persian king Artaxerxes I (ahr′tuk-zurk′seez), who succeeded to the Persian throne in 464 B.C.

Nehemiah left what was a high and secure position to visit the bedraggled Jews of Judea, first using his influence with Artaxerxes to extort permission to fortify Jerusalem against the surrounding enemies. He arrived in Judea about 440 B.C., studied the existing walls, which were virtually worthless, and began a drive to dismantle them and build real ones in their place. With reliance on the good will of the Persian king, Nehemiah faced down opposition from the surrounding peoples who considered that a fortified Jerusalem would be one more step in the direction of the Jewish imperialism they dreaded.

He carried through the task about 437 B.C., and Jerusalem was then once again a fortified city capable of withstanding a siege — at least one that was not very determined. The city so fortified was a tiny one — not more than 100 acres in area. It held the Temple, however, and the rocky strong point ("city of David") where a last firm stand might be made.

Little as it was, it made the Jews feel a nation. They had a capital city that could be defended, a home, however small, in which they could be masters. The great destruction of exactly 150 years before was reversed — except for the fact they had no true political independence.

Really, the Jews were not badly off. For a century following they had virtually no history (usually the sign of peace and prosperity) and lived securely under the Persians. There were not many such centuries in their long and dark history. In this blank interval, Judaism developed considerably, borrowing much from the dominant Persian culture.

The Persian religion was dualistic. That is, it pictured a universe in which there was a principal of good and one of evil, both virtually independent of each other and very nearly equal. The creation of the world, its development and history, were all incidents in the unending celestial warfare between those two principals, each at the head of a separate army of innumerable spirits. Mankind could take part in the battle, fighting on the side of good or of evil.

This view of the universe is an exciting and dramatic one. It gives meaning to life to suppose that an individual man can choose his army and fight for one side or the other. Until the return from exile, Judaism had dealt with a god who was considered the author of everything, both good and evil. After the return, however, a spirit of evil was developed — Satan, which is the Hebrew word for "the adversary." Satan, who was at eternal odds with God, does not appear in the Biblical books that date from the exile or before but begins to appear in those books written during the Persian domination (Chronicles, Job).

Along with Satan, hordes and hierarchies of angels and demons entered into the Judaic view, together with notions of an afterlife, involving rewards for those on God's side and punishment for those on Satan's. Judaism never grew entirely dualistic, however. The spirit of evil was never given any chance of winning out over God. In fact, as is evidenced by the Book of Job, he serves as God's instrument, doing only what he is permitted to do and helping achieve God's purposes by doing so.

8

CANAAN VERSUS GREECE

THE NUTCRACKER

While the Jews were in Babylonian Exile, the Phoenicians stayed at home but remained unreconciled. Tyre, as a result of Nebuchadrezzar's long siege, had gone into deep decline and for a brief period, Sidon had once more become the most important Phoenician city.

When the Persians overthrew the Chaldean Empire, the Phoenicians, like the Jews, were enthusiastic partisans of the newcomers. Unlike the Jews, however, the Phoenicians had something of obvious value they could offer the Persians. They were skilled seamen and had navies at their disposal, while the Persians were a land power without any experience at sea. The Persians might have gained the experience (no people are innately incapable of learning how to handle ships) but it was easier for them simply to make use of the Phoenicians.

Thus, when Cambyses (kam-by′seez), the son of Cyrus, succeeded to the Persian throne in 530 B.C., he at once planned the conquest of Egypt. It was his intention to attack by both land and sea, himself leading the Persian army through Sinai, while the Phoenician navy carried soldiers to the mouth of the Nile and, if necessary, up that river.

The task was not difficult and in 525 B.C. Cambyses won Egypt after a single battle. The land was easily pacified and Cambyses could not help but long to extend his conquests farther, either south or west. To go southward up the Nile into the vast interior of Africa would have meant marching into the unknown, and after some probing ventures, he backed away.

Westward, things looked better. The distances were equally long but they could be covered by sea, and the Mediterranean was familiar from end to end, whereas the jungles of the upper Nile were not. Here, however, Cambyses met a human obstacle. The greatest city west of Egypt was Carthage and, fearing that it was at Carthage that Cambyses aimed, the Phoenician admirals called a halt. They informed Cambyses that they could not, and would not, fight against their own kinsmen.

Without a fleet Cambyses would not move westward across the Libyan desert and his conquest of Egypt was left a dead end. Before he could decide what to do next, he died in 522 B.C. His successor, Darius I (who was to give final permission for the rebuilding of the Temple at Jerusalem), maintained the Persian hold over Egypt but was not interested in further conquests in Africa. His eyes were turned toward Europe, and here the Phoenicians could serve him with enthusiasm.

For centuries the Greeks and Phoenicians had disputed the mastery of the Mediterranean. The Greeks held the eastern half and the Phoenicians the western; but now the Phoenicians saw the chance — with the aid of their Persian employers — to seize it all.

At first Darius attacked directly those sections of Europe north of Greece itself, but a direct confrontation was inevitable sooner or later. Included in the Persian Empire were the

Ionian (Greek) cities along the western shores of Asia Minor. Of these the largest was Miletus (my-lee′tus). In 499 B.C. the Ionian cities revolted and appealed for help to the Greek mainland across the Aegean Sea. The city of Athens, of which Miletus had originally been a colony, responded with some ships and, for a while, the Greeks were victorious.

It was a foolhardy venture, however, that could not in the long run succeed against Darius. To make matters worse, the Greeks could not remain united (it was the curse of their history). The cities quarreled among themselves and some withdrew their naval contingents. Darius, meanwhile, organized his own fleet, made up of Phoenician ships, and in 494 B.C., just off Miletus, there was a naval battle in which the Greeks, far outnumbered, were defeated.

As a result of this defeat, the revolt was crushed. Miletus itself was taken and sacked, and the eyes of the vengeful Darius turned toward the Greek mainland, particularly Athens, from which help had come. Darius made use of his Phoenician ships and sailors to conquer the islands in the Aegean Sea one by one and to subdue the regions immediately north of Greece proper, including Macedonia, a Greek-speaking kingdom in the hinterland, behind the northwest corner of the sea.

A small punitive expedition was landed near Athens in 490 B.C. but here Darius found he had underestimated the job. He had not allowed for cavalry and, in a straight battle between footmen, the advantage was on the side of the more heavily armed Greeks. At the Battle of Marathon, the small village near which the Persians had landed, the Greeks utterly defeated the Persian invaders. Darius died in 486 B.C. before he could set a second and larger expedition under way, and that was left to his son Xerxes I (zurk′seez).

In 480 B.C., gathering a large and well-equipped army, Xerxes crossed the Hellespont and marched through Thrace, then southward into Greece. All northern Greece quickly fell into his hands, and when he forced his way through the narrow pass at Thermopylae (ther-mop′ih-lee), Athens itself had to be evacuated. Nothing was left in Greek hands but the southernmost peninsula, the Peloponnesus, and even that would very likely fall if the Greek fleet could be destroyed. It was the Greek fleet, then, that was Xerxes' crucial objective, and the Greek fleet was all that stood between the Greek cities and conquest.

The Greek ships, far outnumbered by the fleet of the invaders, were afloat in the narrow waters between the island of Salamis (sal′uh-mis) and the mainland, just west of Athens. To the Persians they appeared trapped, for there were only two ways out of the strait and both openings were plugged by the Persian fleet.

But the Persians, with the Phoenician ships serving as their sea-going cutting edge, could threaten only the Greeks in Asia Minor and in Greece itself. Westward, particularly in Italy and in Sicily, there were Greek cities that rivaled those in Greece proper and that were distant enough to be safe from the great Persian power. The Greek cities of the west, however, had a great enemy close at hand. This enemy was the city of Carthage, which was every bit as Phoenician as its mother city, Tyre, and every bit as determined to destroy the Greeks.

It was in Sicily that the Greek-Carthaginian crunch came. For over half a century now, the two peoples had held opposite ends of the island — the Greeks in the east, the Carthaginians in the west — and there had been a steady conflict over it. The desultory war remained inconclusive, but in 480 B.C. a marvelous chance dazzled the Carthaginian policy-makers.

The moment came partly because the Greek cities in the west, like those in the east, could almost never unite, even in the face of a common enemy. In Sicily, for instance, two of the Greek cities, Acragas (ak′ruh-gas) (the modern Agrigento) and Himera (him′uh-ruh), were at odds. Acragas was on the south-central shore of the island, Himera on the north-central shore. The two cities were about fifty miles apart and each was at very nearly the western limit of the Greek-controlled portion of the island. Farther west were no Greeks, only Carthaginians.

The fortunes of war favored Acragas and the Himerans were defeated. The ousted Himeran leaders could think of nothing better to do than to appeal to the Carthaginian enemy, and Carthage was delighted with the pretext. Not only could they drive eastward with the loud claim that they were selflessly righting a wrong, but they could do so at the very crisis and climax of Greek history. The armies of Persia were swooping down on Greece itself, which could therefore do nothing to help the Sicilian Greeks. At the same time, if Carthage now drove eastward in Sicily, the cities there could not help the Greek mainland.

It seems very likely that Greece's enemies, east and west, were acting in careful concert, for both were greatly benefited. In fact, we might look at events in 480 B.C. as a gigantic nutcracker movement of Canaanite versus Greek, with the Tyrian jaw on the east and the Carthaginian on the west five hundred miles apart — not bad for the military technology of the time.

A Carthaginian fleet, under the leadership of Hamilcar (huh-mil′kahr), carried a sizable army to the bases in eastern Sicily, and sent it marching to Himera, whose ousted leaders had requested help. From the opposite direction there came a Greek army from the most powerful Greek city on the island — Syracuse, on the east coast.

It was clear that a decisive battle by land would be fought at Himera and at just about the same time as a decisive battle was going to be fought by sea at Salamis. The dramatic tale told later by the Greeks was that both battles took place on the very same day — about September 20, 480 B.C.

What happened? In the east the Persian fleet advanced confidently to attack and crush the Greek fleet, with a strong Phoenician contingent enthusiastically leading the advance on the right flank, the position of honor. But again, as at Marathon ten years before, the Persians had miscalculated. The narrowness of the sea front available to the ships made mere numbers of little importance. Indeed, the too-numerous Persian ships tended to get in each other's way. Then, too, the Greek ships were more maneuverable and the Greek warriors better armed.

The Athenians marked out the Phoenicians for their prey. Moving in rapidly, they deftly cut them off from the rest of the battle line and forced them up against the shore. All along the line, the Greek ships won and the day ended in a great victory for them. The Persian fleet, Phoenicians and all, was smashed.

In the west, according to the tale told by the Greeks, Hamilcar, on the eve of the battle, decided to sacrifice to the gods of his Greek enemies in order to persuade them to withhold their support from their people. He sent for a contingent of friendly Greeks to guide him in the techniques of the sacrifice. The Syracusan command intercepted the request and a party of Syracusan horsemen were sent to the Carthaginian camp in the guise of those who were to help with the sacrifice. The Syracusans were allowed to enter, and at the very altar at which the sacrifice was supposed to be performed, they killed Hamilcar, spread a swath of destruction, and set fire to the Carthaginian ships.

It was the signal for battle, but the Greeks had an initial advantage and the Carthaginians a disheartenment. (It may be that the Greek tale is a distortion and that Hamilcar deliberately sacrificed himself to his own gods when the battle was going badly in order to bring about a reversal. If so, this maneuver failed.) Whatever the true facts behind Hamilcar's death, the battle of Himera ended in a complete Greek victory.

Thus, by land and sea, both jaws of the Canaanite nutcracker closing in on the Greeks was broken. The Greeks were able to go onward in independence and prosperity to raise their civilization to a pitch of glory such as the world had never seen before.

SICILY

After the Greek victory at Himera, one might expect that the Carthaginians would be driven from Sicily altogether, but they were not. As always, the Greek cities would not cooperate among themselves, so that the Carthaginians were able to hold on to their fortresses in western Sicily against the divided enemy.

For about seventy years, however, they were content to do no more than this, expending their energies at sea and replacing the eastern Canaanites of Tyre as the great sea adventurers of their time.

There is a tale that they sent an expedition beyond the Strait of Gibraltar under an admiral named Hanno (han′oh), who may have been the son of the Hamilcar who died at the battle of Himera. It was Hanno's purpose to explore and colonize the western shores of the Atlantic. He may well have touched the Canary Islands and reached the Gulf of Guinea. He seems to have sailed eastward along the southern shores of the African bulge, assuming it would carry him back to the Red Sea. When, at the Cameroons, the coast turned southward again, he gave up and returned to Carthage. Another Carthaginian fleet under Himilco (hih-mil′koh) explored the Atlantic shores of Spain and some tales have him sailing far westward into what we now call the Sargasso Sea.

While Carthage was flourishing, the Greek cities of Sicily continued to feud among themselves. Near the western tip the situation that had once involved Acragas and Himera was now to be found in connection with Selinus (sih-ly′nus) and Segesta (sih-jes′tuh). The former was on the north shore and the latter on the south shore. The proximity of Carthaginian bases did not prevent them from fighting each other bitterly and continuously. Segesta, which was the weaker and was getting the worst of it, looked abroad for help.

She appealed to the Athenians, who were then the strongest naval power in the Greek world and engaged in a war to the death with Sparta. It seemed to Athens that a victory in Sicily and the establishment of bases there might provide them with important sources of supply. In order to accomplish that, however, the Athenians would have to defeat Syracuse, which was on the side of Sparta. In 415 B.C. the Athenians sent an expeditionary force against Syracuse. Largely through the incapacity of its leaders, the Athenian force was utterly destroyed and the crucially weakened Athens was never to recover.

Segesta was now worse off then before. Athens had failed her, and Syracuse, backed by winning Sparta, was her enemy. There was no Greek city anywhere to which Segesta could appeal, so in 409 B.C., she sent out a cry for help to Carthage. One of the chief Carthaginian leaders at the time was Hannibal (han′ih-bul), a grandson of the Hamilcar who had died at Himera. Under his influence, Carthage agreed to answer the appeal.

The Carthaginian expeditionary force disembarked at Motya (moh′tee-uh), a strongly fortified post they held at the westernmost tip of Sicily. From there they marched directly to Selinus, catching it by surprise. After days of hand-to-hand fighting in the streets of the city (with a Syracusan relief force arriving too late) Selinus was taken and destroyed, its people slaughtered or carried into slavery.

Nor was Hannibal done. From Selinus he marched his men to Himera, sixty miles northeastward. There, three quarters of a century before, his grandfather had died, and he wanted revenge. To be sure he was at a disadvantage, for he had no fleet (it had remained behind at Motya) and the Syracusans had one. The Syracusan fleet was in Greek waters, though, helping the Spartans against declining Athens.

The Syracusan fleet was recalled and for a while it looked as though it might lift the siege of Himera. Hannibal, however, feinted toward Syracuse and the Greek ships scurried eastward to protect their city. Before they could return, Himera had been taken and destroyed. According to the later Greek horror tale, Hannibal, in order to appease his grandfather's spirit, had three thousand prisoners sacrificed with appropriate religious rites at the spot where Hamilcar had died.

Hannibal returned to Carthage, then, his purpose accomplished. Success, however, breeds on itself. The Carthaginians, having tasted blood, wanted more. In 407 B.C. Hannibal was sent back to Sicily along with his cousin Himilco. The westernmost Greek city still standing was now Acragas, forty-five miles southeast of the ruins of Selinus. In 406 B.C. Acragas was placed under siege, and in the course of that siege Hannibal died.

The siege then settled down to a matter of supplies with Syracusan ships feeding the citizens of Acragas and Carthaginian ships supplying the besiegers. After nine months it was the besiegers who won out and Acragas was taken. The next goal was Gela (jee′luh), also on Sicily's southern shore, forty miles east of Acragas. That was taken in 405 B.C. along with Camarina (kam″uh-ree′nuh), some twenty miles still further along the coast.

This unbroken string of Carthaginian victories was raising considerable discontent among the people of Syracuse, who were quite ready to believe their generals to be incompetent or traitorous or both. In the turmoil a certain Dionysius (dy″oh-nish′us), who had been a civil service clerk and who was an effective orator, put himself at the head of the dissidents. Before long he had maneuvered the generals into retirement and himself into a position of supreme power.

He could not prevent the loss of Gela and Camarina, but he recognized the need for a breathing space, and he signed a treaty with Carthage in 405 B.C., recognizing its conquests and handing over the western third of the island to her. Carthage,

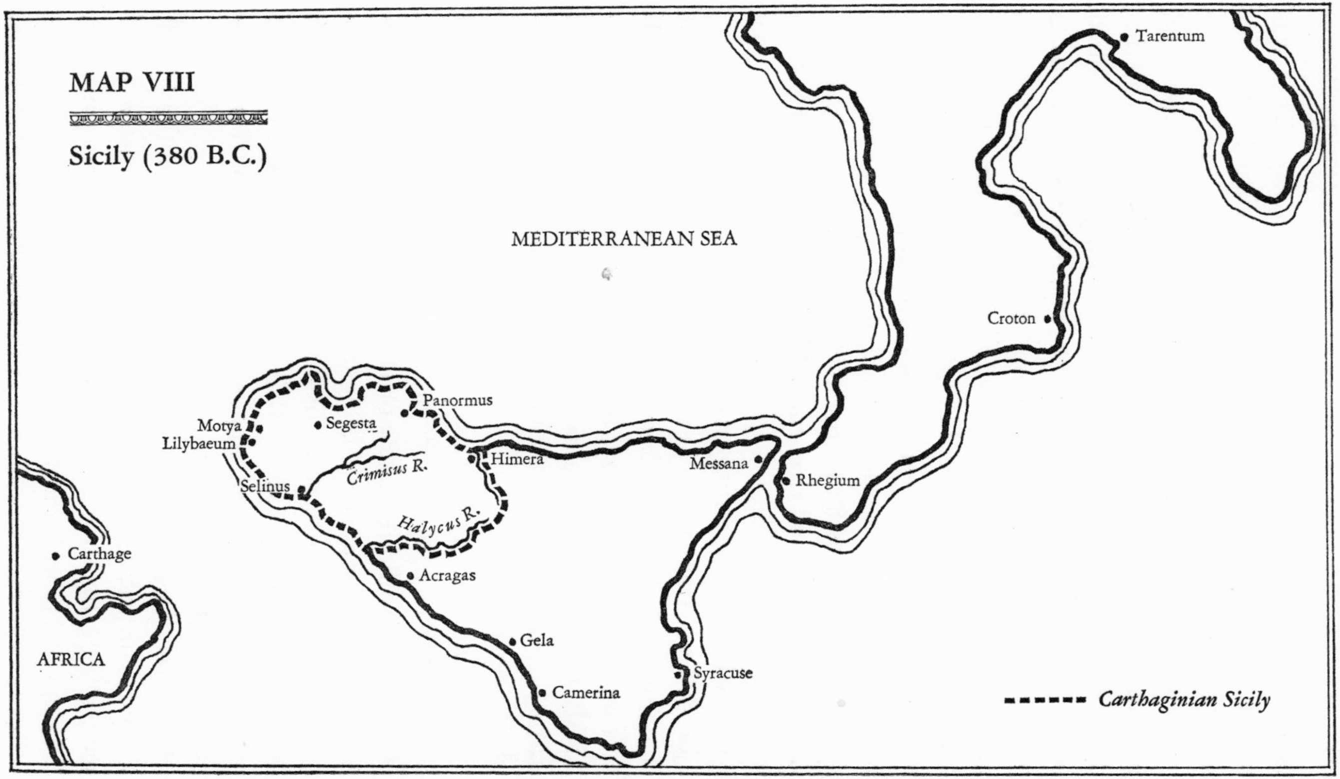
MAP VIII
Sicily (380 B.C.)
MEDITERRANEAN SEA
Tarentum
Croton
Panormus
Motya
Lilybaeum
Segesta
Himera
Messana
Rhegium
Crimisus R.
Selinus
Halycus R.
Carthage
Acragas
Gela
AFRICA
Syracuse
Camerina
Carthaginian Sicily

naturally, was satisfied and retired into inactivity. That was exactly what Dionysius had hoped for: his virtual surrender had bought him time.

Dionysius fortified an island in the Syracusan harbor and built up a strong following about himself. He put down all disaffection in the city and took over neighboring cities. He hired mercenaries, organized an army in which the separate parts were trained to act in coordination, and was the first to make use of the catapult, which seems to have been invented in his shipyards. The catapult could throw large rocks long distances and was the deadliest form of artillery used prior to the invention of gunpowder. It meant Dionysius would be able to lay siege to walled cities far more effectively than others had been able to do so. With all this, and with an increased fleet both in number of ships and in the quality of the individual ship, too, Syracuse became the strongest city in the Greek world.

In 398 B.C. Dionysius was ready. At the head of the largest Greek army that had yet been seen in Sicily, 80,000 foot soldiers and over 3000 cavalry, he drove westward, pursuing the quickly retreating Carthaginians into their far-west stronghold of Motya. Around Motya the Greek army spread out and established siege lines.

Motya was actually an island, set in an excellent harbor, and the Carthaginians were confident that, firmly held, it could not be taken. They did not know of Dionysius' catapults. All Dionysius needed was a way of bringing them close to the fortifications and for that purpose he began to build a mole; that is, to fill in a section of the sea so that a land connection could be built between Sicily and the small island. Over this he intended to drag his catapults.

When the Carthaginian fleet attempted to relieve the island, Dionysius turned his catapults on them and, under the volley of heavy stones, the surprised and disconcerted sailors panicked. The ships had to withdraw.

Finally, the mole was built and the catapults moved across.

With them there came tall structures which could be pulled to the wall and from the top of which armed men could hurl their missiles into the fortress. Even so Motya held out, until a surprise night attack by Dionysius' men turned the trick. The fort was taken and the men who were captured were either slaughtered or sold into slavery.

All that was left to the Carthaginians now was a section of Sicily's northwestern coast, including their long-time post at Panormus (puh-nawr′mus), the modern Palérmo, and their allied city of Segesta. With Motya gone it seemed likely that these might not stand, but winter had come. Dionysius returned to Syracuse to prepare for the next year's campaign and, in the interim, Carthage bestirred herself. A new expeditionary force under Himilco was landed in Panormus and took the field.

Quickly the Carthaginians spread out once more over the westermost end of the island. Some four miles south of the devastated island of Motya, Himilco founded a town called Lilybaeum (lil″uh-bee′um), which he fortified and made into a stronger base than even Motya had been.

Himilco then advanced eastward all the way to Syracuse itself and placed it under siege. Dionysius seemed helpless to stop him. He was a master at siegecraft and proficient at surprise attack, but battles in the open field seemed to be beyond him and he never let himself be drawn into one.

Dionysius held out. Despite considerable unrest at home, he managed to keep control over the Syracusan citizens and waited. Eventually, pestilence began to ravage the Carthaginian besiegers, and then Dionysius was ready with his surprise attack by land and sea. It worked perfectly. Both Himilco's army and his navy were battered, and the Carthaginians were forced to flee westward. With this, Dionysius' first Carthaginian war came to an end in 392 B.C. The Carthaginians were hemmed in at the western end of the island about their post at Lilybaeum and all the rest of the island was now under Dionysius' control.

It meant Dionysius was strong enough to look outside Sicily. He sent an army into the Italian toe and by 387 B.C. controlled it almost entirely. He established colonies and trading posts along the shores of the Adriatic Sea, one almost as far north as modern Venice. He exerted a dominating influence over the Italian heel and even over the strip of coast across the sea from that heel (the modern Albania).

One might almost speak of a Syracusan Empire in the 380s, but now Dionysius became too sure of himself. In 383 B.C. he attempted to take over Segesta. Since that city had been under Carthaginian control for a quarter of a century, Carthage reacted violently.

Near Panormus in 379 B.C. Dionysius suffered a sizable defeat and was forced to sue for peace, pay a huge indemnity, and allow the Carthaginians to extend their power about thirty miles westward all along the line.

Again Dionysius prepared for revenge, and in 368 B.C. he went to war against the Carthaginians for the last time. Again he drove westward to the ultimate tip of the island and again he settled down to a siege of the great new strongpoint of the Carthaginians, Lilybaeum.

But luck had deserted him. Lilybaeum could not be taken and Dionysius was forced to sit on the shore helplessly and watch a sea battle in which the Carthaginian ships destroyed his fleet. Clearly, he was going to have to sue for peace and salvage whatever he could.

Yet even so, he had one last bit of triumph. It seems that Dionysius was a tragic poet of some caliber. He often entered his poetry in the various contests held in Greece but had never won first prize — although he sometimes won third prize and occasionally even a second. Even as the fact of defeat was made clear to him at Lilybaeum, he received the news that one of his dramatic poems, "Ransom of Hector," had won first prize. That seemed to compensate for everything. With defeat staring him in the face, he still held a wild celebration, at which he drank far more than was good for him. He sickened almost at once and died, leaving it to his son to make the peace.

Dionysius' son was not equal to the task of controlling Syracuse and its dominions in Sicily and Italy. Confusion and anarchy gripped Sicily and Dionysius' short-lived empire fell apart. To make matters worse, the Carthaginians supported factions among the Greeks, always choosing their faction in such a way as to best perpetuate disorder and weakness among their enemies.

By 344 B.C. Greek Sicily was in chaos. Each city had its own military despot and all alike were on the point of calling to Carthage. Carthaginian forces were laying siege to Syracuse, with Greek factions actually helping them. Syracuse had to appeal to the Greek city of Corinth to send them a general of character and ability about whom the various parties might rally.

By an extraordinary coincidence, such a man was on the spot. He was Timoleon (tih-moh′lee-on), a firm fighter and a staunch idealist. He accepted the task of straightening out the mess in Sicily and, at the head of a thousand men in ten ships, sailed to Rhegium (ree′jee-um) at the tip of the Italian toe.

There he was met by a hostile Carthaginian fleet which demanded he return to Corinth. Timoleon asked to have the matter discussed before the city council of Rhegium. While Timoleon delayed the discussion with every parliamentary trick he could think of, his ships set sail. He himself sneaked away just in time to catch the last ship as it made ready to depart. The Carthaginians, catching on too late, set off in pursuit, but not in time to catch them.

Once he was in Sicily, Timoleon began the systematic extension of power at the expense of those Greek leaders who were appeasing the Carthaginians. Cleverly, he rallied Greek patriotism about himself, until the Carthaginians who were laying siege to Syracuse, fearful that the Greeks on their side might at any moment join the Greeks fighting them, decided to leave. Timoleon found himself in control of all of Syracuse and then proceeded to put anti-Carthaginians in control of other Greek cities.

Carthage had to do something, and in 339 B.C. a large expeditionary force was sent into Sicily. Later Greek reports placed it at 70,000, though this was probably exaggerated. Timoleon did not dare allow the Carthaginians to reach Syracuse. His only course was to hasten westward with what force he could gather and hope against hope that somehow he could blunt the Carthaginian drive.

His forces were far inferior to the Carthaginians in number, but luck was on his side. The Greeks reached the high ground overlooking the Crimisus River (krih-my′sus), only forty miles east of Lilybaeum, at a time when a mist obscured the river itself. This meant the Greeks could not see the Carthaginian forces at the river, but neither could the Carthaginians see the Greeks on the high ground.

The Carthaginians began to ford their way across the river, unaware that they were in the presence of the enemy, and when the mist lifted, there they were — partly across. The cavalry and part of the elite troops were on the Greek side, but the main forces were still on the far side. Timoleon grasped the situation at once and ordered an attack.

The Greeks outnumbered that part of the army within reach and destroyed them. By the time the main Carthaginian forces had managed to struggle across the river, a vicious thunderstorm broke, with the wind from the east. The rain was driving into the faces of the Carthaginians. Gradually they were forced back toward the now-swollen river and when they finally broke, many of them found death in the torrent. It was a complete victory for the outnumbered forces of Timoleon.

Timoleon might have followed up this victory and attempted to drive the Carthaginians out of Sicily altogether, but he did not let success tempt him into folly. There were still hostile factions in his rear, and any setback, even a small and temporary one, would ruin his base. He returned eastward, therefore, and continued his task of organizing the Greek cities into peaceful union. Once that was done, he made no attempt to establish himself as tyrant, but retired to a role as private citizen and died soon after.

INTERLUDE

While Canaanite power in the form of the city of Carthage was supreme in the western Mediterranean and while it kept the Greeks in Sicily constantly occupied, the Canaanite homeland continued more or less peaceful and prosperous under Persian rule. The Phoenician fleet continued to be used by the Persian kings, who desperately kept the petty wars boiling on the Greek mainland in order to prevent any one Greek city from growing too strong. This made the Phoenician cities useful to the Persians and they were allowed many privileges, including self-rule under kings of their own.

The Persian Empire, however, was going through a period of weakness, and Greek armies roamed at will in Asia Minor, setting Persian power at naught, and humiliating the empire's prestige. In 404 B.C., when the Persian king, Darius II, died, Egypt seized the chance to throw off Persian domination and establish native rule once more.

The example was not lost on Persia's western provinces in Asia. Since the central government could not protect Asia Minor from Greek incursions, those provinces broke away and began to shift for themselves. Artaxerxes II, who had succeeded Darius II, seemed to be presiding over the dissolution of the Persian Empire.

But in 359 B.C. Artaxerxes II died and was succeeded by his son Artaxerxes III, a ruler of quite a different sort. Energetic and forceful, he decided at once to restore Persian power and to do it by reestablishing the central authority over the too-powerful regional governors. He ordered all the governors to dismiss their private armies (consisting largely of Greek mercenaries) and, in combination with those who submitted, attacked those who did not.

Once that was done, he set about reconquering Egypt. His first attempt, in 351 B.C., too hastily prepared, failed, and seemed to have made matters worse, for the failure stirred up the Phoenician cities to revolt. One of the leaders in the revolt was Tennes (ten′is), king of Sidon.

Artaxerxes III, not daunted, prepared to send a larger and more formidable force westward. In 345 B.C. he was ready and his army began to move. At this, Tennes' nerve failed. He sent secret emissaries to negotiate a surrender. His treachery ruined the Phoenician cause but did nothing to ameliorate Artaxerxes' anger. Sidon was taken and sacked and Tennes, despite his last-minute switch to the Persian side, was executed. Artaxerxes then went on to reconquer Egypt in 343 B.C. and for a short while it seemed that the Persian Empire was as strong as it had ever been.

Through all these troubles, the Jews, clustered about Jerusalem in the interior, managed to avoid trouble. They did not join any revolt and they did not meddle with politics. It was an interlude in which the Jewish people seemed to exist in a cloister, removed from the world. All that can be said about them is that the Second Temple stood and that the line of high priests, unbroken from the time of Zadok, continued to officiate. Jeshua, the high priest who presided over the dedication of the Second Temple, was succeeded by his son Joiakim (joy′uh-kim), who was followed in lineal order by Eliashib (ee″ly-ash′ib), Joiada (joy′uh-duh), Jonathan, and Jaddua (jad′dyoo-uh).

In later centuries stories were told concerning Jewish dangers in the nearly two-century interval during which these high priests ruled in Jerusalem. This may have been inspired by memories of Artaxerxes' vengeful forces sweeping along the sea to destroy Phoenician cities and reconquer Egypt. Thus, the Biblical Book of Esther tells how the Jews were in danger of being wiped out in the reign of Xerxes I; and the apocryphal Book of Judith has Judea ravaged by an army under a general named Holofernes, which was the name of one of Artaxerxes' generals. Both the Book of Esther and the Book of Judith, however, are fictional and in no way reflect any known historical fact.

TYRE'S LAST STAND

But a thundercloud was deepening in Europe. Macedon, a kingdom in the north of Greece, was experiencing an astonishing rise in power. Until 356 B.C. it had made only the smallest mark in history, but in that year, when Artaxerxes III was just beginning his rule in Persia, Macedon came under the control of a new king, Philip II. Philip reorganized the Macedonian army and introduced the "phalanx," a close-set rank and file of heavily armed men who had learned, by continual drill, to handle long spears to perfection, so that the entire group resembled a marching porcupine.

Little by little, through the use of bribes, of lies, and of military action when all else failed, Philip gained control of Greece. By 338 B.C. he was the acknowledged leader of the entire mainland except for the now-impotent Sparta. It was at just about this time that Artaxerxes III was assassinated and Persia was forced to go through the uncertainties of a disputed succession.

Philip II was planning to use the combined Greek forces, in alliance with his own superb Macedonian army, in a major assault on the Persian Empire, but in 336 B.C. he, too, was assassinated. That might have ended things, were it not for the fact that succeeding to his throne was his twenty-year-old son Alexander, one of the great captains of all time, who was soon to earn the title of Alexander the Great.

Acting quickly, the young Alexander brought back to heel all the tribes and cities who took Philip's death as a signal to revolt. One blow at any one target was all he needed, and within a year he had restored Philip's full power and was ready to cross into Asia Minor and make the assault on Persia, which was now under an amiable but weak ruler, Darius III.

In 334 B.C. Alexander brought his army into Asia Minor and defeated the local provincial forces there. He spent the winter and next summer crossing Asia Minor and then in October 333 B.C. defeated a larger Persian force in the southeastern corner of that peninsula. Darius III fell back to the Tigris-Euphrates.

Alexander did not follow at once. It was his purpose first to secure the entire Mediterranean coast so that he would leave no navy to threaten his line of communications. For that purpose, he had to have the Phoenician cities.

At first he had no trouble. The Phoenician cities had not forgotten Artaxerxes' brutal conquest a dozen years before and had no intention of sacrificing themselves for Persia. They surrendered readily to Alexander and were well treated.

The men of Tyre, however, were of another mind. Alexander had a small army and it seemed almost impossible that he could remain standing once Persia turned its full strength on him. Tyre did not feel in the mood to undergo another Persian revenge once Alexander had been taken care of. Besides, Alexander had no navy and without a navy what could he do against Tyre? Had not Nebuchadrezzar tried for thirteen years without one, two and a half centuries before, and failed?

So Tyre tried to play both sides. They offered to submit to Alexander but only as a matter of form, without actually allowing Alexander to put a contingent of his Macedonians inside the city. The Tyrian king, Azemilkos (az″uh-mil′kos), sent a deputation making this offer and asking Alexander to pass onward.

But this was precisely what Alexander could not be satisfied with. He wanted the city itself; he wanted the naval base; he wanted control of the Phoenician ships. He therefore asked for permission to enter the city, and was refused.

Alexander had no choice. In December of 333 B.C. he settled down to a siege. In all the unbroken series of victories he had so far experienced and was yet to experience, this siege of Tyre was Alexander's most difficult task. He had no navy and Tyre had many ships. They could provision themselves forever and outwait Alexander, for the longer Alexander waited, the greater the danger that Carthage would join her own ships to those of the mother city and that the Persians would bestir themselves and march to Tyre's relief.

Alexander could only do his best. If he left Tyre unconquered behind him, he would suffer a terrible blow to his prestige and, considering that he was the head of a small army in a vast empire, the matter of prestige might be all that was protecting him. Furthermore, a proud Tyre, aware of having successfully defied Alexander, would not hesitate to use its fleet against him.

There was only one thing Alexander could do. He had to build a half-mile mole to connect Tyre with the mainland, as Dionysius had done at Motya sixty-five years before. Tyre was closer to the mainland than Motya had been, but the sea was deeper here and Tyre was stronger. Grimly Alexander began to build the mole and, as grimly, the men of Tyre prepared to prevent the building. Alexander's first attempt was frustrated by fire-ships and by Tyrian raids. Alexander set about building a bigger and wider mole that could be better defended.

Even Alexander might in the end have failed had it not been for the inability of the Phoenician cities to act as a unit. When those ships of the Phoenician fleet, which were manned by citizens of the cities that had submitted to Alexander, heard the news of the submission, they went over to Alexander's side. Suddenly Tyre found itself outmanned at sea. Nor could Carthage come through with help in time.

The Tyrians nevertheless had no thought of surrender. They got as many as their women and children out of the city and off to safety in Carthage as they could. Unable to risk a sea battle, they drew what remained of their fleet in about the city and prepared for an all-out defense.

Bit by bit Alexander's will had its way. The mole was completed. His siege machines were brought up to the wall, and the wall was attacked and battered. The Tyrians fought back with superhuman courage at every point, both at the wall and within the city. Finally, however, in August 332 B.C., the last of the city was taken and, after nine months, the siege was at an end.

Eight thousand of the Tyrians were slain, 30,000 sold into slavery. The city itself survived and even flourished at times but it was never again to be able to take independent action or to engage in battle on its own. Nor was there ever to be another king of Tyre; Azemilkos was the last.

Tyre had even ceased to be an island. The sea silted about the mole that Alexander had built and the rock is now at the tip of a peninsula that is a mile wide. With the Phoenician cities passing from the scene as independent entities, the only remnant of ancient Canaan that was left proud and strong was Carthage, far across the sea.

As for Alexander, he could move again. With Tyre safely in his pocket, with a navy at his command and none left for Persia, he could continue to march southward to take what remained of the Mediterranean provinces. He anticipated no resistance and he certainly met with none in Judea.

Very likely he bypassed Jerusalem without even knowing it existed — or caring. Josephus, a Jewish historian who wrote four centuries later, tells a story, however, that is not to be found in any of the Greek accounts but is designed to redound to Judean prestige.

He says that during the siege of Tyre, Alexander demanded Jewish help — in itself unbelievable since Alexander could scarcely need the help of a tiny, vegetating city — which was refused, and that after the siege was done, he intended to punish Jerusalem in consequence (as if he would waste his time when all Egypt was beckoning to him). Outside Jerusalem, says Josephus, Alexander was met by the high priest, Jaddua, in full panoply at the head of the assembled priesthood. At this Alexander dismounted and bowed, explaining to the general at his side that he had seen a figure just like this in a dream. He then entered Jerusalem in peace and left the Jews to live under their own laws. Whether this happened or not, Jerusalem was not touched by Alexander's passage.

Gaza, however, proved an unpleasant surprise for the conqueror. This ancient fortress of the Philistines, 150 miles south of Tyre, was well fortified and supplied and was under the command of a eunuch named Batis (bat′is), who was utterly loyal to the Persian cause.

The city was situated on a hill and was two miles from the sea, so that the direct help of the ships — now Alexander's — was not to be expected. Alexander, however, was not going to leave this citadel in his rear, either. He could not drag his machinery through the deep sand or up the steep hill, so he prepared to manufacture a pathway across the sand as, at Tyre, he had built one across the sea.

All through the months of October and November 332 B.C., he had sloping ramparts built up against the walls. Across these he dragged his catapults and other siege engines. Between the action of the engines battering the wall and sappers digging underneath, breaches were made, and eventually the town was taken by storm.

The slaughter that followed was worse than that at Tyre, for Alexander, who had not expected resistance, was growing less patient with delay. There is even a tale that he had thongs passed through the heels of the brave Batis and dragged him alive behind his chariot around the walls of Gaza, in imitation of the atrocity offered Hector's body by Achilles in the *Iliad.*

That, however, was the end of western resistance to Alexander. From Gaza he passed into Egypt, which capitulated without a struggle. Then and only then was he ready to pursue Darius into the heart of his empire. He defeated Darius in the Tigris-Euphrates valley in 331 B.C. and absorbed all the vast Persian Empire under his own rule.

In 324 B.C. Alexander returned to Babylon, where his mind was occupied with vast projects. There was some expectation that he would attempt the conquest of the Arabian coast, or move westward to take over Carthage. But if he had plans, they went for naught. On June 11, 323 B.C., he died of fever in Babylon.

9

GREECE TRIUMPHANT

THE FRAGMENTS OF EMPIRE

Alexander had not had time, in his short life, to consolidate his huge conquests. He had left no heirs of any worth, and too many generals of far too much worth, so his empire fell apart. A dozen generals wrangled among themselves, all trying to inherit the imperial mantle, all determined that none other should, each seizing this part or that.

The general who most quickly lowered his sights and decided to settle for a single province was Ptolemy (tol′uh-mee). On Alexander's death, he took over the rich province of Egypt and made up his mind to attempt nothing more, except perhaps to extend his powers over enough of the adjacent regions to make his Egyptian heartland secure.

At the opposite extreme, striking most pertinaciously for the entire empire, was Antigonus (an-tig′oh-nus). Although one eyed, and already about sixty years old when Alexander died, he was the most forceful and energetic of the entire bunch.

Antigonus and his loyal and equally energetic son Demetrius (dih-mee′tree-us) fought all over Asia, and by 316 were so far successful as to be master of virtually all the Asian part of Alexander's empire. Indeed, the only Macedonian generals who remained beyond their grasp were Ptolemy, who ruled in Africa, and two others, Cassander (kuh-san′der) and Lysimachus (ly-sim′uh-kus), who ruled regions in Europe, north of Greece. These now formed an alliance against the dangerous Antigonus.

Antigonus chose to tackle Ptolemy first and advanced down the eastern shore of the Mediterranean, so that once again war came to the ancient land of Canaan. Ptolemy reacted vigorously. He sent expeditionary forces to the island of Cyprus and to Greece and Asia Minor in order to keep control of the sea for himself and to endanger Antigonus' line of communication. Having done what he could in this direction, he hastened back to Egypt and prepared to meet Antigonus' armies in battle.

Antigonus' army was led by his son Demetrius, then twenty-five years old, brave, and eager. Under his command were 11,000 footmen, 2300 horsemen, and 43 elephants.

The use of elephants in warfare had been an Indian device and Alexander had come upon them unexpectedly in his last great battle, fought on the banks of the Indus beyond the boundaries of Persia. As in all his battles, regardless of surprise or disadvantages, Alexander had won. Nevertheless, although he had beaten the elephants, his generals were impressed by them. The elephant was the nearest thing one could find in the animal kingdom to a modern tank. They could be tamed sufficiently to allow men to mount and guide them, and they had a most daunting effect on those who faced them for the first time.

For over a century, because they seemed so overwhelming a force in theory, they were used in battle. And yet in practice, they proved of surprisingly little value. The basic trouble was that they were too intelligent to sacrifice their lives uselessly, differing in this respect from horses and men. When the enemy seemed too dangerous to attack, elephants would retreat hastily and then they would prove more dangerous to their own side than to the other.

Demetrius brought his army, elephants and all, to Gaza, where twenty years before Alexander had been victorious in the second of his great sieges. There, in 312 B.C., Ptolemy brought up a numerically superior army and a quality of seasoned generalship that more than compensated for Demetrius' youthful verve.

Perhaps Demetrius expected the elephants to overcome Ptolemy's advantages. If so, he was disappointed. Ptolemy placed iron hurdles in the field at irregular intervals and waited for Demetrius' attack. The elephants were driven forward but, as they cannot jump, when they came to the hurdles they saw no purpose in trying to make their way either over them or around them. They stopped dead and could not be made to advance. That reduced the morale of Demetrius' army and when Ptolemy's men counterattacked, they broke and Demetrius was forced into a hasty retreat. Antigonus' greatest opportunity for uniting the entire empire under him had failed.

Ptolemy, in order to prevent Antigonus from making a second attempt, razed the fortifications of the strong points in Judea and Syria, a mild form of a "scorched-earth" policy. To make assurance doubly sure, Ptolemy sent an allied general, Seleucus (sih-lyoo′kus), eastward with an army, urging him to take the Tigris-Euphrates valley for himself, knowing that this would force Antigonus to face east as well as south. This last strategy worked out perfectly. Seleucus took Babylon and Antigonus did indeed have to split his forces.

In 311 B.C. Antigonus was forced to agree to an uneasy truce. Antigonus was frustrated to a degree. Time was passing, year after year, and he could never quite seize the fruit of united empire which seemed to dangle so close now and then. By 307 B.C. he was seventy-five years old and he dared wait no longer.

Desperate to be a ruler and not just a general, and unable to wait for the ever-receding day when he could win total victory, he finally adopted the title of "king" over those portions of Asia which were under his rule.

This move had to be countered. Ptolemy promptly called himself king of Egypt, Seleucus called himself king of Babylonia, Cassander called himself king of Macedonia, and Lysimachus called himself king of Thrace. Other smaller kingdoms were also established and the breakup of Alexander's empire thus received a kind of official recognition.

Egypt was to remain under the descendants of Ptolemy for nearly three centuries, and this is the era of "Ptolemaic Egypt." The descendants of Seleucus were to rule over sections of Asia with less well defined boundaries, and the lands they controlled are called the Seleucid Empire.

The kings continued to fight among each other as endlessly and viciously as they had done when they were only generals. The final battle came in 301 B.C. at Ipsus (ip′sus) in central Asia Minor. Ptolemy did not take part but the other allied kings, Cassander, Lysimachus and Seleucus, defeated Antigonus, who was now eighty years old but still fighting like a fury. He had to be killed in that battle; nothing else would stop him. Demetrius, unable to rescue his father, fled. He eventually recovered some power and temporarily made himself king of Macedonia, but he was never again to be a threat in Asia.

With Antigonus gone, the remaining generals settled down to their fragments, and while the wars did not stop, they decreased greatly in intensity.

Fragments or not, all the shores of the eastern Mediterranean — from Sicily, eastward through southern Italy, Greece, Asia Minor, Syria, Egypt and Libya — were under a ruling class that was Greek in language and culture. Although the great Greek cities of the past — Athens, Sparta, Thebes, and the rest — were receding into the background, Greece, in terms of its culture, was triumphant.

THE JEWS UNDER THE PTOLEMIES

After the Battle of Ipsus, the victorious allies divided the empire outside Egypt. Cassander, who had Macedon, added Greece to it. Lysimachus, who had Thrace, added western Asia Minor. Seleucus took all the rest of Asia, including all the vast areas east of the Tigris River.

In point of area, the Seleucid Empire looked very impressive on the map, almost as though it represented all of Alexander's empire but for some fringe areas. However, the eastern provinces were never more than loosely held and it was Syria and the Tigris-Euphrates that made up the core of the kingdom.

Seleucus established a capital city in each of the two major portions of his empire. Immediately after taking Babylon in 312 B.C. he established a new city, Seleucia (sih-loo′shee-uh), named for himself, on the banks of the Tigris, just north of Babylon on the Euphrates. The growth of this new city, Greek in culture, meant the inevitable decline of Babylon, which faded gradually into a village and eventually into nothing at all.

In 300 B.C. Seleucus established his second capital on the Orontes River (oh-ron′teez) in northern Syria. There, near the northeast angle of the Mediterranean, he built Antioch (an′tee-ok), named for his father. Antioch eventually became the largest city in the Seleucid dominions in time and the Syrian province gradually became the chief Seleucid stronghold. It is sometimes convenient to speak of the Seleucid Empire as "Syria," therefore.

Seleucus dated his laws from 312 B.C., the year in which he had taken Babylon. The Jews of Babylonia naturally adopted this chronology, which is referred to as the "Seleucid Era." What made this important is that the Jews everywhere began to use this chronology even in places and at times when they were not Seleucid subjects. Since the Jews were gradually scattered through all the Mediterranean area, while retaining a certain cohesiveness, the use of the chronology was spread by them beyond its natural boundaries in space and time, giving it a greater longevity and importance than might be expected.

Historians, you see, sometimes have difficulty in determining the dates of events where these are given in terms of some obscure chronological system. If the same event can also be found dated by some better-known and more widespread system, everything in the obscure chronology (including events not otherwise dated) will become clear. The Seleucid Era, because it was spread far and wide by the Jews, became of prime value as a standard chronological reference in this respect.

Ptolemy, who had not been present at the climactic battle at Ipsus, was left out in the cold. None of the portion that Antigonus ruled had been assigned to him. He was left only with what he had: Egypt, Cyprus, and a precarious section of southeastern Asia Minor. With this he was not content. As long as he did not control the Asian approaches to Egypt, he was threatened from that direction. In the confusion that followed the Battle of Ipsus, therefore, he seized what he could of the neighboring sections of Asia.

He and Seleucus did not actively fight over it. The memory of having been comrades in arms under Alexander once and allies against Antigonus later seems to have kept them at peace. Still, there was some minor maneuvering for advantage in Syria and certain sections owed allegiance now to Seleucus and now to Ptolemy. In the end, though, what had once been Canaan, including the small land of Judea centered about Jerusalem, became Ptolemaic. It was to remain Ptolemaic for a century, and for the Jews of Jerusalem, at least, it meant that, after a generation of turmoil in the surrounding regions, there was a return to the placid existence that had proceeded under the Persians.

Ptolemy and his immediate successors were well aware that

they ruled a kingdom that was overwhelmingly Egyptian, with only a small Greek ruling class in the cities, largely in Alexandria. They attempted therefore to keep the sensibilities of their Egyptian subjects in mind, bent to their religion and customs in many ways, and behaved in some fashions much as once the pharaohs had behaved.

This, of course, did not please the average Greek, who felt a hearty contempt for things Egyptian (a contempt that was returned). The Ptolemies who had to try to balance Greek versus Egyptian found it useful to have a third force, widely different from either, to help maintain the balance. The Jews were perfect here, since they were equally alien to both Greek and Egyptian.

Jews were encouraged to emigrate into Egypt and to settle in Alexandria, the city which had been founded by Alexander the Great during his brief stay in Egypt, and which now served as the Ptolemaic capital. Eventually, Alexandria became the great polyglot metropolis of the ancient world, with its population divided into almost equal thirds among Greeks, Jews, and Egyptians, each living under its own customs and laws, and each strongly suspicious of the other two.

Ptolemy I abdicated in 285 B.C. in favor of a younger son who ruled as Ptolemy II. In 283 B.C. the old no-longer-king died in peace at the age of eighty-three, the wisest and happiest of all Alexander's generals. When he died, Seleucus I remained alive, the last of Alexander's generals to survive. Unlike Ptolemy I, he did not retire in old age but kept on ruling and fighting. When he died in his turn in 280 B.C. — forty-three years after the death of Alexander, whose statue, Seleucus said, he could never pass without shuddering — it was at the hands of an assassin, one who happened to be Ptolemy I's oldest son.

Ptolemy II fought two wars with the descendants of Seleucus I. They were fought over the disputed areas in Syria and Judea where the two kingdoms bordered each other on land. There was a First Syrian War from 276 to 272 B.C. and a Second

Syrian War from 260 to 255 B.C. These were inconclusive, but on the whole the advantage lay with the Ptolemies and Judea remained firmly Ptolemaic.

The Jews survived these early wars with very little trouble. They were not involved or particularly victimized, since it was one of those periods in history where battles were confined to the maneuverings of armies, each side finding trained soldiers too valuable to risk foolishly, so that there was much striving for position and relatively little bloodshed.

In fact, all one can say of Judean history under the first Ptolemies is that Simon I became high priest about 300 B.C. and was succeeded by Onias II about 250 B.C. Beyond Judah, there were two other important colonies of Jews. In the Tigris-Euphrates there was a colony that had existed there since the exile under Nebuchadrezzar, three centuries before. Outside the mainstream of events, they remained there little disturbed. The second colony, of course, was the much newer one that existed in Alexandria.

It was the Alexandrian colony, however, that introduced a new difficulty to the Jewish world. Hebrew, you see, had disappeared as the language of the ordinary Jew at the time of the exile. In the Tigris-Euphrates the Jews began to speak the Aramaic that was the common language of the merchants of the western reaches of Asia. When they returned to Judea, they continued to speak Aramaic. Aramaic, however, was a language closely related to Hebrew. It was not at all difficult for an Aramaic-speaking Jew to learn Hebrew also, so that the holy writings of the Bible could still be read by them.

Because of this, there was little pressure to translate the Biblical writings into Aramaic. Indeed, the feeling existed among many of the Judean Jews that it would be most impious to have the holy books appear in any language *but* Hebrew, since they believed (with the usual self-assurance of early peoples) that Hebrew had been the language of God and of original mankind. The fact that Hebrew was no longer the language of ordinary life in Judea was, if anything, all to the good in that case, since that made Hebrew a holy language reserved for holy things.

But then what of the Jews in Alexandria and the smaller, but growing, colonies of Jews in other cities of the Greek world? The Greek culture was extraordinarily attractive, and Jews who were born and bred in Greek cities could often speak no language but Greek. To them the Biblical books were items that could neither be read nor understood. Despite Judean prejudices, therefore, there arose among the Alexandrian Jews a strong pressure toward the translation of the Bible into Greek.

This pressure was encouraged by the Ptolemies. Under Ptolemy I and, even more so, under Ptolemy II, Alexandria was made the intellectual capital of the world. It contained a Museum, which was the closest ancient approach to what we would now call a "research institution," and an enormous Library, the greatest before the invention of printing. It was a Ptolemaic ambition, apparently, to gather all knowledge into Alexandria and they did not limit this to Greek learning. They encouraged and even possibly supported the translation of the Jewish scriptures into Greek.

Therefore, somewhere about 270 B.C., the Biblical books began to appear, for the first time in history, in other than their original language. Later tradition embellished this appearance of the first foreign translation of the Bible. Ptolemy II was supposed to have sent for scholars from Judea. The number of scholars was supposed to have been seventy (or seventy-two) so that the translation was eventually called the Septuagint, from a Latin word for "seventy." What's more, the tale goes on, each of the seventy (or seventy-two) translated the Bible separately and independently, and when the translations were compared, all were found to be identical. (This was a transparent attempt to show that the Greek version was as inspired as the original Hebrew since, without divine intervention, seventy independent versions couldn't possibly have been identical.)

Actually, the translation was not a very good one. There were many errors, and modern translations of the Bible must bypass the Septuagint and go back to Hebrew versions. This does not alter the fact that the Septuagint was *the* Bible of ancient times. It was the only Bible available to non-Jews and to many Greek-speaking Jews, too, and this strongly affected the history of the world.

The translators of the Septuagint, whoever they were, must have been deeply immersed in Greek culture, and this showed itself in their Greek version of Hebrew phrases. The most important example involves a passage in the seventh chapter of Isaiah, the one where the prophet assures King Ahaz that the attacking forces of Israel and Syria will be destroyed. In part he says (according to the New English Bible, a 1970 translation): "A young woman is with child, and she will bear a son, and will call him Immanuel." Exactly what Isaiah meant by that is very controversial, but he made use of the Hebrew word "almah," which is translated as "young woman."

During the exile, the Jews were strongly stirred by messianic hopes and there was a search through all the historical and prophetic writings for any passages that might be interpreted as divine indications of the coming of a Messiah. This verse in Isaiah was one of those seized upon. The mysterious remark about the birth of Immanuel was maintained to be a prophetic reference to the coming of a Messiah, an ideal king who would defeat the Gentile kingdoms and establish a righteous world-kingdom with its capital at Jerusalem.

In the Greek tradition it was common to think of ideal kings as divine, as being sons of one or another of the gods, as having been begotten by a god upon a woman who, sometimes, had not had relations with any mortal man and who could thus be considered a virgin. To men imbued with notions gathered from Greek literature (even if they were Jews by religion) it seemed fitting to translate the Hebrew word "almah" into the Greek word "parthenos" ("virgin") if the verse were to keep its messianic implication.

The Greek verse made it possible to think of the Messiah as a divine Son of God. It was the Septuagint version of the Bible that influenced the early Christians, and in the King James Version of the Bible, for instance, the passage is given as: "Behold, a virgin shall conceive, and bear a son, and shall call his name Immanuel." *

All things considered, then, it is easy to argue, from the standpoint of its effect on future history, that the most important event in the entire three-century existence of Ptolemaic Egypt was the publication, in Alexandria, of the Septuagint.

Ptolemy II, the genial patron of the Septuagint, died in 246 B.C. and was succeeded by his son, who reigned as Ptolemy III. The Seleucid monarch of the time was married to a sister of the new Egyptian king, this being a condition of the latest peace treaty between the two powers. Once Ptolemy II was dead, however, the Ptolemaic princess was sent away and eventually killed, together with her son, by a competing queen.

This was the occasion for the Third Syrian War, in which the angry Ptolemy III, seeking vengeance for the death of his sister, won a complete victory and marched as far as the Tigris-Euphrates itself. This was the high point of the power of the Ptolemaic kingdom.

It was also the high point of the happy peace of the Jews under enlightened Ptolemaic rule. Ptolemy III, like his father and grandfather, was very conscious of ruling over people of disparate religious beliefs. Like them, he tried to be king of them all. On his way back from Babylon, therefore, he stopped off in Jerusalem in 241 B.C. and laid gifts on the altar of the

* When, in the nineteenth and twentieth centuries, newer translations tried to replace the word "virgin" with the more correct "young woman," many Christians, who were emotionally committed to the mistranslation, were shocked and horrified.

Temple in Jerusalem in careful obedience to the ritual as prescribed by the priesthood.

AGATHOCLES

While Greece and all the east were upset by the hurricane of Alexander the Great and his successors, the Greek cities of the west, such as Syracuse, remained untouched. And while the Phoenician cities went down, while Tyre was devastated, the Tyrian colony of Carthage continued its proud existence — stronger and wealthier than ever.

To be sure, the great victory of Timoleon on the Crimisus River had forced Carthage on the defensive in Sicily, but she could afford to bide her time. From past history she could be quite certain that the Greek factions would fall out and that one side or another would appeal to her for help. And whichever side appealed, she would answer, for as long as she kept Greek fighting Greek she paved the way for her own eventual triumph.

It happened as Carthage knew it would. After Timoleon's death, Syracuse and other cities came under the control of oligarchs, and against them, as was inevitable among the Greeks, there arose demagogues, who made use of the resentment of the mob to try to rise to power themselves.

In Syracuse there lived one Agathocles (uh-gath′oh-kleez), the son of a potter. He had married a wealthy widow, who supplied him with funds, and he had a great deal of native charm and daring. He began to agitate and intrigue for the downfall of the oligarchs. Twice he was exiled but he gathered an army outside of Syracuse, not hesitating to use funds supplied him by the Carthaginians, and 317 B.C. finally took over the city.

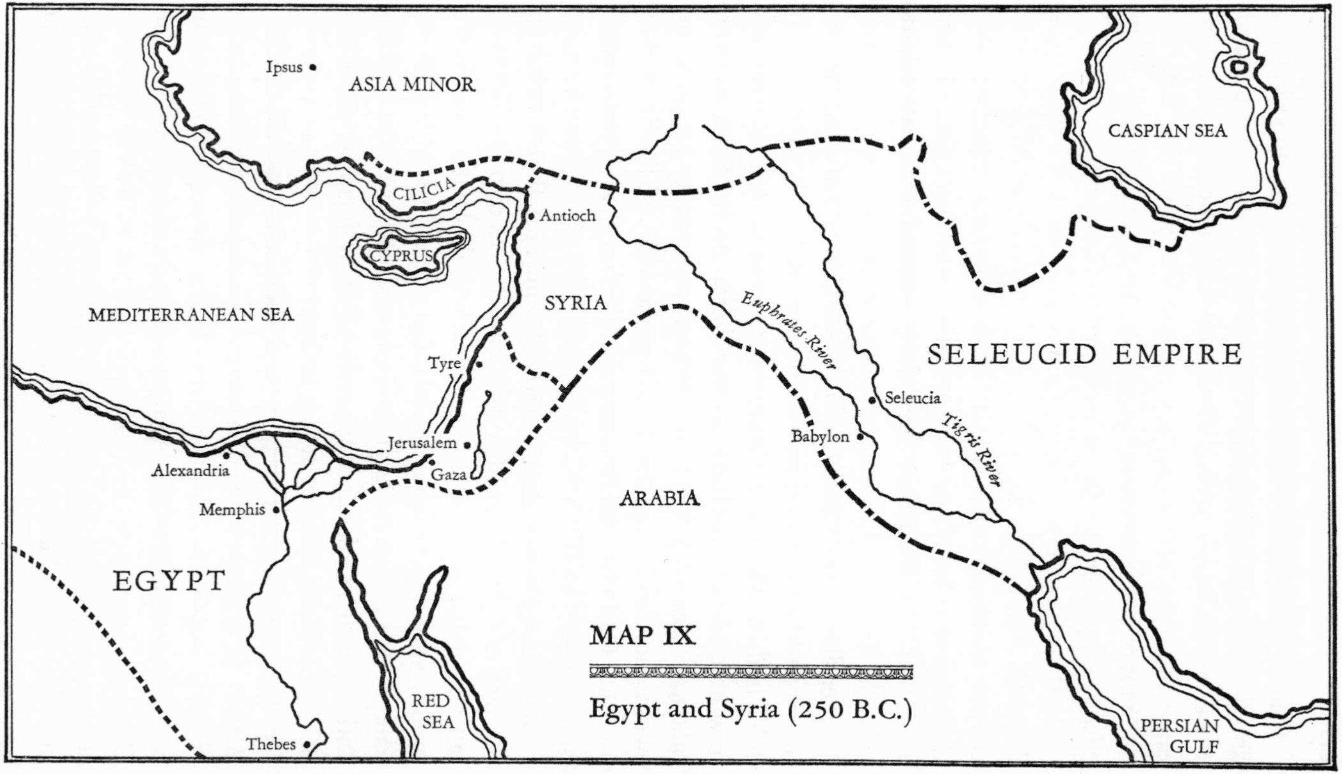

MAP IX

Egypt and Syria (250 B.C.)

Once in power, he visited slaughter upon the opposing faction until his rule was undisputed. He then began to expand his power as, a century earlier, Dionysius had done. Finally, there came the moment Carthage was confidently waiting for. The remnant of the faction overthrown by Agathocles, unable to oppose him by their own force, appealed to Carthage.

Carthage answered gladly. In 311 B.C. she sent a large expeditionary force into Sicily under a general named Hamilcar. On the south central coast, a Greek army was smashed. The Carthaginians hastened eastward and, as on a number of occasions before, placed their men down around the city of Syracuse.

In earlier sieges Carthage had failed, but this time, her victory looked certain. Greek morale was at rock bottom. Agathocles had overdone his bloody suppression of his enemies and now he could count on friends nowhere. And if Syracuse were taken, it was very likely that the three-century struggle between the Greeks and the Carthaginians would finally be over and that Carthage would then control all of Sicily for an indefinite period.

Sheer desperation gave Agathocles an idea that seemed, on the face of it, to be suicidal. But since it was also suicidal to do nothing and since, all things being equal, Agathocles always preferred action to inaction, he moved forward with demonic energy. His idea was simply to gather whatever forces he could and force or sneak his way out of the besieged city, leaving behind a skeleton force sworn to hold out as long as possible. He, his men, and his ships would then make a foray on the African coast and, by endangering Carthage, force that city to recall its expeditionary force from Sicily. The gamble seemed to have zero chance, but Agathocles was a born gambler. The Carthaginian fleet was blockading the port so tightly that a rat couldn't have slipped out, but Agathocles counted on their being overconfident. He held his own ships in readiness and waited.

Some merchant ships, Agathocles knew, were on their way and would attempt to run the blockade. When they did arrive, the Carthaginian ships rowed carelessly toward them, intending to intercept the cargo, but leaving a large gap in the cordon about the city. Agathocles' ships set out at top speed. By the time the Carthaginians reversed direction, they were too late to catch him and, what's more, the merchant ships then managed to row into port and bring in the supplies. The Carthaginians, snapping for each in turn, had lost both.

Agathocles, having escaped the ships of the enemy, managed to make his way safely across the Mediterranean, landing his ships on the African coast in 310 B.C. Since he had too few troops to send some inland and leave others to guard the fleet, he carried audacity a step further by burning the ships and informing his men that their only chance to return home safely was to win victories. He then marched them to Carthage and encamped on the outskirts.

The Carthaginians could scarcely believe their eyes. Their secure and peaceful city had never before been threatened and their suburban villas and orchards had drowsed in perpetual serenity — till then. They had to assume that their army in Sicily had been destroyed, as in no other way could they account for a Greek force in Africa.

Hastily they sent messengers to Sicily to find out what had happened and to recall any men who might have survived. Meanwhile, they scraped up a ragtag collection of men to send against Agathocles. These were easily wiped out by the trained Greek infantry, but meanwhile the city was pulled into shape to withstand a siege, at least until the Carthaginian army returned.

Return it did, and the Greek army in Africa was ultimately defeated. Long before that, however, Agathocles had had ships built and had himself returned to a Syracuse that was no longer under siege and to whom he was now a hero.

By 306 B.C. the Carthaginians were willing to sign a treaty in which their dominion in Sicily was restricted to what it had held in the time of Dionysius and Timoleon. Agathocles' daring gamble had paid off.

For the remaining twenty years of his life, Agathocles consolidated his power in Sicily and in neighboring regions of Italy. Syracuse prospered and it was for all the world like a return to the days of Dionysius except that Agathocles, although just as tyrannical, was more charming.

In 289 B.C. Agathocles died, and his death (like that of Dionysius) was followed by another period of confusion and anarchy. Certain Italian mercenaries that Agathocles had kept as a bodyguard seized the town of Messana (meh-say'nuh) in the corner of Sicily adjacent to the Italian toe. They called themselves Mamertines ("sons of Mars"), and made life hideous for surrounding areas by their depredations. Once again the Carthaginians quietly waited their chance.

PYRRHUS

But meanwhile, a new factor appeared in the west. In central Italy, on the Tiber River, there was a city called Rome. According to legend, it had been founded four and a half centuries earlier in 753 B.C. but until the time of Alexander the Great, its history was a blank as far as the Greek world was concerned.

In the time of Alexander, however, the Romans had begun fighting a series of strenuous wars against another central-Italian people called the Samnites — and won. By 290 B.C., just at the time that Agathocles was reaching the end of his astonishing career, all central Italy was Roman.

Furthermore, as it happened, Rome had developed a remarkably flexible system of government that enabled it to rule efficiently over allies and colonies, and bring them enough prosperity to reduce the likelihood of revolt. It was rare that any enemy could persuade a town dominated by Rome to revolt against it, with the result that Rome's efforts were unified and strong. It could not be diverted and it could survive adversity. That, combined with a trained army quick to adapt its tactics to changing circumstances, made it the most formidable nation in arms the ancient world had yet seen.*

The first portion of the Greek world to appreciate the effect of this new phenomenon on the stage of world history were the Greek cities that dotted the coast of southern Italy. The chief of these was Taras, better known to us by the Roman version of its name, Tarentum (tuh-ren′tum).

It did not take long for Tarentum to realize that it was not facing an ordinary "barbarian" power, and that by its own strength it could never hold off Rome, as for so long it had held off the forces of other native Italian cities. Clearly, Tarentum realized, it needed help from outside.

This was the time when Macedonian generals with advanced military techniques, such as the use of the phalanx and of corps of elephants, were ruling the east. The nearest of these was Pyrrhus (pir′us), who ruled over Epirus, a section of northwestern Greece just across the strait from the Italian heel. To Pyrrhus, Tarentum appealed for help in 281 B.C.

Pyrrhus, a dashing adventurer, responded gladly and came to Italy with 25,000 men and a number of elephants. Twice, once in 280 B.C. and once in 279 B.C., Pyrrhus met the Romans. Twice his elephants trundled into the Roman lines and twice the phalanx managed to push forward by sheer weight. Twice the Romans were forced to abandon the field in defeat, but only after having inflicted such losses that Pyrrhus ruefully realized that unless the war came to a quick end, he would be left without an army. (It is from this that the phrase "Pyrrhic

* For the early history of Rome, see my book *The Roman Republic* (Houghton Mifflin, 1966).

victory" arose.) But the Romans wouldn't make peace as long as Pyrrhus kept a single soldier in Italy, and Pyrrhus, weary of fighting Romans, gladly answered a call for help from Sicily.

There Syracuse and other Greek cities were in utter disarray because of the Mamertines, and Carthage, taking advantage as always of Greeks in trouble, had advanced eastward and was again laying siege to Syracuse. Pyrrhus landed on Sicily's eastern coast, proceeded to Syracuse, and easily broke the Carthaginian siege.

There now came to pass for the first and only time in history war between Carthaginian and Macedonian. In a way, it was a second round of Canaan versus Macedon, if we consider Alexander's siege of Tyre to have been the first round. On land Pyrrhus had it all his own way, for the Carthaginians were by no means Romans. Pyrrhus marched westward, all the way to Lilybaeum and only that westernmost fort remained in Carthaginian hands by 277 B.C.

Lilybaeum, however, was as impregnable as Tyre had been, unless Pyrrhus, like Alexander, managed somehow to gain control of the sea. It occurred to Pyrrhus that, with ships, he could repeat Agathocles' trick of landing in Africa, and with a stronger army. But where was he to get the ships? The Sicilian cities had them but they had grown tired of Pyrrhus' hard-driving methods and they were satisfied merely to have the Carthaginians driven back. They refused to help Pyrrhus further, and he left Sicily saying with a sigh (according to some reports), "What a battlefield I am leaving for the Romans and Carthaginians!" Pyrrhus returned to southern Italy, where he was needed badly. In his absence, the Romans had been surging southward again and Tarentum was calling loudly for help.

In 275 B.C. Pyrrhus fought the Romans for one last time. By now, though, the Romans had worked out methods for countering the elephants and for fighting the phalanx. Pyrrhus' tiring phalanx could barely hold its own against the grim Roman legions and the Macedonian general had finally had enough. He returned to Greece. His departure sealed the fate of the Greek cities in Italy. By 270 B.C. all southern Italy, without exception, was controlled by Rome.

Sicily, however, remained. Its problem continued to be the Mamertines. A certain young man named Hiero (hy′uh-roh), who had fought with distinction under Pyrrhus against the Carthaginians, was placed at the head of Syracusan forces. In 270 B.C. he defeated the Mamertines at Centuripae (sen-tyoo′-rih-puh), about sixty miles southwest of Messana, and then again at Mylae (my′lee), twenty miles west of the city.

The Mamertines fled back to Messana and Hiero might have taken it, but for the fact that the Carthaginians, as always, moved to weaken Syracuse. Hiero was forced to return to Syracuse to block them. The grateful Syracusans made Hiero their king, and he reigned as Hiero II (for an earlier Hiero had ruled the city not long after the Battle of Himera, two centuries before).

By 265 B.C. Hiero had consolidated his rule and, gambling on Carthage remaining quiet for a while, raised a large well-equipped army and made ready to march on Messana. The Mamertines knew they needed help but were in a quandary. To whom ought they to appeal? Some among them wanted to call to those who never failed to help against Syracuse — the Carthaginians. Others, however, recalling the Italian origins of the Mamertines, wanted to appeal to the great new power of Italy — Rome.

In the end, both factions won out. Appeals were sent out by the Mamertines to both parties, and both responded. Carthaginian forces entered Messana to strengthen its defenses against the Syracusans, even while a Roman army (leaving Italy for the first time in Rome's history) landed south of Messana. Hiero found the Romans to be the closer enemy and offered them battle.

The Romans accepted the offer and promptly dealt the Syracusan army a hammer blow such as they had never felt at the hands of the Carthaginians. Hiero needed no second taste. He recognized at once that with the Romans it was useless to fight, and being unable to beat them, he joined them.

In 263 B.C. he made a treaty with Rome. For the remainder of his long reign (which lasted fifty-five years altogether) he left all fighting to the Romans and Carthaginians. He remained a loyal ally of Rome and under him Syracuse had its last period of reasonable independence.

10

CANAAN VERSUS ROME

HAMILCAR BARCA

The wars between Rome and Carthage, which the Romans called "Punic wars," after the name they gave the Carthaginians in their language, were the greatest seen up to that date. The fighting was not as spectacular, perhaps, as the gigantic marches and victories of Alexander the Great, but then neither Rome nor Carthage was quite the pushover Persia had been. Nor could the battles between Rome and Carthage be compared to the stately dances between the Macedonian armies in the east. The war in the west was for blood, with both sides in a win-or-die mood and with Rome never and Carthage hardly ever willing to make peace after a reverse or two, as the Macedonians always were.

Carthage was by far the richer and larger city. At its peak it had a population of 700,000 and in the third century B.C. it may well have been the largest city in all the Mediterranean world. What's more, it had a navy and Rome had none.

On the other hand, Carthaginian allies were always restless and resentful, so that Carthage could never safely conduct a war near home, whereas Roman dominions were rock hard. Carthage fought largely with mercenaries, who could become dangerous if not paid, whereas Rome fought with citizen soldiers, who did not fight for pay.

The Carthaginians tasted the quality of Roman fighting early in the game. In 264 B.C. the Romans, having defeated Hiero, turned against the Carthaginians who were actually occupying Messana and drove them out. That began the First Punic War. For a while, the situation seesawed, but then the Romans, growing steadily stronger, began to win. The Carthaginians ruefully learned they were now fighting an enemy worth far more than the Syracusan forces they had so long battled, and even more dangerous than Pyrrhus had been.

Even so, Carthage might well have felt they had nothing to fear through any local defeats in Sicily. After all, they had been defeated there often in the past, without ever having been totally driven off the island — for they controlled the sea.

But the Romans saw that, too. Making use of Greek shipwrights, they learned how to build ships and how to fight with them. By 260 B.C. they had actually made of themselves, in only four years from a standing start, a naval power on a par with the Carthaginians. To the astonishment of the Carthaginians, the Romans began to win victories at sea, and Carthage was forced to recognize that a whole new dimension of danger faced them.

The Romans did more. With ships at their command, they could now repeat the tactics of Agathocles under far more favorable circumstances. They did not have to sneak out of blockaded harbors; they did not have to work with inadequate numbers of ships and men. A large fleet of 330 ships was sent to Sicily, and then to Africa, where it landed in 256 B.C. after defeating a Carthaginian fleet that had tried to stop it.

The African expeditionary force, under the leadership of the Roman general Marcus Atilius Regulus (reg′yoo-lus), now prepared to do what Agathocles' much smaller force had not quite been able to manage — to take Carthage.

It did not seem he would have any trouble. Agathocles' incursion sixty years before had taught the Carthaginians nothing. Carthage still lay nearly defenseless, surrounded by wealthy suburbs inhabited by men who knew nothing of fighting and who could only surrender at the approach of the hardened Romans and hope they could escape with their property, or at least their lives. The city itself, trembling and in panic, was placed under siege, and it made ready to surrender.

They asked Regulus for terms and Regulus, confident of success, laid it on heavily. Not only would Carthage have to surrender Sicily to the Romans, but all the other west Mediterranean islands as well. She would also have to give up her fleet and pay an enormous indemnity. The most catastrophic defeat could not have resulted in harsher terms, and so Carthage decided she might as well fight. Her inhabitants were, in the last analysis, Canaanites, and by long tradition Canaanites fought to the last man when truly pushed. Regulus had truly pushed.

As luck would have it, there was, within the city, a mercenary named Xanthippus (zan-tip′us). He was of Spartan ancestry and, although it was now a century and a half since Sparta had dominated Greece, the military tradition still survived among its descendants. He offered to lead the Carthaginian forces, insisting that the Romans were being poorly handled and were winning only because the Carthaginians had not yet really fought.

The Carthaginian leaders were only too willing to let the Spartan do what he could, and Xanthippus gathered all the mercenaries at hand, together with such elephants as were available. (The Carthaginians used elephants native to northern Africa, a small species now extinct.) He determined to try what audacity could do in a war in which audacity had so far been demonstrated only by Romans.

Xanthippus attacked suddenly. The Romans, who were expecting only surrender, were caught completely by surprise. What's more, it turned out that Xanthippus was right and that Regulus was not, after all, a capable general. The Roman army, outnumbered and outgeneraled, was just about destroyed and Regulus was taken prisoner in 255 B.C. It was the greatest Roman land disaster of the war and Carthage was saved. The war returned to Sicily, where Carthage fought Rome both by land and sea, holding out with Canaanite stubbornness at all points, but slowly giving way before a Roman stubbornness that was at least as great.

Carthage might not, in the end, have lasted as long as she did, were it not for the fact that a greater leader than Xanthippus appeared — and a native Carthaginian, too, not a mercenary. His name was Hamilcar, a name that crops up several times in Carthaginian history. This Hamilcar, the greatest of them all, is distinguished from the rest by the surname Barca (bahr'kuh). This may be a true family name or it may be a nickname, for it means "lightning" and Hamilcar Barca was remarkable for the speed and force of his strokes.

It was Carthage's supreme misfortune that Hamilcar Barca was born too late. He was only a boy of six when the First Punic War had begun. When he was old enough finally to have demonstrated his abilities and to be placed in command of the Carthaginian forces in 247 B.C. (even then, Hamilcar was only in his early twenties) the war was all but lost for Carthage. In Sicily only Lilybaeum and Drepanum (drep'uh-num), fifteen miles apart on the far western coast, remained in Carthaginian hands.

To divert attention from these, Hamilcar Barca effected a landing on Sicily's north coast, in a mountainous region near Panormus, and made that a center for skillful guerrilla raids that drove the Romans to distraction. For years he fought off all Roman attempts to dislodge him, and in this one man the Romans found a greater and more pertinacious enemy than in all of Carthage besides.

But Hamilcar Barca could not be everywhere. The Romans, who had already lost several fleets at sea, either to Carthaginian action or to storms — which had also destroyed several Carthaginian fleets — made one last effort. They built another fleet and, in 241 B.C., off the western edge of Sicily, managed to defeat the Carthaginian fleet once again, and now Carthage finally lost heart and gave up.

The trouble was that the war had been lasting a quarter-century, and Carthage, its trade ruined, was being impoverished. Rome, a farming nation with little or no overseas trade, could keep on fighting in Sicily and on the sea forever, but Carthage could not. The Carthaginian merchants decided to cut their losses and ask for terms, even though Hamilcar Barca was still undefeated in Sicily.

By the terms of the peace Carthage gave up all of Sicily to Rome. She gave up even the fortified towns of Lilybaeum and Drepanum, which Rome had not been able to conquer, and the mountain strongholds from which Hamilcar's guerrillas had never been driven. And thus, finally, the Romans accomplished what no Greek — not Dionysius, not Agathocles, not Pyrrhus — had ever been able to do. They drove the Carthaginians completely out of Sicily forever.

For Carthage the First Punic War was a disaster for a greater reason than the mere loss of Sicily. It had left Carthage in a state of bankruptcy. The treasury was empty, what money she could scrape up had to be earmarked for the Roman victors, and Carthage found herself unable to pay her mercenaries who had fought for her so long and so ably.

The mercenaries might conceivably have waited for their money if Hamilcar had been kept in command, for they trusted the young general and he had promised to take care of them. The merchants who ruled Carthage, however, distrusted

Hamilcar for the very brilliance he displayed. They feared he might take over the government and end their own corrupt and thoroughly selfish rule. They therefore removed him from his command.

At that the mercenaries, surmising they would get no money out of the merchants ever, revolted and prepared to take by force that which they felt to be theirs by right. They swept through the countryside, occupied the nearby coastal towns of Utica and Hippo, which lay west of Carthage, and by 239 B.C. had Carthage itself virtually under siege.

The merchant princes, certain that to give in to the mercenaries at this stage would mean an inevitable and indiscriminate slaughter, bowed to what had to be and decided that even Hamilcar Barca was the lesser evil. He was recalled to command. Reconciliation was by now impossible. Matters had gone too far and Hamilcar had to defeat the mercenaries if Carthage was to remain standing. He proceeded to do that with characteristic energy and brilliance.

A river separated Carthage from the main body of besieging mercenaries. Under certain wind conditions that river could be crossed. Hamilcar seized the appropriate moment and, with all the men he could raise — 10,000 of them plus 70 elephants — he splashed across and caught the unprepared mercenaries from the rear. In a second battle he feinted retreat, lured the mercenaries into a forward rush, and caught them in the flank with the very troops that had earlier seemed to be in flight. Such mutineers as remained were penned up in Tunes (tyoo′neez), a suburb of Carthage (and one which eventually grew to be the modern Tunis). There Hamilcar blockaded them and, in the end, annihilated them. Within the year Carthage had weathered its danger.

That is, the city had, but not all its dominions. Rome had been watching with grim interest as civil war further weakened its enemy. On the island of Sardinia, which had been Carthaginian for three centuries, the occupying army, also mercenary, had joined in the revolt. With Hamilcar victorious in Africa, it seemed clear he would take his troops to Sardinia and clean out the rebels there, too. Nervously the rebels in Sardinia appealed to Rome for protection, and that was what Rome was waiting for. Like Carthage, Rome liked to perform her aggressive acts under the color of helping some pitiful suppliant.

Using the appeal as an excuse, Rome instantly demanded that Carthage cede them not only Sardinia but the island of Corsica, to its north, as well, and in addition pay a further indemnity. The appalled Carthaginians were helpless. A quarter-century of war, ended by the devastation of the mercenary depredations, had made it impossible for them to present even the barest show of force. They had to give in.

It must have been at this moment that Hamilcar conceived his all-embracing hatred of Rome. What the Romans had done and won in the First Punic War, they had done and won in open combat, and they had taken blows as well as given them. What they now did, wresting two islands out of a beaten and helpless enemy, with no shadow of justification except that they had the naked power to do it, was cowardly and despicable. Hamilcar determined to spend his life evening the score.

But how? Only one realm remained Carthaginian outside northern Africa. That was the southern coast of Spain. It was to Spain that Hamilcar intended to go. There he would find hardy tribes who would make first-class fighting men, and who were separated from Rome only by land so that he would not need the navy Carthage no longer had. What's more, he would be far away from Carthage with its appeasing merchant princes, who thought far more of their money bags than of the city.

Nor would it be difficult to go there. The Carthaginian rulers would be only too glad to get rid of him and send him far away and hope that he would die before he ever came back. As for Rome, it knew that Spain was rich in minerals, and Hamilcar could go under cover of developing mines that would help pay the Roman indemnity. The Roman rulers were by no means strangers to greed.

In 235 B.C., then, Hamilcar Barca went to Spain and established his base at Gades (Cadiz) — as far as possible, to begin with, from the unwanted attentions of either Carthage or Rome. With him went Hasdrubal (haz′droo-bul), his son-in-law. With him also went his nine-year-old son, Hannibal. This, too, was a common name in Carthaginian history, but there had never been, nor was there ever to be, another Hannibal like Hannibal Barca. It had not originally been Hamilcar's intention to take the child, but Hannibal had pleaded earnestly for permission to go. Hamilcar finally gave in on condition that the boy swear eternal enmity to Rome. (Hannibal himself, many years later, told of this.)

Hamilcar made no attempt to conquer the Spanish tribes outright. That would have involved him in endless battles and probably in eventual failure. Instead he won them over by adopting their customs and marrying a Spanish woman. He became one of them. When he did have to fight a tribe, he offered generous settlements after a minimum of fighting, so as to make allies at once of those he had defeated. As a result, he finally extended his control as far eastward as Lucentum (lyoo-sen′tum), the modern Alicante, some 400 miles eastward along the coast from his original base at Gades. That had taken him nearly eight years and in 228 B.C., he died in the course of military operations, apparently while crossing a river.

THE SON OF HAMILCAR

Hamilcar was only forty-two years old at the time of his death, and his premature passing might well have brought an end to all his far-sighted planning had not his son-in-law, Hasdrubal, taken over and moved in the footsteps of his predecessor. Hasdrubal continued the policy of conciliating the Spanish tribes and of fighting as rarely and as mildly as possible. About 225 B.C. he founded a new city on the Spanish coast some fifty miles south of Lucentum. It was a "new Carthage" and was called by a name which to the Romans became "Carthagena" (kahr″thuh-jee′nuh).*

By now, though, the expanding Carthaginian realm in Spain had attracted the attention of two Greek cities along the northwestern coasts of the Mediterranean Sea. One was Massalia and the other was Saguntum (suh-gun′tum), which was located on the Spanish shore only about 160 miles north of Carthagena.

Both cities were economic rivals of Carthage and both were accustomed to view it as a traditional enemy. Both had allied themselves to Rome as soon as it was clear that Rome was the strongest power in the west, and now both clamored at the Roman doorstep with news of the dangerous Carthaginian advance in Spain.

In 226 B.C. a Roman mission was sent to Spain and Hasdrubal felt it prudent to agree to a thus-far-and-no-farther agreement. He accepted the Iberus River (igh-beer′us), the modern Ebro, as the northern limit of Carthaginian power. This was not entirely satisfactory for Saguntum, since the Iberus River runs eastward into the Mediterranean some ninety miles north of that city. The agreement meant it would be a Greek enclave surrounded by Carthaginian power. Nevertheless, since the agreement satisfied Rome, there was nothing Saguntum could do about it.

Then, in 221 B.C., Hasdrubal, the worthy successor of Hamilcar, was killed by an assassin. Again it seemed as though the Carthaginian plan might shiver to destruction, but again there

* The city still exists under the name of Cartagena, thus preserving the memory of the vanished Carthage. Another city of the same name exists in the New World, on the Carribbean shore of Colombia.

was a worthy successor, and even a more than worthy one. The successor was the son of Hamilcar Barca, Hannibal, who had now spent eighteen years in Spain and was twenty-six years old.

Hamilcar Barca might well have been the greatest Carthaginian warrior in its history had it not been for his son, for Hannibal surpassed him completely. The two formed a combination of a remarkable father followed by a more remarkable son, matched by no others in history but Philip of Macedon and his son Alexander the Great.

Hannibal proved to be the greatest leader of armed men ever produced by any of the peoples who could trace their ancestry back to the ancient land of Canaan. It was not just that he was a military genius of the first rank — with few in history his equal and none, perhaps, his clear superior (not even Alexander) — but he had the ability to gain the love of his men. He dressed and lived like an ordinary officer; he was brave in the field, taking risks coolly, and could withstand all the privations of a hard campaign uncomplainingly. He built an army of the most disparate groups, united by nothing but his leadership, led them for years through victory and hardship, and never at any time was there even a whisper of revolt against him. It was as though his men always knew that without him they would be destroyed at once and that only in his shadow was there safety, so wherever he led, they followed. Perhaps the greatest testimony to the greatness of Hannibal is the fact that we hear most about him from the Romans, whom he almost destroyed, and though he was the most terrible enemy Rome ever had, the Roman historians praise him.

As soon as Hannibal took over in 221 B.C. on the death of Hasdrubal — to the unanimous, enthusiastic acclaim of the army, which already knew his quality — he began to organize it into a superb fighting unit. He had good material to work with. The Spanish infantry was steady as a rock. He had slingers from the Balearic Islands who could hit their targets with pellets of stone or lead with greater accuracy than archers could. He had Numidian horsemen from North Africa who may well have been the best cavalry of their time. He also had a number of the North African elephants from what is now Morocco, but these were not terribly much larger than horses and only a third the weight of the gigantic elephants of tropical Africa.

Within a year Hannibal's rapid strokes completed the task of bringing under Carthaginian control virtually all of Spain south of the Iberus, and he next prepared to put into action, at last, the plan conceived by Hamilcar and carried on by Hasdrubal. That was nothing more nor less than to lead an army out of Spain, eastward across Gaul and over the Alps, down into Italy itself, in order to fight the Romans on their own territory.

This involved enormous problems. Could he really catch the Romans unprepared? Hannibal was sure he could, for the Romans were busy fighting the Gallic tribes in northern Italy and were not looking very closely at distant Spain. Could he keep his troops supplied over the long march? Again Hannibal was sure he could. He could live off the country and, to make up for inevitable loss of men by death and desertion, he could probably get reinforcements from the Gallic tribes between Spain and Italy — tribes who had cause to fear and hate Rome.

What Hannibal feared most was Carthage itself. The appeasing merchant princes in control couldn't possibly be expected to take the risk of declaring war on Rome. It would be necessary to force their hand by making Rome take the initiative. The means to do so were at hand, for the city of Saguntum was stuck like a Greek raisin into the Carthaginian coast of Spain.

In 219 B.C. Hannibal deliberately broke the treaty with Rome and laid siege to Saguntum, demanding its surrender. The men of Saguntum immediately appealed to Rome, and a Roman commission was sent to Spain to remind Hannibal that the city was a Roman ally. Hannibal treated the Romans with studied insult, telling them to take their complaints to Carthage, hoping that this would force the short-tempered Romans into declaring war at once. To Hannibal's chagrin, the Romans actually went to Carthage.

Hannibal sent messengers speeding to Carthage ahead of the Romans in order that they might rally the war party in the city and delay conciliation as long as possible. Sure enough, while the Romans were still talking angrily in Carthage, Saguntum finally fell after a siege of eight months. There was the usual sack and massacre, which Hannibal did not try to lessen since he was intent on angering the Romans. Hannibal confiscated the gathered wealth of the city and sent it to Carthage in order that it might be passed around as bribes where it might do the most good in manufacturing hawkish sentiment.

The result was that when the Roman envoys finally declared that Carthage must choose either peace or war, the Carthaginians, fired by the victory and soothed by the gold, told the Romans to choose whichever they pleased. The choice was war, and in 218 B.C. the Second Punic War began.

At the end of May of that year, Hannibal left Carthagena with 90,000 infantry, 12,000 cavalry, and a number of elephants. Behind him he left his brother, Hasdrubal Barca, in control of Spain with 15,000 men. Hannibal marched rapidly, fighting off the hostile tribes between Spain and Italy in as gingerly a fashion as possible. When his own men finally realized he was leading them to Italy, some quailed, so he allowed the fearful to leave — lest their cowardice infect the rest of the army.

He reached the Rhone River and crossed it before the Romans were sure he had left Spain. Indeed, a Roman force which was sent westward to Spain landed at the mouth of the Rhone en route, and its general was horrified to find that Hannibal was directly to the north, 350 miles east of the Iberus, and making for the Alps. He hurried back to Italy.

Hannibal was racing now. He had to get across the Alps and into Italy before the coming of winter made the mountains absolutely impassable. If he was caught north of the Alps by winter, the Romans would have time to prepare and, perhaps, to hunt him down.

He marched northward along the Rhone River to avoid any fight with the Roman army to the south — there must be no battles with the Romans till his army was in Italy — then he turned eastward, reached the Alps, and spent fifteen days crossing the mountains. In doing so, he had to fight two battles with the tribesmen (winning both, but at considerable loss). He also had to withstand the hardships of the gathering cold, the snow that was beginning to fall, the dangerous trails and declivities.

Yet he made it. Five months after he had left Carthagena, he found himself, at the end of October, in the plains of northern Italy.

It did not seem an enviable position, however. Somehow, he had managed to bring all his elephants across Gaul and over the mountains, but he had lost two thirds of his men and most of his horses. Now he was in Italy with only 26,000 men, facing the Romans, who could have put many times that number of men into the field. What's more, Hannibal was without bases, without any line of communications, without reserves. Surely Hannibal had merely committed elaborate suicide. It seemed the Romans had only to find him and crush him.

HANNIBAL AT WAR

This the Romans proceeded to try to do. A Roman army was sent northward to destroy him. The first skirmish took place near the Ticinus River (tih-sy′nus), which flows into the Po River from the north. The overconfident Romans, foreseeing no trouble, attacked heedlessly and were astonished to find themselves slammed back across the Po River. They rallied at the Trebia River (tree′bee-uh), which flows into the Po from the south.

Grown a little more prudent, the Romans waited for reinforcements. Calmly, almost contemptuously, Hannibal stood aside and let the reinforcements arrive. The more Romans, the greater the victory. The reinforced Romans now stood to the east of the Trebia River, while Hannibal was on the west.

Hannibal sent a detachment of cavalry across the river with instructions to behave like an isolated group of horsemen unaware of the presence of the Romans. This they did, and when the Romans attacked, they fled in simulated panic back across the river. It was winter now and the waters were icy, but the Romans, anxious to take care of the horsemen, plunged into the water after them.

It was one thing to send a few horses splashing across a cold river; it was quite another thing to have thousands of footmen do so. The Romans emerged from the river, soaked and freezing; the few cavalry they were pursuing faded away to right and left; there in front of them, unexpectedly, was Hannibal's entire army — dry and confident.

Caught at a disadvantage, the Romans nevertheless fought heroically, but Hannibal used his cavalry and his elephants like a master, feeding them into the fight exactly where and exactly when they would do the most good. Most of the Roman army was destroyed and the Gauls of the region, learning of the magnificent victory and scenting revenge over the Romans, who had so few years before defeated them and occupied the Po valley, went over to Hannibal.

While the Romans tried to recoup their strength, Hannibal remained in camp for the winter. Then, in the spring of 217 B.C., he marched his army across the Apennines, 275 miles to the vicinity of Lake Trasimenus (tras″ih-mee′nus) only 100 miles north of Rome. The winter and the mountain march in the spring were by no means easy. All his elephants but one were lost. At one point in the march, the army had to spend four days crossing a marsh with no really dry ground at any point. In the increase in pestilence that followed, Hannibal himself caught an infection that cost him the sight of one eye.

At Lake Trasimenus Hannibal noted a narrow road skirting the lake, a road that was hemmed in by hills. He knew that a new Roman army was almost upon him, so he placed his own men behind the hills and waited. The Roman army came snaking along the narrow road in the morning and a light mist helped keep them in ignorance of the waiting enemy. When the Romans were spread out completely into a long, narrow line along the road, Hannibal's army came down all along that line and simply slaughtered them. The Roman army was wiped out at almost no cost to Hannibal.

There was now no army between Hannibal and Rome. There might have been the temptation to march directly on Rome, but if so, Hannibal resisted it. He had no siege machinery and the Roman walls were strong and the Roman will indomitable. If he sat down outside Rome, his army would wither away.

Hannibal's only chance was to rouse all Italy against Rome. The Italians had been slowly conquered over the past century and they still lacked Roman citizenship. If they thought the Romans were defeated, they might strike for their freedom and this Hannibal would offer them, not Carthaginian conquest in its turn, but self-rule.

The first of his victories — the double battle at the Po — had brought over the scarcely conquered Gauls, but even the second, at Lake Trasimenus, had not brought over the longer-quelled Italians. He needed a third. For a while it looked as though the Romans would not give it to him, for the wiser heads among them counseled they ought to avoid a fight and let Hannibal wither away. That was a hard tactic for a proud people used to victory, and they were soon persuaded to try again.

Hannibal continued to march southward along the length of

Italy in an insulting display of contempt for Rome's might, and in 216 B.C. still another Roman army, the largest yet, set out in pursuit. They caught him at Cannae (kan′ee), near the Adriatic Sea and nearly 200 miles southeast of Rome.

The Roman army outnumbered Hannibal nearly two to one — 86,000 to 50,000 — and was spoiling for a fight. Hannibal, despite his numerical disadvantage, was willing to humor them. Hannibal's infantry was pushed forward in a semicircle and when the Romans attacked, it slowly stepped back, first into a straight line and then into a backward semicircle.

Through it all, though, the flanks of Hannibal's army did not move. The forward-rushing Romans did not care about the flanks, apparently. The enemy center seemed to be caving in and it seemed that one more push would cause the line to break and that Hannibal would then be destroyed. But Hannibal knew exactly what he was doing. He kept his men under firm control and let the line bend backward until the furious Romans were in a sack surrounded on three sides by Hannibal's army. Then, and only then, did Hannibal give the signal. The flanks closed in and the Carthaginian cavalry, circling wide, came down on the tightened opening of the sack to prevent all escape.

Again the Romans were simply slaughtered. The Battle of Cannae was perhaps the greatest example in all military history of a complete victory over a great fighting force by a numerically weaker enemy. The whole difference was made up by the military genius of a single man, Hannibal.

He had fought the Romans four times — Ticinus, Trebia, Trasimene, Cannae. He had faced a larger Roman force each time. He had won a greater victory each time. The Romans, who were unbeatable for centuries before Hannibal and were again to be unbeatable for centuries after him, were simply straw men to Hannibal, and it is for this reason that he is sometimes claimed to be the greatest general who ever lived.

At the moment that Hannibal won the Battle of Cannae, it

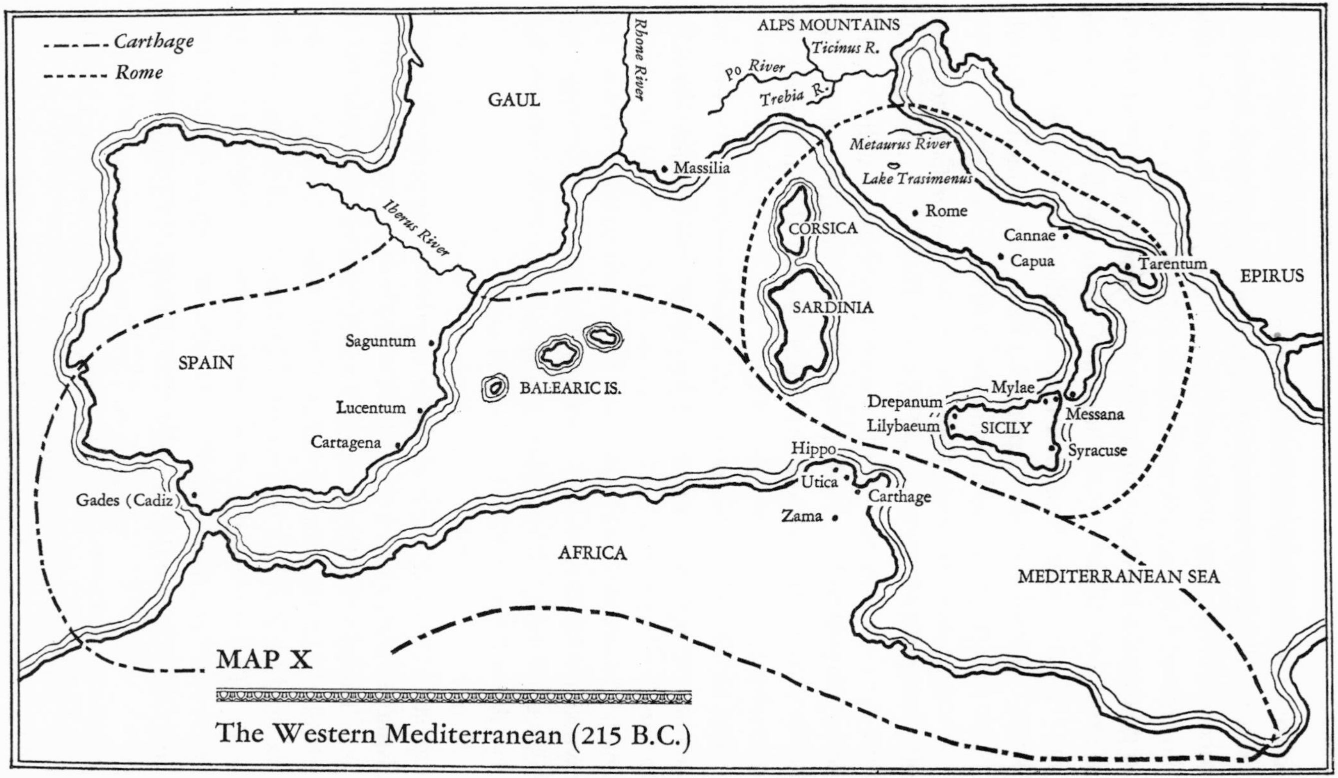

MAP X

The Western Mediterranean (215 B.C.)

looked for a moment as if the entire plan, worked out by his father and carried through so magnificently by himself, would succeed. With that gigantic victory, the Roman system in Italy did indeed begin to crumble. Some of the Italian cities began to go over to his side. Not many, but some, and even that was as great a moral defeat for Rome as Cannae had been a military one. What's more, Hannibal received the defection of the important coastal city of Capua (kap′yoo-uh), which he could use as a secure base for the winter of 216 B.C.

It might seem to some that immediately after Cannae, Hannibal ought to have marched directly on Rome, but he could not. The Roman walls still stood; the Roman will — which *never* showed to better advantage than in the aftermath of that battle — was still indomitable; and Hannibal still lacked the equipment to carry through a siege.

But he had a seaport now. What he needed was reinforcements. He needed new men, fresh men, trained men, devoted to the Carthaginian cause, for most of his own veterans were dead. To be sure, he made use of Italians who came over to his own side and, driven by his genius, they never failed him, but he needed more. He needed supplies; he needed siege machinery. All of it could come from Carthage.

None of it did. Where Rome, after Cannae, displayed a will and strength that showed them worthy of victory, Carthage displayed a meanness of spirit that proved them worthy of defeat. The merchant princes who ruled the city were dominated entirely by distrust of Hannibal and by the fear that his victories might make him all-powerful at home to their own detriment. They argued that his victories proved he needed nothing, so let him go on to win more. But Hannibal was only the greatest general who ever lived — nothing more. He was not a god, and he could not command the Romans to meet him in battle. Nor, without reinforcements, could he afford to take their fortified points one after the other.

The Romans, having learned their lesson, never again fought

Hannibal in the open field in Italy. They circled around him, nipped at his heels, struck and run, but never faced him head on. Instead, they began to fight at the periphery. Despite the danger at home, Rome sent armies abroad to reduce Syracuse (which had switched to the Carthaginian side after the death of Hiero) and to invade Spain. The Carthaginian government, fearful for the loss of the Spanish silver mines, sent reinforcements there rather than to Italy.

For years Hannibal, ever faithful to his faithless city, fought in Italy, with declining hopes — waiting for reinforcements that never came, waiting for a break in Roman will that never came, waiting for a chance at another battle that never came. In 212 B.C. Hannibal was in the extreme south of Italy, capturing some of the Greek cities. In 211 B.C., as a gesture, he marched to Rome itself and, it is said, threw a spear over its wall with his own hands. But it was just a gesture; he still could not mount a siege and he could only march away again.

Hannibal had to look to Spain where his brother Hasdrubal was in charge. If Carthage itself would do nothing for him, surely Hasdrubal would. In 208 B.C. Hasdrubal, in response to his brother's call, decided to repeat Hannibal's feat of ten years before. He dodged the Romans, marched his army across Spain and Gaul, clambered over the Alps, and descended upon Italy.

At last Hannibal had his reinforcements — provided he could join his brother. Hannibal, however, was in the south, while Hasdrubal was in the north of Italy. Hasdrubal sent messages to Hannibal setting a marching plan and a meeting place. Through a series of accidents, the messengers were taken and the messages fell into the hands of the Romans, so that they knew where Hasdrubal was going to be and Hannibal did not — and that was the turning point of the war.

The Romans combined their forces, daring to leave Hannibal unguarded, and met Hasdrubal's forces on the banks of the Metaurus River (meh-taw′rus), about 120 miles northeast of Rome near the Adriatic. Hasdrubal tried to avoid battle but couldn't find a ford across the river at his back and wasted time looking for one. When he did find one, it was too late. The Romans were upon him, he wasn't ready, and the inevitable end was a complete Roman victory.

Hasdrubal died with his army, and the news of this reached Hannibal in a horrible manner. The Romans cut off Hasdrubal's head, carried it southward, and threw it into Hannibal's camp. Hannibal must have known then that the last hope was gone, but he would not give in. He retired to the Italian toe and held out there for four more years; and even then the Romans dared not attack him directly.

But a new Roman general had arisen, Publius Cornelius Scipio (sip′ee-oh), son of the general who had faced Hannibal on the Ticinus River. The father might have died in that battle if the son — only nineteen years old at the time — had not rescued him. Scipio's father died in 211 B.C. fighting in Spain, and his son took over. Showing great talent as a general, he completed the conquest of Spain in 206 B.C., the year after Hasdrubal's disastrous battle at the Metaurus River.

Scipio was now the most popular man in Spain, although the older generals and Roman leaders opposed him, much as the Carthaginian leaders opposed Hannibal. Scipio remembered the feat of Agathocles a century before and of Regulus a half-century before and suggested that an army be sent to Africa.

When the Roman government refused to assign an army for the purpose, Scipio asked for volunteers and got them by the thousands. In 204 B.C. he sailed for Africa. Once he got there it was the turn of the Carthaginian home front to begin cracking. West of Carthage was the land of Numidia (nyoo-mid′ee-uh), where modern Algeria is located. It was the source of the best cavalry in the Carthaginian army and its king, Masinissa mas″ih-nis′uh), had led them in Spain. Now, when Scipio landed, Masinissa led his Numidians into the Roman camp.

It was quickly apparent to Carthage that it could not withstand the Roman-Numidian combination and that their only hope lay in the man of genius it had mistreated for so long. The Carthaginian government delayed matters as long as possible, treating with Scipio and even going so far as to accept peace terms he offered — which were quite reasonable ones. Meanwhile, though, they sent for Hannibal, and Hannibal, ever faithful, answered the call.

As soon as Hannibal landed with his army in Africa, the Carthaginians denounced the peace terms they had accepted and made ready for war. They expected miracles of Hannibal and laid their burden on his shoulder. Hannibal accepted the load but even for him it was too heavy. The 24,000 men he had brought with him were Italians, for the magnificent army with which he had begun his career was long since dead. He himself was old and weary and he was facing now a better general than any he had yet met. It was Scipio versus Hannibal, and the final battle was fought on October 19, 202 B.C., at Zama (zay′muh), a town about 100 miles southwest of Carthage.

Hannibal had eighty elephants, more than he had ever commanded in any previous battle, but they were worse than useless to him. He began the battle with an elephant charge, but the Romans stood firm and sounded trumpets, which promptly frightened some of the elephants back into Hannibal's cavalry, throwing it into confusion. Masinissa's horsemen charged at once and completed the removal of the far-inferior Carthaginian cavalry. (As a result of the failure of the elephants in this battle, they were never again used in western warfare.)

It was then the turn of the Romans to advance, guided by Scipio's master hand. The Carthaginian front-liners, green men, fled, and only the third line, composed of the men who had fought under Hannibal in Italy, remained steadfast. They were outnumbered, however, and they went down. In his entire career, Hannibal lost only one pitched battle, but it was the Battle of Zama that he lost — and that outbalanced all his victories.

There was nothing left. Carthage had to surrender unconditionally and the Second Punic War was over. The great scheme invented by Hamilcar Barca ended in failure — but not through the fault of the Barca family. Had Hannibal had a government behind him that knew how to exploit victories — had he been born a Roman, for instance — he might have conquered the world.

AFTER ZAMA

By the treaty of peace, signed in 201 B.C., Carthaginian power was broken forever. She was not wiped out completely, as some vengeful Romans would have liked, because Scipio held out against a too cruel peace, but it was bad enough. Carthage's territory was limited to the area immediately around the city (equivalent to the northern half of modern Tunis). She gave up Spain, Numidia, her fleet, her elephants. She had to pay a large indemnity and agree to place her foreign policy under the control of the Romans.

Once the treaty was signed, Hannibal was made head of the Carthaginian government. This was made possible by Scipio. Many Romans wanted Hannibal surrendered to their vengeance, but Scipio insisted on respect for a foe of genius who, at least, had always fought fair, and in this he won out for a while.

All Hannibal's ability was now turned to the way of peace. Over the next five years he reorganized Carthaginian finance, increased efficiency, and managed affairs so well that the city soon felt the pulse of restored prosperity. It was even able to begin paying off the indemnity to Rome.

Romans could view this only with chagrin and extreme hostility. Few of them could forgive Hannibal and soon they were regretting having let themselves be swayed by Scipio's nobility. In 196 B.C. a Roman mission was sent to Carthage and it accused Hannibal of planning a new war and demanded that he be given up. Hannibal managed to escape to the east — where enemies of Rome still existed and were still powerful.

While Rome and Carthage were locked in their epic struggle, the kingdoms in the east had not seriously intervened. Philip V of Macedon had given Hannibal some help and had even sent a small contingent of men to fight at Zama against the Romans. It wasn't enough to help Hannibal, but it was enough to earn the undying hatred of Rome.

The Ptolemies of Egypt, on the other hand, maintained a friendship with Rome. As for the Seleucid Empire, the farthest east, it seemed completely unaware that Rome and Carthage existed, and its attention was fixed on Asia.

In 223 B.C., while Hannibal was still in Spain, a nineteen-year-old youth had succeeded to the Seleucid throne and reigned as Antiochus III (an-ty′oh-kus). It was his ambition to re-create the empire of Alexander and with this in mind, he began to expand Seleucid territory in Asia Minor.

In 221 B.C. Ptolemy III died and was succeeded by his son, who reigned as Ptolemy IV. At once Antiochus decided to gain revenge for the victories of Ptolemy III by taking advantage of the confusion invariably attendant on the beginnings of a new reign. He set about seizing as much of the Ptolemaic dominion as he could. He marched his army down the Mediterranean coast and began to win victories over local garrisons at once. Over the next four years almost all of what had once been Canaan was in his hand.

Ptolemy IV, however, bestirred himself in 217 B.C. and gathered together a large army that included 73 of the small North African elephants. He did not have to go far. At Raphia (ruh-fy′uh), on the very border of the Sinai Peninsula, the army of Antiochus was waiting. Antiochus' army was not quite as large as Ptolemy's, but the former had 102 of the larger Indian elephants.

It was the one important battle fought in history in which

there were Indian elephants on one side and African elephants on the other. Since Antiochus' elephants were both more numerous and larger, they drove Ptolemy's elephants back when the crunch came. That, however, did not decide the battle. It was Ptolemy's men who defeated the Asians, and Antiochus was forced to retreat in a great hurry, leaving Judea and Phoenicia in Ptolemaic hands.

There is an apocryphal book of the Bible (Third Maccabees) which purports to tell what happened immediately after the battle. The story goes that Ptolemy IV, flushed with victory, entered Jerusalem in order to conduct a sacrifice as his father had done. Unlike his father, however, Ptolemy IV wanted to enter the sanctuary of the Temple, where only the high priest might enter. He was not allowed to do so by popular indignation and divine intervention and he returned to Alexandria, vowing revenge. In Alexandria he decided to shut up all the Jews in the hippodrome and force them to face drink-maddened elephants. The elephants were, however, driven back by divine intervention upon the Egyptians themselves.

This need not be taken seriously. Third Maccabees is clearly a work of fiction designed to encourage Jews in times of persecution by telling of miraculous rescues in the past. Ptolemy IV, whatever his faults, can be acquitted of any design to profane the Temple or to perpetrate the mass killing of Alexandrian Jews.

Antiochus may have been humiliated by the Battle of Raphia and the failure of his Egyptian campaign, but he bounced back. From 209 B.C. to 204 B.C. he ranged at the head of his armies in the eastern provinces, bringing back to allegiance lands as far as India.

If Antiochus were aware that while he was engaged in mighty marches over vast stretches of land, Hannibal was trying to keep his army in being in Italy's toe and Scipio was completing the conquest of Spain, he might well have scorned such small matters. He took to calling himself Antiochus the Great.

And then came what seemed a lucky break for him in the west. In 203 B.C. Ptolemy IV died and his seven-year-old son succeeded as Ptolemy V. It seemed quite likely that under the rule of a child, Egypt would be in chaos. Antiochus at once made an alliance with Philip V of Macedon to attack Egypt together and split the loot.

But even as the two powers were making their plans for a simultaneous attack on Egypt, the Battle of Zama took place and Rome was victorious. Her baleful glance now looked across the strait separating the Italian heel from Macedon. Philip, mindful of the Macedonian contingent that had fought on the losing side at Zama, abandoned the Egyptian project and turned to face Rome, which sent an army into Macedon in 200 B.C. Had Antiochus had good judgment at this point, he would speedily have come to the aid of Macedon against the common danger. By that time, however, he was involved with Egypt and could not bring himself to give up the campaign.

Indeed, in 200 B.C., the very year that war between Rome and Macedon started, Antiochus III won a great battle at Panias (puh-ny′as), twenty-five miles north of the Sea of Galilee. The Battle of Raphia, fought seventeen years earlier, was avenged and its results reversed. All of Judea and neighboring regions were lost to the Ptolemies forever, and fell into Seleucid hands. Since the Jews had guessed Antiochus would be the winner and had supported him, they were treated well and did not suffer by the change in control — at least, not then.

Nor did Antiochus try to take over all of Egypt after all. He saw better pickings elsewhere. By 197 B.C. the Romans had defeated Philip V of Macedon and forced that nation to accept a peace that was to keep them powerless. Antiochus, far from being concerned that by failing to help Macedon he had contributed to the growing strength of Rome, saw in the event a chance to scavenge territory for himself. He began to take over territory in Asia Minor in actions which until then would have meant war with Macedon.

But now the small kingdoms of Asia Minor appealed to the new power, Rome. Rome sent a warning to Antiochus to cease and desist, but the now-victorious monarch who thought of himself as "the Great" paid no attention. Instead, in 196 B.C., he sent troops into Europe to take further advantage of Macedonian weakness.

Then, in 195 B.C., Hannibal arrived. Driven from Carthage by the Romans, he landed in Tyre, visiting the mother city for the first time in his life. But his intention in going east was not a matter of sentiment. His own enmity to Rome had not died, and he was seeking Antiochus III, the one man left in all the world who had armies capable (perhaps) of resisting the Roman colossus.

Hannibal and Antiochus met at Ephesus (ef′uh-sus) on the western shore of Asia Minor, and Hannibal suggested that while Antiochus continue his campaign in Greece, he himself be entrusted with an army to take back into Italy. Antiochus lacked the vision to do as Hannibal suggested or, perhaps, felt he himself was sufficient to take care of the upstart westerners. Meanwhile, the Carthaginian government, aware of Hannibal's plans and terrified lest this bring retribution on themselves, played the coward and informed Rome.

The Romans promptly sent a mission to Asia Minor to try to learn the intentions of Antiochus and Hannibal and to warn them off. Antiochus would not be warned. He sent more troops into Greece and ordered Hannibal to Tyre to collect a Phoenician fleet for use in the Aegean.

Unfortunately, the self-assured Antiochus underestimated the Romans. His expeditionary force to Greece was too small and too laxly led. They were defeated by a Roman army at Thermopylae (ther-mop′ih-lee) in 191 B.C., while Hannibal found himself unable to enter the Aegean Sea because of the resistance of ships from the Greek island of Rhodes, which feared Antiochus more than it feared Rome.

Antiochus, in chagrin, left Greece for Asia Minor but the Romans followed. In Asia Minor the Romans defeated him again at Magnesia (mag-nee′zhuh) in 190 B.C., even though the Seleucid army was the larger in numbers and included elephants and camels. There is a story that before the battle Antiochus asked Hannibal if he thought the army was large enough for the Romans and Hannibal, surveying the quality and distribution of the forces, said dryly, "Even the greediest Roman couldn't ask for more."

The Battle of Magnesia was the end for Antiochus and, indeed, of any chance of ever stopping the Romans. Antiochus accepted Roman terms and evacuated Asia Minor. As part of the terms, the Romans demanded the surrender of Hannibal, but Antiochus, anticipating this, had the decency to warn Hannibal to leave in time.

Hannibal took ship for Crete, and then traveled to Bithynia (bih-thin′ee-uh), a kingdom in northwest Asia Minor. Bithynia asked for his services because they were fighting a neighboring kingdom, Pergamum (pur′guh-mum), which was a Roman ally. With Hannibal's help, Bithynia began to win and Pergamum shrieked loudly for Roman help.

Down came the Romans. Bithynia dared not imitate Antiochus and Hannibal knew that this time he would be surrendered. It was 183 B.C., thirty-five years since he had crossed the Alps. He was sixty-four years old, worn out and tired, and all there was now left in life for him was imprisonment, display to the mocking, reviling Roman populace, and, undoubtedly, execution.

He saved the Romans, and himself, that trouble. Saying "Let us now put an end to the great anxiety of the Romans, who have thought it too lengthy, and too heavy a task, to wait for the death of a hated old man," he took poison. And so ended one of the most remarkable men in history and very possibly the greatest general who ever lived.

11

THE MACCABEES

HELLENIZATION

At the time of the death of Hannibal, it seemed that the people of the old land of Canaan were in the last stages of inconsequentiality and would henceforth be nothing more than a cipher in history. In the west there was still Carthage, but it was now merely a city with some surrounding countryside, utterly in the power of Rome. In the east there was Tyre, still alive and trading, but utterly in the power of whatever monarch controlled the immediate area.

And there were the people of the interior, behind Tyre, who seemed less important still. And surely among the least inconsequential of all would seem to have been tiny Judea. What was the situation in Judea in 183 B.C., the year in which Hannibal died?

The high priests of the old line of Zadok, which dated back to

Solomon's Temple, still held their state in Jerusalem. In 219 B.C., during the last years of Ptolemaic dominion, Onias II died and Simon II became high priest. He is known to later generations as Simon the Just and received an eloquent tribute in the fiftieth chapter of the apocryphal Biblical book Ecclesiasticus. In 196 B.C., at about the time Judea passed under Seleucid dominion, Simon's son Onias III became high priest. He, too, is pictured as having been pious and devout.

Judea itself was confined to a small inland region bordering on the northwestern shores of the Dead Sea, with Jerusalem as its only city of note and with an area all told of only about 750 square miles. To its north, where once Israel had been, was Samaria, and with the Samaritans the Jews maintained a deadly hostility, each considering the other to be a set of pernicious heretics. To the south of Judea lived the descendants of the Edomites who had moved northward into land that had once been southern Judah and which was now Idumea. Between Jews and Idumeans there was also a deadly enmity.

To be sure, the Jews were not confined to Judea. Many of them colonized Galilee, the region north of Samaria. It had once made up northern Israel but in these latter days was so full of non-Jews that it was called "Galilee of the Gentiles" by the conservative and disapproving Jews of Judea itself. Then, of course, there were the Jews of the "Diaspora" (or "Dispersion"); that is, those who dwelt outside the borders of the land that had once been promised to Abraham. There were the Jews of the Tigris-Euphrates, of Alexandria, of the Greek cities in Asia Minor and elsewhere.

To all Jews, however, wherever located, Jerusalem and its Temple remained at the center of their national consciousness. At the time of the great festivals, Jerusalem was crowded with Jews from all over the Near East, coming to sacrifice. The development of Judaism was by this time almost complete. Virtually all the books of the Old Testament had by now been written.

Yet Judaism faced a new danger. The old Canaanite idolatries were long gone, but a new and even more attractive idolatry existed. Since the time of Alexander, Greeks had penetrated all the Mediterranean world and wherever they went they carried Greek culture with them. They were a city people, too, and wherever they went, they founded cities. In Judea and surrounding lands, the penetration by the Greeks had been slow under the Ptolemies, but when the Greek-loving Seleucid kings took over the trend accelerated.

And those who were not Greeks by race (or "Hellenes," as the Greeks called themselves) nevertheless hastened to adopt Greek culture. They became Hellenized and the process of Hellenization became a dominating force in all the Mediterranean. Even the rough Romans of the west felt the force of Hellenization; and Scipio himself, the conqueror of Hannibal, was a leader of those who would adopt Greek ways.

The Jews were not immune. Many Jews, not only in Greek cities far from Jerusalem but even in Judea itself, adopted Greek ways of life while paying lip service to the older and less sophisticated notions of Judaism. Other Jews, however, particularly in Judea itself, clung entirely to the old ways and abhorred Greek notions.

The stage was set for a quarrel between these two kinds of Judaism, but anyone looking at the world in 183 B.C. could not possibly have foreseen that such a struggle could have any importance or that it could have any possible effect outside Judea. The thought that the struggle would end by having world-shaking effects and that it would dictate the nature of the religions that would dominate the world in centuries to come would have seemed utterly unbelievable.

Yet it happened; but so slowly that for centuries no one could possibly have noticed that anything important was taking place.

It began with the failure of Antiochus III. The large indemnity he had agreed to pay the Romans following his defeat was more than he had in his treasury. To get the money, he had to squeeze the rich temples of his land. It was while he was trying to carry the gold out of one of the temples in a far province that the rioting peasantry killed him in 187 B.C.

He was succeeded by his son Seleucus IV, who found the Seleucid realm weakened by defeat and plunder and the far-eastern provinces, so painstakingly retaken by Antiochus III, falling away again, this time permanently.*

Seleucus IV attempted to lead a quiet and unadventurous reign, since the land needed time for recovery. He still needed money, however, as his father had, and one of the obvious sources was the Temple in Jerusalem. Seleucus sent an official named Heliodorus (hee″lee-oh-daw′rus) to see what could be done in that direction.

The tale of what follows is told in the apocryphal book of Second Maccabees in a garbled fashion. What may very likely have happened was that Onias III, the high priest, managed to make a deal with Heliodorus. He bribed Heliodorus generously, giving the underling a part in order to avoid having to give the master the whole. Heliodorus knew that he was risking his neck if what he had done was discovered, so he arranged to have Seleucus IV assassinated in 175 B.C.

But Seleucus IV had a younger brother Antiochus, who had been born in Athens and who, after his father's defeat, had been sent as a hostage to Rome. The younger Antiochus was kindly treated there and conceived an admiration for Rome. He was also (perhaps because of his pride in his Athenian birth) an enthusiast of Greek culture. On hearing of his older brother's assassination, Antiochus left Rome and made his way to Antioch. Once there, he had no trouble seizing control and beginning his reign as Antiochus IV.

Antiochus IV was a capable man who dreamed of restoring the Seleucid Empire to the strength from which the Roman de-

* For the subsequent history of these eastern provinces, see my book *The Near East* (Houghton Mifflin, 1968).

feat had toppled it. To do this — the old story — he needed money. Among the sources of funds was still the Temple at Jerusalem. Onias III, who represented the more conservative factions of Judaism, was still high priest and Antiochus IV viewed him with disfavor. This might have been simply the result of the old man's stubborn refusal to part with Temple money, or perhaps Antiochus had heard rumors of the deal with Heliodorus. Then, too, Antiochus may well have thought his kingdom would be stronger if all its people were united in Hellenic culture, and the stubborn adherence of Onias III to conservative Judaism may have bothered him.

In any case, when Onias' brother Joshua approached Antiochus with suggestions of a deal, Antiochus listened. The suggestion was that Antiochus appoint Joshua as high priest in place of his brother. Joshua would then allow Antiochus a generous supply of the Temple funds. (In return, Joshua would have the prestige and power of the high priesthood and — as both men knew — a chance to enrich himself, as any high priest could do if he were a little unscrupulous.) To tempt Antiochus further, Joshua played up to his known pro-Greek proclivities by offering to encourage the Hellenization of the Jews. As a demonstration of his sincerity in this direction, he had changed his name from the Hebrew "Joshua" to the Greek "Jason."

Antiochus agreed to the deal. Onias III was taken off to house arrest in Antioch, and Joshua-Jason became high priest. Joshua-Jason promptly began to live up to his part of the bargain. Antiochus got his money and Joshua-Jason established a gymnasium in Jerusalem. At the gymnasium young men could exercise, Greek fashion, in the nude, and the more modish of the young Jews flocked to it. (And Joshua-Jason, who controlled the gymnasium financially, reaped generous profits.)

The conservative Jews were horrified by the arrest of Onias III and by the rifling of the treasury, but the gymnasium shocked them most of all. Not only was public nudity considered an abomination, but young Jews who wished to exercise often wore false foreskins to avoid advertising the fact that they were circumcised — thus denying the very mark of Judaism.

But Joshua-Jason had merely taught others to take the same route as himself. A cousin of his named Onias, who took the Greek name of Menelaus, offered Antiochus a still higher bribe if he were made high priest in his turn. Antiochus obliged in 172 B.C. and in succeeding years the Temple and the people were looted indeed.

When the depredations of Onias-Menelaus became plain, old Onias III, who was looked upon by all conservative Jews as the only legitimate high priest, had the courage to denounce the matter publicly, and then took sanctuary in a Greek temple in a suburb of Antioch. Onias-Menelaus, however, seems to have persuaded the Seleucid commander in the district (with bribes, perhaps) to induce Onias III to leave the sanctuary by giving an oath for his safety. Once Onias III was out of the temple, he was promptly murdered. This was in 170 B.C.

There was chaos in Judea among those factions supporting this high priest or that, but this was of little moment to Antiochus IV. The Hellenization of the land seemed to be progressing favorably and he had the money he needed from the Temple at Jerusalem and from other sources. He could now buy arms, pay soldiers, and begin the Seleucid comeback. He intended to begin the comeback by taking over Egypt, which was now under the rule of Ptolemy VI, an amiable person but a complete incompetent.

Antiochus IV had no trouble at all. He was a good general and he had a good army. Brushing aside feeble Ptolemaic resistance, he marched to Memphis, the ancient capital of the Egyptians, and in 170 B.C. had himself declared king of Egypt. He then took his army to the Ptolemaic capital of Alexandria and, in 169 B.C., placed it under siege.

While the siege was under way, however, news reached Antiochus that in his absence Joshua-Jason had attempted to take the high priesthood from Onias-Menelaus by force. Jerusalem was in a state of civil war and the Seleucid army, almost 350 miles west of its own borders, could not afford to have its line of communications threatened.

Furious, Antiochus IV hastened back to Judea and punished the troublesome Jews by occupying the city, entering the Temple himself at the head of an armed contingent, and dragging off all the valuables he could find. For the moment, Jerusalem was stricken and quiet.

In 168 B.C., then, Antiochus IV returned to Egypt, where he had as little trouble as before and where he once again resumed the siege of Alexandria. By now, however, the Ptolemies had squealed for help to Rome, which promptly answered the call. Outside the walls of Alexandria a Roman ambassador approached Antiochus IV. Antiochus recognized him as an old friend and approached gladly to greet him; but the old friend was an official emissary from Rome now and he had only one thing to say: either Antiochus was to leave Egypt, or to accept war with Rome. Thunderstruck, Antiochus IV asked for time to consider. The Roman drew a circle in the ground around the king and said, "Decide before you leave the circle."

Antiochus dared not face Rome. Though his entire army was around him and though it had marched victoriously through Egypt, and though it was sure to take Alexandria, he and all his men had to back down in the face of a single unarmed Roman. There are few humiliations in history as dramatic as this one.

We can imagine Antiochus' angry frustration as he retreated, his need to get back at something or someone. Perhaps the news reached him that the Jews were jubilant over the state of his affairs, as well they might be in view of the troubles he had visited on them by his manipulation of the high priesthood and by his looting of the Temple.

In any case, Antiochus IV determined that, though the Romans might humiliate him, the Jews would not. On his return to Antioch in 167 B.C. he resolved to put an end to Judaism altogether. Let the Jews become Greeks and loyal subjects! It did not seem to him (probably) to be much of a task. Men such as Joshua-Jason and Onias-Menelaus seemed only too eager to be Greek, and they commanded sizable factions among the Jews.

Consequently, Antiochus ordered that the Temple in Jerusalem be made Greek and that within it there be erected a statue representing Zeus (with whom Yahveh was to be identified) and that on its altar there be sacrifices offered in Greek fashion. What's more, copies of the Jewish Scriptures were to be destroyed, Jewish dietary regulations ended, the Sabbath abolished, and the practice of circumcision forbidden. Those Jews who accepted Hellenization were to be left in peace as loyal subjects of Antiochus. For the first time in history a persecution began that was religious, and not national, in character.

JUDAS MACCABEUS

Words cannot describe the horror felt by the conservative Jews. Nebuchadrezzar, four centuries before, had merely destroyed the Temple, but Antiochus had desecrated it with idols and swine's flesh. Nebuchadrezzar had merely taken away the Jewish land, but Antiochus was taking away their ideal. The conservative Jews prepared to resist and to retain their way of life, even to death by torture.

Such deaths took place, according to the tales told later in Second Maccabees. Grisly tales of martyrdom, of Jews dying under torture rather than agreeing to taste swine's flesh, are recorded there. These were the first martyr tales in the Judeo-Christian tradition and formed a precedent for later examples.

It was during this period of trial that the books of Daniel and of Esther were written with their (fictional) tales of the dangers and sufferings undergone by Jews under previous oppressors and of how these were overcome by faith and courage. The apocryphal books of Tobit and Judith were written in similar fashion. None of these were intended to serve as sober history (though they were taken as such by the pious of later ages) but as devices for stimulating and encouraging resistance. And eventually, the resistance ceased being that of passive acceptance of torture and death and became the active return of violence for violence.

This new turn of events began with an aged priest Mattathias (mat″uh-thy′as). He and his five sons left Jerusalem and retired to the comparative safety of a small town named Modin, seventeen miles to the northwest, which was outside Judea proper. According to Josephus, the great-great-grandfather of Mattathias was named Hashmon, so that Mattathias and his descendants are sometimes called the Hasmoneans. On the other hand, the third of his five sons, who was to turn out to be the most famous of them, was Judah Makkabi, or in Greek form, Judas Maccabeus (joo′das mak″uh-bee′us). The surname may mean "the Hammerer," from his later victories. In any case, the family has come to be better known as "the Maccabees" (mak′uh-beez) in consequence, and the apocryphal books written about the events of this time, whether sober history in the case of First Maccabees, dramatized history in the case of Second Maccabees, or fiction in the case of Third Maccabees all received this name.

The spark that initiated the Jewish rebellion against the Seleucids was set off by an officer of Antiochus who came to Modin to enforce the new laws. He asked Mattathias, as a prominent Jewish leader, to set a good example and to carry through a sacrifice to Zeus in the manner required. Mattathias refused. When another Jew offered to fulfill the royal command, Mattathias, in a rage, killed the Jew and the Seleucid officer.

There was then nothing to do but to leave Modin hastily.

Mattathias and his sons made for the Gophna hills, some dozen miles northeast of Modin. Other Jews, who resented the new laws, came to join him there and in no time a guerrilla band had been formed. Mattathias died very soon after the flight to the hills and the band came under the command of Judas Maccabeus.

Joining the Maccabee standard were bands of "Hassidim" (or, in the Greek version of the name, "Hasideans"), a term which means "the pious ones." Their sole concern lay in religion and they were uninterested in politics. It was only when the practice of Judaism was outlawed that they were willing to resort to violence, but under those conditions they were fanatical fighters indeed.

The Gophna hills lay in Samaritan territory, and the Seleucid governor of the region, Apollonius (ap″uh-loh′nee-us), moved quickly to nip the revolt before it got very far. Apollonius was, in all likelihood, overconfident. He must have been convinced he could easily handle a few rebels and he marched forward carelessly. Judas' men lay in ambush and swarmed down at the proper time. Apollonius' men were scattered, Apollonius himself killed, and Judas took Apollonius' sword for use in later battles.

This victory encouraged the conservative Jews in Jerusalem and placed the pro-Hellenizers there in difficulties. Matters grew still worse for the latter. A larger Seleucid force was sent out in 166 B.C. to occupy Jerusalem and end the annoying revolt. Again Judas Maccabeus and his men lay in ambush, this time at Beth-horon (beth-hawr′on), twelve miles northwest of Jerusalem. The second Seleucid force was also trapped and destroyed.

By now the Jewish guerrillas had made a first-class nuisance of themselves, but Antiochus IV could not turn his full attention to them. He needed money, money, money and he had to get that somewhere in the east, where the provinces had declared themselves independent and where tax collections had dried up. Off he marched eastward, leaving the small Jewish war band to the attention of his minister, Lysias (lis′ee-us.)

In 165 B.C. Lysias assembled a strong army at Emmaus (eh-may′us), fifteen miles west of Jerusalem and eleven miles west of the Maccabean stronghold at Mizpeh (miz′peh). Judas held his ground and remained on the defensive. With only 3000 men he had to.

But the Seleucid army could not wait. If the rebels would not come out to fight, they would have to be flushed out. Its commander made a mistake, however; he divided his forces and sent only part to Mizpeh. That was what Judas was hoping for. With the enemy divided, Judas raced his men to Emmaus, where he attacked and defeated that part of the Seleucid army that had remained there. With that done, Judas whirled on the contingent that was returning fruitlessly from Mizpeh. For the third time, the Seleucids had been defeated.

Later in the year Lysias tried once more, sending a troop around Judea into the friendly land of Idumea and then attacking toward Jerusalem from the south. The watchful Judas stopped him at Beth-zur, sixteen miles southwest of Jerusalem, and defeated him again.

By now, successive victories had brought enough of the Jews to the side of the Maccabees to make it possible for the guerrillas to enter Jerusalem. Seleucid forces and their Hellenized Jewish sympathizers still controlled the fortified portions of the city, but the Maccabees were able to seize the Temple.

Judas Maccabeus proceeded to rededicate the Temple, purifying it from its Seleucid profanation. He chose priests who had never compromised with the Seleucid authorities, tore down the altar on which swine had been sacrificed to Zeus, and buried the stones. A new altar was built, new vessels supplied, and proper sacrifices performed. The anniversary of the dedication of the Temple in 165 B.C. is celebrated to this day by the Jews, as the eight-day feast of Hanukah ("dedication").

Judas Maccabeus by no means considered this a final victory. It was merely an item. He had as his ambition the liberation of all Jews everywhere in the land that had once been Canaan. He led his army across the Jordan and northward, while his brother Simon, with another troop, took the route northward along the coast. Both defeated Seleucid contingents, enrolled fighters from among the Jewish population, and established strongpoints. By 163 B.C. the Seleucid power south of Damascus had been reduced to tatters and far off, in what is now central Iran, Antiochus IV died, possibly from tuberculosis. Despite his very real ability, his reign had been a disaster.

The death of Antiochus IV did not end Seleucid attempts to repress the Maccabean revolt. Antiochus' nine-year-old son reigned as Antiochus V, with Lysias as his minister. In 162 B.C. yet another Seleucid army advanced to the attack. It was the strongest yet, and once again it attacked from the south, moving through Beth-zur. It had at least one elephant moving with it.

In a battle at Beth-zechariah (beth″zek-uh-ry′uh), five miles north of Beth-zur, the Maccabeans were forced back. Eleazar (el″ee-ay′zar), one of the brothers of Judas, fought his way to the elephant, thinking that it carried the king in person. He stabbed it in the abdomen and killed it, but the dying elephant fell on Eleazar and crushed him — and it did not, after all, carry the young king.

Eleazar's feat did not turn the tide of battle and for the first time, in the face of overwhelming strength, Judas was defeated. He brought what he could save of his forces back to the Gophna hills, where he and his family had first sought refuge five years before, and the Seleucid forces reoccupied Jerusalem. This time, however, they were careful to make no attempt to interfere with the Temple services. Lysias' moderation was the result of trouble at home. Other generals were trying to seize control of the kingdom from Lysias, while Demetrius, a nephew of Antiochus IV, was grabbing at the throne itself.

Lysias therefore, in an effort to end the Judean revolt which was sapping his strength, offered a compromise. He would grant the Jews complete religious freedom if they would accept Seleucid political sovereignty. The Hassidim, who were interested only in Judaism as a religion, accepted this and retired from the battle. This meant that Lysias had gained his point, for without the Hassidim, Judas' remaining forces were too weak to offer resistance and he could only maintain himself in the Gophna hills and await events.

In the Seleucid wars that followed, both Antiochus V and Lysias were killed, and Demetrius I ruled in their place. With Judea quiet, he attempted to restore the situation as it had once been, with the appointment of a high priest who would control Judaism in the Seleucid interest — at least to a reasonable degree. He appointed Eliakim (ee-ly′uh-kim) as high priest; Eliakim, a Hellenizer, preferred to be known by the Greek name of Alcimus (al′sih-mus). Since Eliakim-Alcimus was of the old Zadokite line of priests, the Hassidim accepted him.

Now there was left only the small band of irreconcilables in the Gophna hills. Demetrius might have ignored them, but apparently Judas was attempting to interest Rome in the Jewish plight, and the Seleucid king decided to clean them out before it occurred to Rome to interfere. Demetrius therefore sent his general Bacchides (bak′ih-deez) with a strong force from Jerusalem toward the Gophna hills.

Battle was joined eight miles north of Jerusalem in 161 B.C. Judas, whose forces now were less than a thousand strong, was overwhelmed. He himself died on the battlefield and the few survivors scattered. Two of his brothers, Jonathan and Simon, who were among those survivors, managed to take Judas' body away from the battlefield and bury him in the family tomb at Modin. Thus died the most remarkable Jewish fighter since the time of David eight centuries before.

INDEPENDENCE!

The Maccabean revolt appeared over. A few men lurked in the southern desert with Jonathan, the younger brother of Judas Maccabeus, but they were powerless and could be ignored. The moderate policy of Lysias and Demetrius I had worked where the stern force of Antiochus IV had failed.

The revolt had nevertheless accomplished one purpose: the Temple was Jewish again and the Seleucids made no attempt ever again to interfere with the ritual. This meant that Judaism had been saved and that — alone — meant that Judas' stand, though it had ended in defeat and death, was nevertheless of crucial importance to world history.

On the other hand, the danger was not entirely over. Judaism might have been saved only to die more slowly. The high priest, Alcimus, did all he could to Hellenize the religion. He died in 159 B.C. — the last high priest who was in any way Zadokite — but Hellenization continued after him. And it might have succeeded had the Seleucid kingdom remained a stable and effective governing force. What prevented the withering of Judaism was not so much what the surviving Maccabees could do, but the continuing dynastic struggle among the Seleucids. Demetrius I was constantly fighting rivals for the throne and when he was forced to pull soldiers out of Judea, Jonathan and his small band automatically began to increase in numbers, and expanded to fill the vacuum.

Demetrius made the best of it. In 157 B.C. he appointed Jonathan to the post of royal governor and allowed him to enter Jerusalem and rule Judea, provided he acknowledged Seleucid sovereignty. Jonathan agreed to that, accepting the reality of power and letting the appearance go.

In 152 B.C. an imposter, Alexander Balas (bay′las), who claimed to be a son of Antiochus IV, obtained the backing of Ptolemaic Egypt and launched a civil war against Demetrius I. Jonathan remained shrewdly uncommitted for a while, allowing both sides to bid for his services. Demetrius offered Jonathan rule over wider areas and Balas offered to appoint him high priest. Jonathan accepted both offers.

In that year of 152 B.C., then, Jonathan donned the robes of the high priesthood and for the first time in nine centuries an individual who was not descended from Solomon's high priest, Zadok, officiated in the Temple.

Finally, when Jonathan had to choose, he came down on the side of Balas. The choice seemed a good one, for in 150 B.C., in a final battle between the two claimants, Balas was victorious and Demetrius I was killed.

In 147 B.C., however, the son of Demetrius arrived in Syria and attacked Balas. The son was Demetrius II and he, of course, was hostile to the Maccabeans, who had supported — and were, perforce, continuing to support — Balas. An army loyal to Demetrius encamped in what was once the land of the Philistines and challenged Jonathan to battle. Jonathan, in that same year, accepted the challenge and the battle was fought in Azotus (uh-zoh′tus), the Biblical Ashdod.

For the first time the Maccabean army was large enough to fight as something more than a guerrilla force — to fight an organized battle rather than instituting a surprise attack from ambush — and it won. The Maccabees under Jonathan now controlled land on both sides of the Jordan over an area of some 800 square miles.

In 145 B.C. Demetrius II finally defeated Balas in battle and drove him to flight and eventual death, but by then the Seleucid monarchy was a worthless toy. The civil wars that had been nearly continuous since the death of Antiochus IV, eighteen years before, had seen a steady shrinkage of the dominions of Antioch. All the east, even including the Tigris-Euphrates valley, was now part of the independent kingdom of Parthia (ruled by a people akin to the Persians). Only Syria remained to the Seleucids.

Demetrius II found his power so limited that he could no longer mount a real offensive against the Maccabean forces. In fact, he needed help against his own enemies. Jonathan offered such help, suggesting that he send a band of seasoned Jewish mercenaries to serve Demetrius if the king would hand over the fortified posts surrounding Jerusalem. Demetrius agreed, accepted the forces, used them to establish his power firmly in Antioch, and then refused to give up the fortified posts.

The angry Jonathan waited for the inevitable — more dynastic troubles. In 143 B.C. a general named Tryphon (try′fon), making use of a young boy who was hailed as the son of Balas and given the title Antiochus VI, rebelled against Demetrius II. Jonathan threw his support to the new claimant at once.

But Tryphon wearied of the indirection of having to act under cover of a boy and planned to kill Antiochus VI. To do so, however, might have risked the good will of Jonathan, who was, at the moment, his strongest supporter. Tryphon therefore planned to plunge the Maccabean power into confusion in the most direct possible way first. He invited Jonathan to a conference in the royal city of Ptolemais (tol″uh-may′is), eighty-five miles north of Jerusalem. Jonathan, apparently flattered to be treated with considerable respect by the Seleucid power, allowed himself to be lured into the city with a very small band of men. He was captured and killed in 142 B.C.

But one Maccabean brother remained — Simon. He reclaimed Jonathan's body and buried it in the family tomb, then once more approached Demetrius II, who still maintained a force against Tryphon. Simon offered him an alliance against Tryphon in exchange for recognition of complete Judean independence. The deal was made, and 142 B.C. marked the moment when for the first time since Nebuchadrezzar's destruction of Jerusalem, 445 years before, there was an independent

Jewish state. Simon ruled both as king (though he did not use the title) and high priest.

Almost at once Simon began to strengthen himself. In 141 B.C. he took over the fortified posts in Jerusalem so that at least the capital city was entirely free of the foreign soldiery. He also took the coastal city of Joppa to give the newly independent kingdom a foothold at sea.

Meanwhile, Demetrius II had gained very little from the concession he had made to Jonathan. Attempting to gain further power for a showdown with Tryphon, Demetrius went eastward to increase his dominions and tax power there, as Antiochus IV had done a generation before. Demetrius fared just as badly; he was beaten by the Parthians and taken into imprisonment in 139 B.C.

In 137 B.C., however, a brother of Demetrius II defeated Tryphon and assumed rule himself as Antiochus VII. Antiochus VII was the last Seleucid ruler to show any vigor at all, and he made up his mind to reestablish power over Judea. Once again, the Maccabean forces faced Seleucid invasion. In the first skirmish, the Judeans, under two sons of Simon, John Hyrcanus (hur-kay′nus) and Judas, were victorious, and Antiochus VII resorted to more indirect means.

Simon had a son-in-law, Ptolemy, who coveted power for himself and who was quite willing to play along with Antiochus. In 134 B.C. Ptolemy invited his father-in-law and brothers-in-law to a banquet. Simon came, so did two of his sons, but not John Hyrcanus. After Simon and his sons had taken enough drink to be harmless, Ptolemy had them disarmed and murdered. Thus died Simon, the last of the five sons of Mattathias the priest, eight years after he had assumed the rule and thirty-three years after the beginning of the Maccabean rebellion.

John Hyrcanus, the remaining son of Simon, took to the hills with a guerrilla band to fight Ptolemy, who, in his turn, called Antiochus VII to his aid. In 133 B.C. Antiochus invaded Judea and, after a prolonged siege, took Jerusalem. However, what

Antiochus needed (as every Seleucid had since the Roman defeat a half-century before) was money. John Hyrcanus bid higher than Ptolemy and so Antiochus turned Jerusalem over to the Maccabean. Ptolemy had to flee the land and John Hyrcanus was accepted as ruler in place of his father.

In 130 B.C. Antiochus VII marched off east to try once again to conquer the lost provinces and he died in battle there the next year. Although the Seleucid kingdom managed to continue a kind of moribund life for over half a century more, never would the Judean kingdom have to worry about it again. The generation-long Judean struggle for freedom of conscience (the first such war in history) was won and, indeed, had gone far to destroy the Seleucids.

CARTHAGE'S LAST STAND

But if the land of Canaan saw a resurgent people regain independence, the story was otherwise in the great city of Canaanites in the west. After the death of Hannibal, Carthage had continued to try to work out its destinies within the limited area allowed it by the victorious and vengeful Romans. Industriously the Carthaginians struggled to cultivate their fields, sell their produce, invest their profits.

They did this all under the endless harassment of the Numidian king, Masinissa, who had the Romans on his side and who prolonged his life well into the eighties. He raided the shrunken Carthaginian territories and the frustrated Carthaginians could do nothing, for the peace terms forbade them to make war without Roman consent. When they appealed to Rome, they were invariably rebuffed. However outrageous Masinissa's provocations, Rome always backed him and Carthage could do nothing.

Yet Rome was never satisfied. The mere fact that the Carthaginians lived and prospered was an affront to them. One old Roman senator, Marcus Porcius Cato (kay′toh), headed a mission to Carthage in 153 B.C. and was so angered by the sight of its prosperity that thereafter he dinned into the ears of the Roman Senate, at every possible occasion, the refrain, *"Carthaginem delende esse"*; that is, "Carthage must be destroyed." Rome had its chance in 149 B.C., when Carthage, badgered beyond endurance by Masinissa, finally tried to defend itself. At once, Rome declared war.

The frightened Carthaginians backed down immediately and asked for terms. The Romans demanded 300 young men from the best families as hostages. They were sent by the submissive Carthaginians. The Romans next sent an expedition to Carthage and burned whatever shipping they could find in the harbor. They further demanded that the Carthaginians give up all their arms since they were not allowed to make war in any case. The Carthaginians gave up their arms.

The Romans then ordered the Carthaginians to leave the city and retire to villages not less than ten miles from the coast — and here at last the Carthaginians rebelled. If their city was going to be destroyed then they had nothing to live for, and if they were going to die, they might as well take a few Romans along with them.

A maddened Carthage made ready to fight. The very temples became workshops for the making of arms and the women contributed their hair to make bow strings. The Carthaginians fought with absolute desperation: one and all determined to die where they stood rather than surrender — and the astonished Romans found themselves with a major siege on their hands.

For two years the desperate city defied them and in that interval, Carthage's two great enemies, Cato and Masinissa, both died, the former at eighty-five years of age, the latter at ninety. Neither of these cruel old men was able to live to see Carthage destroyed. Both spent their last days watching Roman arms humiliated again by a Carthaginian adversary in a Third Punic War. But in 146 B.C. the inevitable end came. Carthage was taken and burned to the ground. Many Carthaginians chose to die in the flames, fighting to the last. Those that did not were slaughtered and enslaved.

The Romans swore never to allow a city on that site again. To this determination later Roman generations did not adhere, for the site was too good a harbor. A century later, a new Carthage was founded — but a Roman one. The old Carthaginians of Phoenician descent were gone forever. A few Carthaginian villages near by remained for some time and in these the Punic language might still be heard, but gradually they dwindled and died, too. The very books of Carthage were destroyed, so that not even a disembodied voice would remain to speak on the side of that city against the polemics of her Greek and Roman enemies.

But Canaan itself remained. The old Phoenician cities of Tyre and Sidon even had a kind of shadowy independence, thanks to the decline of the Seleucid monarchy, and, of course, there was the rising Maccabean kingdom of the Jews.

THE MACCABEAN KINGDOM

With the decay of the Seleucid monarchy, the Maccabean kingdom went from defense to an imperialist expansion almost without a pause. John Hyrcanus took territory east of the Dead Sea and then, in 125 B.C., conquered Idumea along the western shores of that body of water.

The Judean fight for freedom of conscience showed at once what history was to show frequently in the future — that once the defenders gain their own right to believe as they chose, they are not in the least ready to grant it to others. The Jews forced the Idumeans to accept Judaism at the point of the sword, a dreadful precedent from which many people were to suffer in the future, not least among them the Jews themselves.

John Hyrcanus also invaded Samaria and as early as 129 B.C. had occupied Mount Gerizim, the sacred mount of the Samaritans. On that mountain was the Samaritan temple and this John Hyrcanus callously destroyed — another precedent from which the Jews were to suffer.

In 108 B.C. John Hyrcanus laid siege to Samaria itself, seven miles northwest of Mount Gerizim. It was a largely Greek city and the Samaritans called to their aid Antiochus IX, a shadowy Seleucid who could do very little. The city fell in 107 B.C. By the time John Hyrcanus died in 104 B.C., after an almost uniformly successful thirty-year rule, the Maccabean kingdom, though still small, was the strongest military force in the east.

There was, however, trouble within. Judaism was never a monolithic belief and it split further and further into mutually hostile sects. A basic difference was to be found between the priests and the laymen. The priests were in control of the Temple and of the official ritual, and called themselves Zadokim (followers of Zadok, the first high priest). By way of Greek, this has become "Sadducees" in English.

The Sadducees tended to be fundamentalists in their view of Judaism and accepted only the Mosaic law (the first five books of the Bible). They rejected the accretions that had been collected from Persian and Greek beliefs. Thus, the Sadducees didn't believe in angels, or in the immortality of the soul, or in the judgment day and the resurrection, or even in the Messiah. Moreover, they held to the old traditional rituals of sacrifice and rejected any reforms.

Under John Hyrcanus, the Sadducees succeeded in barring nonpriests from serving on the Sanhedrin, the legislative council that sat in Jerusalem and made decisions on religious matters. These laymen angrily called themselves Perushim ("separated," presumably from the Sanhedrin and from religious influence). This, by way of the Greek, has become "Pharisee" to us. The Pharisees accepted all the colorful additions to Judaism that had been made since the exile — angels, demons, the world after death, the Messiah.*

There was a tendency among the Pharisees to multiply the minutiae of ritual and to adhere to these rigidly. Some among them were apparently proud of their piety, ostentatious about it, and were convinced that this "separated" them (another reason, perhaps, for the name of the sect) from ordinary people. Such views, *not* characteristic of the sect as a whole, were denounced in the New Testament, so that our word "pharisaical" has come to mean "self-satisfied hypocrisy."

In addition there were small ascetic sects, of whom the Essenes are the best known. (The origin of the word is uncertain but may come from a word meaning "healer" because, perhaps, some of them were considered holy enough to cure illness by touch.) They dwelt in communes, from which women were excluded, along the shores of the Dead Sea, in a fashion that was very much like the Christian monks of later times.

John Hyrcanus allied himself with the Sadducees, as was rather natural. The Pharisees, after all, awaited the Messiah and since the days of the exile, it had been maintained that the yearned-for ideal king would be of the house of David. The Maccabees were not descended from the house of David, but were Levites, so from their standpoint, messianism was virtually treason and the Pharisees were potential traitors, one and all.

On the death of John Hyrcanus I in 104 B.C., his older son succeeded as Aristobulus I (uh-ris″toh-byoo′lus). He conquered Galilee, and with him, the Maccabean kingdom reached its fullest extent. He also adopted the name of king and added that to his inherited title of high priest.

He only reigned a year, however, and in 103 B.C. his younger

* Modern Judaism and much of Christianity descends from the Pharisee viewpoint.

brother Alexander Jannaeus (juh-nee'us) succeeded. During his twenty-seven-year reign Judea prospered and remained peaceful and strong. The one untoward event was a revolt of the exasperated Pharisees, who objected to his continuing support of the Sadducees. It wasn't much of a revolt, for all the Pharisees did was to pelt the king with citrons when he was officiating at one of the festivals. The exasperated monarch, objecting to the blow to his dignity, took a bloody revenge, massacring many of the Pharisees.

When Alexander Jannaeus died in 76 B.C., he left behind a wife, Salome Alexandra, and two sons. Salome Alexandra, a mild woman, reversed the policies of the earlier Maccabees and allied herself with the Pharisees, thus bringing internal peace to the kingdom. Furthermore, she separated the state and the Temple by making her older son high priest, as John Hyrcanus II, but keeping the temporal power herself. While she lived the Jews had peace, but the horizon was growing cloudier. Those old adversaries, the Ptolemies and Seleucids, were utter cyphers now and there was only one power in the Mediterranean, that of Rome.

In 133 B.C., when John Hyrcanus I was just starting his reign and the Jews were settling down to their two generations of prosperity, King Attalus III of Pergamum, a kingdom making up the western third of Asia Minor, died. He left his kingdom to the Romans, who accepted it. In this way, the Roman dominions reached Asia for the first time. Gradually, other parts of Asia Minor accepted roles as Roman puppets.

In 88 B.C., when Alexander Jannaeus was at the height of his power, the kingdom of Pontus, in eastern Asia Minor, declared war on Rome — the last attempt of a Greek kingdom to resist the mighty Romans. For a while, Pontus had surprising success but by the time Alexander Jannaeus died, it was clear that Pontus had failed and that all of Asia Minor would pass under Roman influence.

Therefore, this was the very worst time for the Jews to in-

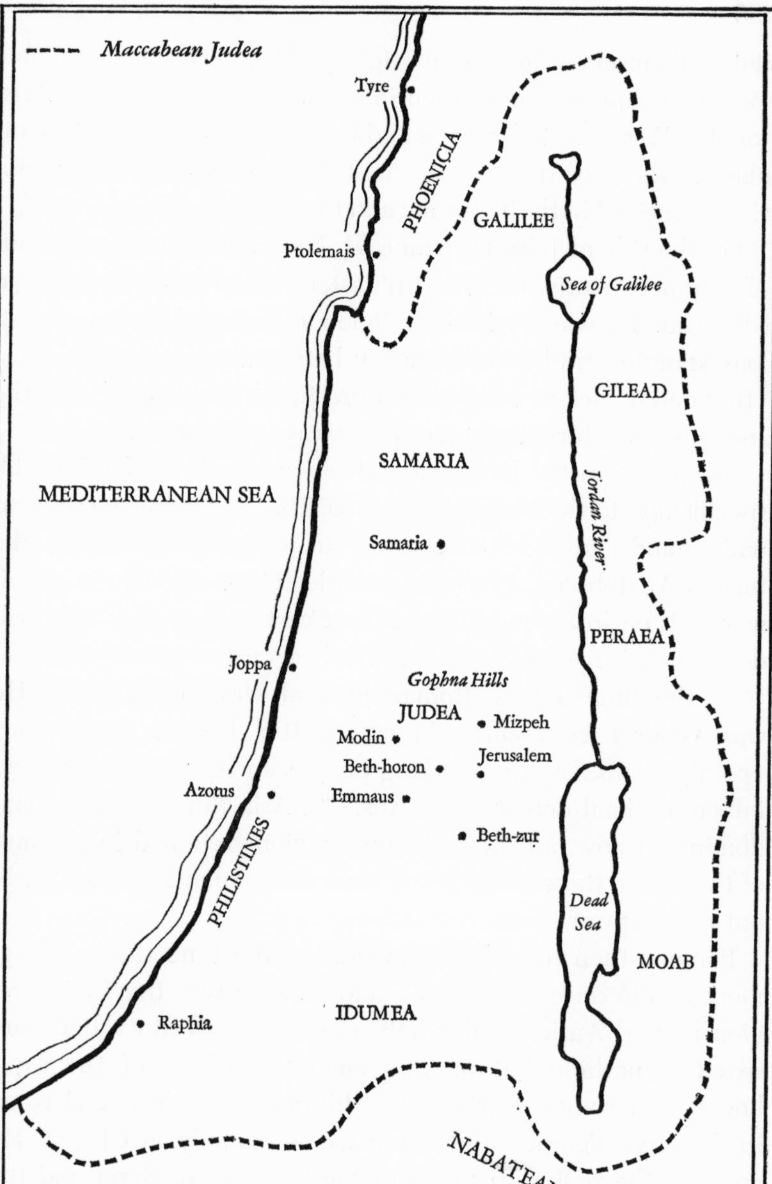

MAP XI

The Maccabean Kingdom (100 B.C.)

dulge themselves in a dynastic squabble. Yet it happened. When Salome Alexandra died in 67 B.C., her younger son, Aristobulus II, supported by the Sadducees, decided to contest his older brother for the throne. Aristobulus won the initial victories and seized both the throne and the high priesthood.

On the side of John Hyrcanus II, however, was the governor of Idumea, Antipater (an-tip′uh-ter), who was himself an Idumean. He was Jewish by religion, of course, but there was a long-standing tradition of enmity between Judea and Idumea (that dated back to when they were Judah and Edom) and the Judeans never forgot that Antipater was an Idumean.

Antipater, on the losing side, decided to call for foreign aid, specifically, to the Nabatean Arabs. The Nabateans were most willing and soon were laying siege to Jerusalem and it was the turn of Aristobulus II to be in trouble. Once one side in a civil war calls on foreign aid, it is almost certain the other side will do so also, if it can. Aristobulus called on Rome for help.

At the time a new Roman general was in the east. He was Gnaeus Pompeius Magnus, better known as Pompey (pom′pee) to English-speaking people. In 65 B.C. Pompey had inflicted a final defeat on Pontus. All Asia Minor was Roman-dominated now, and though some regions retained local kings of their own, these knew better than to as much as sneeze without Roman permission.

Pompey then turned southward. At the time the last fragment of the once-mighty Seleucid Empire was the Syrian region around Antioch. For half a century its history had consisted of nothing but feuding among members of the royal house; now someone who called himself Antiochus XIII ruled in the city. Pompey ended the whole comedy in 64 B.C. He annexed the region to Rome as the Province of Syria and the Seleucid Empire was no more.

And while he was in Syria, he received the petition for help from Aristobulus. At once Pompey sent a messenger to Judea ordering a truce. He then marched into Judea at the head of the Roman army. There was no resistance to speak of until Pompey reached Jerusalem itself. There Pompey occupied himself in a rather leisurely siege, building a ramp along which to move the siege machinery up toward the walls of the central citadel. Pompey made full use of the Sabbath, when the Jews refused to fight unless attacked, to position the machines without disturbance. Then he made the final assault during the Sabbath, too. Jerusalem fell, and with that the Maccabean kingdom came to an end. After less than eighty years of life and only a century after Mattathias had begun the revolt against Antiochus IV, Judea became a Roman province.

Pompey made no attempt to interfere with religion. John Hyrcanus II was confirmed as high priest, while Aristobulus was made prisoner, even though it was the latter who had asked for Roman help. (Pompey may have judged Hyrcanus to be the weaker personality and therefore the safer high priest. It may also be that Antipater, the clever Idumean, had something to do with the decision.) The Samaritans and the Greek cities were removed from Judean control and only the Jewish regions — Judea, Galilee, and Idumea — remained under the control of Jerusalem.

Pompey was curious enough about the odd rites of the Jews to enter the holy of holies in the Temple, the place where only the high priest could go, and that only on the Day of Atonement. Those who opposed Judaism sometimes spread the tale (meant mockingly, perhaps, rather than seriously) that the Jews, so opposed to idolatry, secretly worshiped an ass's head in the sanctuary. Pompey apparently found nothing, but, on the other hand, he emerged unharmed to the surprise of the more pious Jews. Pompey then returned to Rome, taking Aristobulus and his two sons with him.

12

ROME TRIUMPHANT

HEROD

Total Roman control of Asia Minor and the end of the Seleucids did not herald peace in the east, however. To the east of Syria lay the Parthian kingdom, which had been growing steadily more powerful as the Seleucids declined, until it had become Rome's great opponent in the east.

In 53 B.C. a Roman general, Marcus Crassus (kras′us), set out from Antioch to invade and crush Parthia. Instead, it was his own army that was disastrously defeated and he was killed. His lieutenant, Gaius Cassius Longinus (kash′ee-us-lon-jy′-nus), preserved part of the army and labored to save Syria from the Parthian riposte. The Jews favored the Parthians as possible rescuers from Rome, but Antipater, judging the situation accurately, clung to the Romans and kept his province in line.

The Romans recovered and a new man, Julius Caesar (see′-zer), was now on top. Caesar indicated his gratitude for Antipater's loyalty to Rome in the crisis by making him procurator of Judea.* Antipater gave his two sons subordinate positions to himself: the older, Phasael (fay′zay-el), ruled in Jerusalem; the younger, Herod (her′ud), in Galilee.

Caesar also released Aristobulus II and his older son, Alexander, from their Roman captivity in 49 B.C. They at once hastened toward Judea with the intention of trying once again to gain control of the high priesthood at least, but they were headed off by men in the pay of Pompey. By now, Pompey and Caesar were on the point of civil war and the two Maccabeans were thought to be Caesarian partisans. Both were killed.

Alexander, however, had been married to Alexandra, a daughter of John Hyrcanus II and, therefore, his own first cousin. He was survived by a son of this marriage, Aristobulus III. This young man, plus his surviving uncle, Antigonus Mattathias, and the high priest, John Hyrcanus II, were now the only Maccabean males left alive.

Caesar defeated Pompey in Greece in 48 B.C. and the latter fled to Egypt and was killed there. For a while Caesar ruled supreme and then in 44 B.C. he was assassinated. One of the leaders of the assassins, Cassius Longinus, took control of the eastern sections of the Roman realm. That included Judea, and Antipater carefully went along with him again, as he had done in the aftermath of Crassus' defeat.

The chaos in Rome was much greater now than it had been on the earlier occasion and Judea was correspondingly harder to control. One of Antipater's opponents had learned enough from Roman events to try his own hand at assassination and, in 43 B.C., he succeeded in poisoning the procurator. It brought the anti-Roman party nothing to do this, however, for Cassius clamped down hard on the province and Antipater's sons, Phasael and Herod, took control.

But the Roman world wasn't operating in a vacuum. To the

* "Procurator," meaning "caretaker," was the name Romans gave to the ruler of a region that made up only part of a province.

east the Parthians were delighted at the opportunity to take advantage of Rome's internal troubles. They invaded Syria in 40 B.C., took city after city, reached the Mediterranean, and finally marched into Judea. With them was Antigonus Mattathias, younger son of the dead Aristobulus II and nephew of the high priest, John Hyrcanus II.

Phasael and Herod remained loyal to Rome and tried to organize resistance to the Parthians but Jewish sentiment was overwhelmingly pro-Parthian. Phasael was captured by the Parthians and killed himself. John Hyrcanus II was also captured and while he was left alive, his ears were cut off so that, as a physically mutilated person, he could never serve as high priest again. In his place, Antigonus Mattathias was made king and high priest, so that, in appearance, the Maccabean kingdom was restored. It was only in appearance, however, for it could function only as long as the Parthian horsemen remained in the land and Rome was too busy elsewhere to interfere.

Herod, the remaining son of Antipater, was betrothed to Mariamne (mar″ee-am′nee), the niece of Antigonus Mattathias. He and Mariamne fled southward, eluded pursuers with great difficulty, and made their way first to the Nabateans, then to Alexandria, where Queen Cleopatra, of the line of the Ptolemies, still reigned, and finally to Rome.

In Rome Herod proved himself a fit son of his father, for he cleverly worked himself into the good graces of the men who were now in control of Rome. These were Octavian (ok-tay′-vee-an), the young great-nephew of Julius Caesar, and Mark Antony, who had been Caesar's chief lieutenant. Together, in 42 B.C., they had defeated and killed the leaders of Caesar's assassins, including Cassius Longinus, and now were dividing the Roman realm between themselves.

Herod was given more than his father's title. In recognition of his loyalty he was made king, and not only of Judea, Idumea, and Galilee but of Samaria as well. The lands he was to rule were nearly equal to those of the Maccabean kingdom at its height. There was only one catch: he would have to reconquer them for himself. He would only get minimal Roman help, for Octavian and Mark Antony, nominally allies, were already getting ready to fight each other and it was for this fight that they needed their real forces.

Herod landed in Judea in 39 B.C. The Parthians had gone, but the anti-Idumean, anti-Roman Jews supported their Maccabean ruler, Antigonus Mattathias, fervently. For two years the foes battled in Judea. Herod was a capable leader, however, and he could always count on some Roman help. In 37 B.C. the last resistance to him crumbled and he took Jerusalem. Antigonus Mattathias was executed and young Aristobulus III, his nephew, was made high priest.

The next year, however, Herod tired of the arrangement, for it was clearly the high priest and not the king to whom the people turned. He had Aristobulus III executed. Of all the Maccabeans, the only male left was the mutilated John Hyrcanus II who could not serve as high priest.

The Maccabean high priesthood thus came to an end, 115 years after Jonathan, the brother of Judas Maccabeus, had accepted the priestly robes. After 36 B.C. the high priests were neither Zadokite nor Maccabean, but were chosen out of one or another of aristocratic, priestly families of Jerusalem. This meant a decline for the prestige of the high priesthood and of Sadducee power, and a corresponding increase in the hold of the Pharisees on the emotions of the Jews generally.

Herod was now undisputed king of Judea. He was execrated by the anti-Roman Jews as the destroyer of the Maccabean royal house and as the man who had finally riveted the chains of Rome to the land — and for being an Idumean besides. We hear of him in history through the words of his enemies alone, and we think of him as a dark and brutal tyrant, very nearly a madman, in fact. Yet perhaps there is another side to the matter.

Herod strove to rule well and in his long reign of thirty-three years, Judea was at peace and it prospered. What's more, as his father had done before him, he maneuvered the frail bark of Judea skillfully through the dangerous waters of Roman politics. He supported Mark Antony in his struggle against Octavian, but when Antony was defeated in 31 B.C., Herod switched sides with such agility that he gained the favor of Octavian. Octavian now ruled all Rome and was soon to be called Augustus and be considered the first of the Roman emperors.* Thanks to Herod, this change was effected with no harm to Judea.

Herod was a great builder and he beautified the land with structures in the Roman style. Since he was a Jew and carefully adhered to all Jewish ritual (at least while in Judea), he did not neglect the Temple. Indeed, he began rebuilding the Temple, at great expense, to make it more magnificent than it had ever been before — much more so than it had originally been under Solomon.

He favored the Pharisees, since the Sadducees had been too intimately connected with his Maccabean predecessors, and required only that Jews, while retaining full freedom of worship, keep their religion out of politics. Even this may not have been so much a matter of tyranny as a prudent regard for the very real power of Rome and the vengeance it might take if the Jews revolted.

What's more, he married Mariamne (she was his second wife) and by her had two sons, Alexander and Aristobulus. In this way, the bloodline of Idumean and Maccabean were fused. Alexander and Aristobulus were great-great-grandsons of Alexander Jannaeus, at least through their mother.

Yet nothing helped. The Jews would not be mollified, and persisted in hating the Idumean who ruled them. There came to be a new growth of messianism. Now that the Maccabees were gone and that the independent Jewish state was crushed,

* For the story of Augustus and his successors, see my book *The Roman Empire* (Houghton Mifflin, 1967).

increasing numbers of Jews began to await the miraculous descendant of the house of David who would sweep all enemies to one side and establish a mighty world kingdom with its capital at Jerusalem. Almost any brigand, almost any preacher, could claim to be the Messiah, find followers, and start some sort of revolt. Several did so in the reign of Herod and his immediate successors.

Herod had to crush all messianic pretensions at the earliest possible moment, for they were terribly dangerous. If any of them escaped his attention or eluded his forces long enough to grow dangerous and attract the attention of Rome, it might be the end of Judea.

Unfortunately the success of Judas Maccabeus and his followers a century and a half before had destroyed Jewish discretion. Because the early Maccabeans had succeeded against a weakened and declining Seleucid kingdom, too many people felt that only audacity and faith were required to sweep away any oppressor. Too many refused to recognize the reality of a Rome many times stronger and infinitely more determined than the Seleucid kingdom ever was.

Dedicated to this notion, extremist groups flourished in Judea. There were the Cananaeans or "Zealots," who refused to pay taxes to Rome, maintained that any Roman who invaded the Temple precincts ought to be killed, and held that Judea must be freed from Rome by force, if necessary. Herod had their first leader executed without trial, but the movement continued. It even developed an extremist wing, the Sicarii, so called from the small dagger, or "sicarius," they carried. They were terrorists who believed in assassination as an instrument of policy.

Herod stood, alone, between the folly of Jewish patriotism and the deadly risk of Roman retaliation, and his reward was nothing but vilification and the danger of assassination. It is not surprising that as the years went on, he grew ever more suspicious, particularly of possible attempts to use some Maccabean puppet against him. In 30 B.C. he had old crop-eared John Hyrcanus executed. Then, in 29 B.C., in a fit of jealousy, he ordered his wife, Mariamne, executed, too. The unavailing remorse that followed this act, for he apparently loved her dearly, pushed him further into melancholia and suspicion.

He married a succession of wives thereafter (by some counts he is supposed to have had as many as ten), found none of them satisfactory, but managed to beget enough different sons by enough different women to develop a complicated problem of succession.

In his old age Herod's suspicion grew to the level of paranoia. He had a number of his sons executed (to the point where the Emperor Augustus is supposed to have said dryly that he would rather be Herod's pig than Herod's son). Among those he had executed, in 6 B.C., were his two sons by Mariamne.

The younger of these sons, however, left behind small children: three boys and a girl in whom the Maccabean line could still be traced. One of the boys was named Herod Agrippa (uh-grip′uh), having been named in honor of Marcus Vipsanius Agrippa, the son-in-law of the Emperor Augustus and the friend of Herod. On his father's death, four-year-old Herod Agrippa was sent to Rome. There, at least, he was safe during the remaining years of Herod's life. Herod Agrippa's sister was Herodias (hih-roh′dee-as).

In 4 B.C. Herod died. He is sometimes known, to historians, as Herod the Great, partly to distinguish him from his descendants, almost all of whom incorporated the name "Herod" in their own names.

JESUS

Herod left four surviving sons. Two of them, Herod Archelaus (ahr″kuh-lay′us) and Herod Antipas (an′tih-pas), were sons of a Samaritan woman. The other two, sons of two different women, were both known as Herod Philip in the histories, which is a source of great confusion.

In his will, Herod divided his kingdom into three parts. His oldest son, Herod Archelaus, was to rule over Idumea, Judea, and Samaria. Herod Antipas was to have Galilee and a section just east of the Jordan River. One Herod Philip was to have Iturea (it″oo-ree′uh), a mainly non-Jewish region east of the Sea of Galilee. The second Herod Philip was left out.

The will was of no value unless the Emperor Augustus ratified it, of course, and he did so only after considerable hesitation. When he finally did, he removed the title of king. Herod Archelaus was to be merely ethnarch ("ruler of a people") and the other two were to be tetrarchs ("ruler of a fourth"). For this reason the Herod Philip who ruled over Iturea is commonly called Philip the Tetrarch to distinguish him from the other.

Herod Archelaus proved a failure. Despite Augustus' advice that he deal gently with his difficult Jewish subjects and let them have their way whenever possible, the ethnarch took a harsh law-and-order line. The result was that there were constant disturbances among his subjects, who detested him for being half-Idumean and half-Samaritan. Deputation after deputation was sent to Rome by one Jewish faction or another, pleading that Herod Archelaus be removed.

In the end, Augustus saw this as the only hope of establishing peace in the small troublesome province. In A.D. 6* Herod Archelaus was removed from his ethnarchy. He lived on in retirement till his death in 12, while his ethnarchy was ruled by a series of Roman procurators. Herod Antipas continued to rule as tetrarch of Galilee and was politic enough to avoid too serious a confrontation with his subjects — except in one respect.

* Dates that are later than the traditional year in which Jesus was born can be written with the initials A.D., standing for "Anno Domini" or "in the year of the Lord." In this book, however, such years will be written without initials. I will write 10 B.C., for instance, but instead of A.D. 10, I will simply write 10.

His half brother Herod Philip (*not* Philip the Tetrarch, but the other) had married Herodias, the granddaughter of Mariamne the Maccabean. The marriage was a failure. Herod Antipas, who was himself married to a daughter of the Nabatean king, divorced that wife in order to marry Herodias. Herodias' second marriage seems to have been a love match but Herod Antipas may further have calculated that marriage to someone of Maccabean descent would endear him, at least a little, to the people.

It did not. Herodias was the half niece of her new husband, but she had also been the half niece of her old husband, and this had not seemed to bother anyone. However, Herod Antipas had now married his half sister-in-law, and this seemed incest to the more conservative Jews.

Among those who were offended was a revivalist preacher named John, who operated just east of the Jordan in what was Herod Antipas' territory. He preached repentance and a new start, having his followers undergo a symbolic washing in the Jordan to indicate the cleansing away of old sins. He thus came to be known as John the Baptist, "baptist" being from a Greek word meaning "to dip in water."

John the Baptist denounced Herod Antipas for his breach of the Jewish ritual rules against incest and his harsh language was particularly offensive to Herodias. What's more, the Nabatean ruler, offended at his daughter's dismissal, warred against Herod Antipas and defeated him. To be sure, Roman interference kept the defeat from meaning anything, but Herod Antipas was humiliated by it. Between his own feeling that John the Baptist might be in Nabatean pay and Herodias' feeling that, in any case, the preacher's language was insupportable, Herod Antipas had John imprisoned and, eventually, executed.

Another Galilean preacher, who seems to have been a disciple of John to begin with, was Joshua or Jeshua — far better known by the Greek version of the name, which is Jesus. He carried on where John had left off, but since he was discreet enough not to attack Herod Antipas or his wife personally, he was left to himself.

He gathered disciples about him and eventually went to Jerusalem, where some among those who greeted him hailed him as the Messiah. The Jewish priesthood, who wanted no troubles in Judea at this time, felt it necessary to suppress this outbreak of messianism at once. They had reason to feel disturbed, for the situation with respect to Rome had deteriorated badly since Herod's time.

The tolerant and capable Emperor Augustus had died in 14 and had been succeeded by his capable but unpopular stepson, Tiberius (ty-bee′ree-us). Tiberius' chief minister was Lucius Aelius Sejanus (sih-jay′nus), who was strongly anti-Jewish and did not believe in pampering this turbulent province with its Parthian sympathies. In 26 a new procurator was appointed to rule Judea. His name was Pontius Pilate (pon′shus-py′lit), he was a protégé of Sejanus, and he came to Judea determined to stand for no nonsense.

Where earlier procurators had made their headquarters at Caesarea (see″zuh-ree′uh), a city on the Samaritan coast, fifty miles northwest of Jerusalem, Pontius Pilate stationed troops in the capital itself. This meant that the army, with its ensigns bearing the portrait of the emperor, moved into Jerusalem. The excited Jews considered such portraits to be a violation of the commandment against idolatry and protested violently. Matters had reached nearly the level of revolt before Pilate could be persuaded to remove the objectionable ensigns.

It was clear, nevertheless, that Pilate was looking for trouble, and the priestly party was desperately anxious not to give him a chance for finding any.

Jesus, to be sure, preached a mild and gentle doctrine. He abjured the use of force — "resist not evil" (Matthew 5:39) — and advised that Roman taxes be paid — "Render therefore unto Caesar the things which are Caesar's" (Matthew 22:21).

Nor did he himself make any public claim to messiahhood. Nevertheless, the mere hint of messianic claims within Jerusalem might give Pontius Pilate the handle he was seeking, and the priestly party felt it had to take measures.

As it happened, Jesus' mild teachings seem to have alienated some among his followers who expected stronger measures. Traditionally, one of those alienated was Judas Iscariot — "Iscariot" as such makes no sense, but if it is a misspelling for "Sicariot" it may be that Judas was a member of the extremist faction who wanted a Messiah of war and not of peace.

The disillusioned Judas betrayed Jesus' whereabouts to the priestly party, which had him arrested and handed over to Pilate. To the Romans, any Jew calling himself a Messiah (or called so by others) was calling himself (or was called) the king of the Jews, and this was treason. Jesus was therefore accorded the usual treatment assigned traitors under Roman law and was crucified, possibly in 29.

Certain of his followers, however, refused to accept this crucifixion as final. He was still the Messiah, they insisted, the "Anointed One."*

Jesus' followers insisted he was not really dead; that he had risen from his grave three days after the crucifixion, spoken with his disciples, had eventually risen to heaven, and would return again (the "Second Coming") on the Day of Judgment, which was imminent.

Tales were told of his birth in accordance with messianic prophecies in the Bible, of the fact that he was of Davidic descent and born in Bethlehem of a virgin, of escape from dangers, of miraculous healings, and so on. Those who had heard him preach recorded his words as they remembered them (he had left behind no writings of his own) and these were woven into a short biography. Three versions of this biography are

* The phrase "Anointed One" is "Khristos" in Greek, "Christus" in Latin, and "Christ" in English, so the crucified preacher is best known in history as Jesus Christ — that is, Joshua the Messiah.

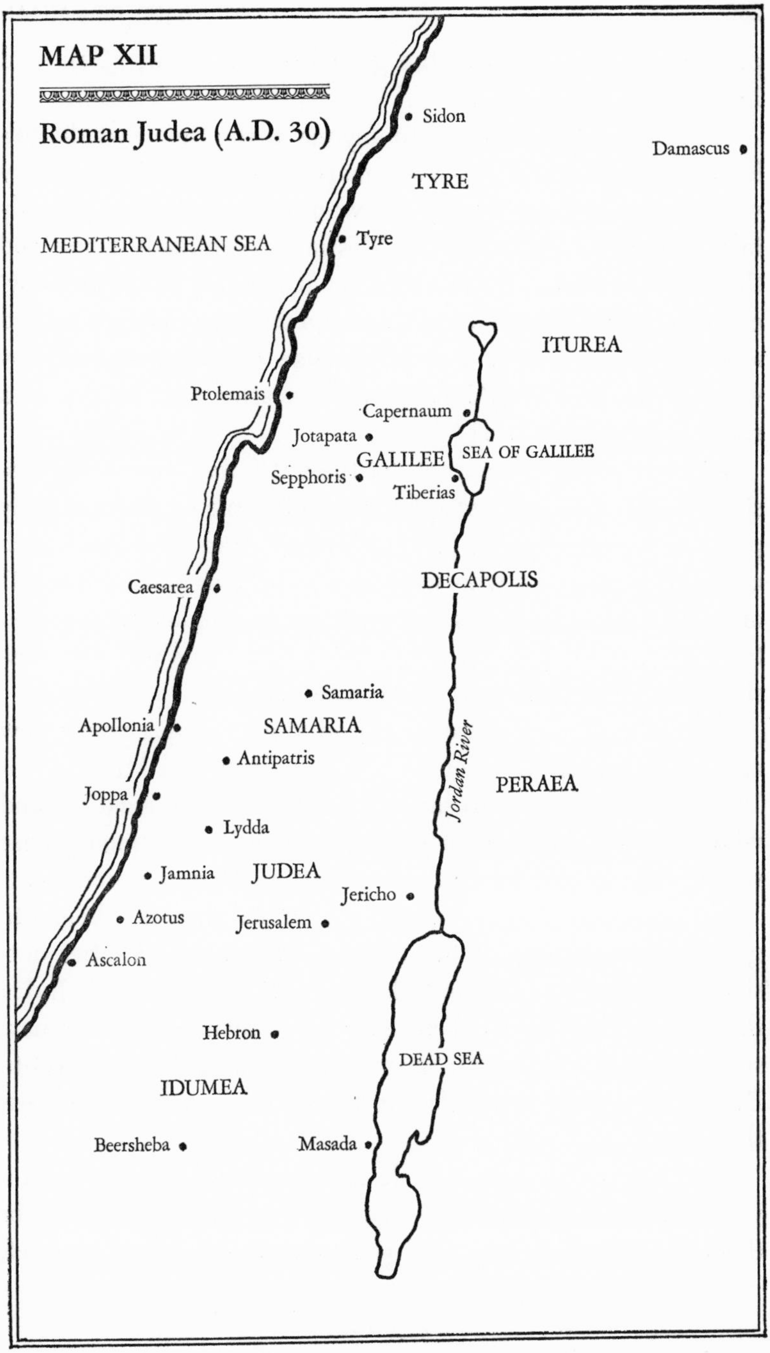
Sidon
Damascus
TYRE
MEDITERRANEAN SEA
Tyre
ITUREA
Ptolemais
Capernaum
Jotapata
GALILEE
SEA OF GALILEE
Sepphoris
Tiberias
Caesarea
DECAPOLIS
Samaria
Apollonia
SAMARIA
Antipatris
Jordan River
PERAEA
Joppa
Lydda
Jamnia
JUDEA
Jericho
Azotus
Jerusalem
Ascalon
Hebron
DEAD SEA
IDUMEA
Beersheba
Masada

MAP XII

Roman Judea (A.D. 30)

preserved in the forms of the gospels of Matthew, Mark, and Luke.*

It could not have seemed to anyone at the time that the followers of Jesus would make any mark at all on the world. They were Jews, quite orthodox Jews, who differed from others only in that they insisted that the Messiah had already come and that the end of the world was close at hand. Most Jews, however, would not accept a Messiah who was apparently defeated and executed without a single stroke on his behalf. They wanted one who would be victorious after the fashion of a super Judas Maccabeus.

When any of the new sect got too vociferous about the messiahhood of Jesus, he was apt to get in trouble with the priestly party — who wanted no Messiah at all — and with the Jewish man in the street — who wanted a victorious one. About 31 one of the followers of Jesus, a man named Stephen, was stoned to death as a blasphemer for insisting that Jesus was the Messiah. He was the first martyr of the new sect.

At the stoning, and strongly approving it, was a young Jew named Saul, who had been born in Tarsus in Asia Minor about 10, who had come to Jerusalem for his religious education, and who was a confirmed Pharisee. He was a leader among those who wished to eradicate the new sect by force, if necessary.

The new sect, despite opposition from the majority, began to spread, and members of the Jewish communities in cities outside Judea became interested. Thus, reports reached Judea that among the Jews of Damascus were members of the new sect. Some time about 35, Saul received permission to travel to Damascus (about 130 miles north of Jerusalem) to suppress these.

In his letters afterward, he describes himself as having had a vision of Jesus and to have been stricken with blindness for three days. As a result, Saul was converted to the new sect,

* A fourth gospel, that of John, was written a generation later than the other three and from a different viewpoint.

becoming as fanatical an upholder of the belief as, earlier, he had been fanatical in opposing it. As a result of the conversion, he grew unpopular indeed with those Jews who had earlier supported him and he was forced to retire to his native Tarsus.

And still the sect spread. There were Jews all over the cities of the eastern half of the Roman Empire, and where a Jewish community existed, there were sure to be those who had been to Jerusalem to sacrifice at the Temple and who came back with the news that the Messiah had arrived and was soon to come again. In Antioch the members of the new sect were therefore referred to as "Messianists," but since it was a Greek-speaking city, the Greek equivalent of the word was used, and they were called Christians.

HEROD AGRIPPA

In Judea conditions continued most turbulent and Pontius Pilate made no effort to smooth matters over. His protector, Sejanus, lost favor with Tiberius and was executed in 31. Thereafter, Pilate had to be more careful, but even so his procuracy was a conspicuous failure and he was finally relieved in 36. Two other procurators followed, neither lasting more than a few months.

Then, in 37, Emperor Tiberius died, and his great-nephew, Caius, usually known by his nickname, Caligula (kuh-lig′you-luh) or "Little Boots," succeeded. At this the Jews could only rejoice, for it was well-known that one of Caligula's boon cronies was Herod Agrippa, a grandson of Herod the Great by his wife, Mariamne the Maccabean. Herod Agrippa was the great-great-great-grandson of Alexander Jannaeus and perhaps he might persuade Rome to treat Judea more leniently.

Indeed, if Herod Agrippa was mindful of his Jewish descent, it would seem he could surely help Judea, for his connections were of the best. As a little boy he had found what was almost a foster-mother in Antonia, the sister-in-law of the emperor, Tiberius. In later life, he became a boon companion of Caligula, so close to him, in fact, that he carelessly hinted it was high time that old Tiberius died so that Caligula could succeed to the throne. Tiberius heard of this and Herod Agrippa found himself in jail. Within six months, however, Tiberius was dead anyway and Caligula at once liberated his friend.

Caligula made Herod Agrippa king of the realm east of the Sea of Galilee that had been formerly held by his half uncle, Philip the Tetrarch, who had died in 34. Herod Antipas, who still ruled in Galilee, was annoyed that his half-nephew should receive the title of king whereas he remained merely tetrarch. He objected and, it might seem, with reason. Caligula, however, saw no need for abstract justice, when his purpose was merely to reward a friend. He removed Herod Antipas from his post and added Galilee to Herod Agrippa's kingdom. Antipas died soon after in banishment.

All this favoritism to Herod Agrippa, however, did not mean the Jews themselves would continue to enjoy the release of tension that had followed Pilate's removal and Tiberius' death. Indeed, a new and most terrible danger arose. Caligula was a flighty young man who had known nothing but luxury for himself and obsequiousness from others all his life. After he had been emperor for seven months (doing reasonably well), he fell seriously ill and it is possible that this illness affected his mental condition, for afterward he grew wildly erratic.

He decided, for instance, to have himself worshiped as a god and to have his image placed in various temples. This was not as horrible in Roman times as it would seem to us today. Many sections of the empire were used to giving rulers divine honors and, in any case, the worship would consist of no more than a ritualized formula of words, a pinch of incense, and that's all. It was very perfunctory indeed.

In one section of the empire, however, the result was turmoil.

To the Jews any worship of the emperor, however perfunctory, was an abomination, and to put his image in the Temple was absolutely unthinkable. It would mean a return to the dread time of Antiochus IV, two centuries before. Caligula, however, was minded to be firm. Judea was the most turbulent province in the empire, and the Jews, of all the inhabitants of the empire, seemed the least assimilable. It was time they were taught a lesson, he may have decided.

In Alexandria, where they were most numerous (outside Judea itself) and most influential, they had been at continuing odds with the Greek population and the Roman authorities. Not only did the Jews refuse to participate in the official religious services of the empire, but they also refused to serve in the army, where unacceptable religious practices would be required of them. In 38 there had been anti-Jewish riots in Alexandria and images of the emperor had been forcibly installed in the synagogues. Caligula saw no reason why this could not be done also to the Temple at Jerusalem.

The emergency brought into momentary prominence the greatest of all the Alexandrian Jews, Philo (fy′loh). Born about 30 B.C., he was the first Jewish philosopher in the Greek sense, the first to try to express Judaism in terms of Greek thought. He was specifically a follower of the Academic school, which dated back to the great Greek philosopher, Plato (play′toh) of the fourth century, B.C. Philo attempted to fuse Moses and Plato, so to speak. This was to be the task of Christianity in the next few centuries and Philo is sometimes called "the first theologian."

In 40, when Philo was an old man in the last year of his life, he undertook to lead an embassy to Rome, where he might appeal to Caligula to rescind his edict that the Temple be desecrated. It is the only event in his life that is clearly known and it was a failure. He returned with nothing accomplished and, not long after, died.

Herod Agrippa was more successful and now he fulfilled the

hopes that had been held out for him. Interceding with his good friend the emperor, he pointed out that any attempt to violate the Temple would surely bring about a Jewish revolt, that the fanatics among the Jews would care nothing for death and would fight like fiends, that the expense in money and in Roman lives simply wasn't worth it. Caligula thereupon reluctantly rescinded the degree.

With Caligula, of course, such an act was no cause for very much relief. The erratic emperor might change his mind at any time and determine on placing his image in the Temple again. In 41, however, Caligula was assassinated and the danger came to an end.

Nevertheless, the crisis proved of fatal consequence to the Jews, for it strengthened the hands of the Zealots, that party of extreme nationalists who called for war against Rome. To nationalist fervor was now added all the religious zeal that had been roused by tales of synagogue desecrations in Alexandria and the attempt to desecrate the Temple itself. And yet for a moment, it seemed that all might be well.

When Caligula died, the assassins found an uncle of his, Claudius (klaw′dee-us), in hiding and promptly proclaimed him emperor. Claudius was the son of the Antonia who had once treated young Herod Agrippa as her protégé. Thus, the Jewish king was the friend of the new emperor as he had been the friend of the old. What's more, Claudius had led a retired life and had no notion of how to behave in connection with public matters, and the smooth Herod Agrippa advised him and helped him over the initial hurdles. The grateful Claudius therefore appointed Herod Agrippa king of the entire realm that had once been ruled by Herod.

For the last time Judea bore the appearance, at least, of independence and greatness and, indeed, for a short time, the land stood at the peak of prosperity, and was materially better off than ever it had been since the days of Solomon nearly a thousand years before.

Herod Agrippa I scrupulously adhered to all the tenets of Judaism, hoping to make the Jews forget that it was only through his grandmother that he was a Maccabean. The Jews were more sympathetic to him than to his grandfather, perhaps because of Herod Agrippa's services in Caligula's time. At any rate when, during a Passover feast, Herod Agrippa wept that he was not a full Jew by birth, the spectators, weeping in sympathy, are supposed to have called out that he *was* a Jew and their brother.

He displayed his Jewish zeal by taking action against those who maintained the messianism of Jesus and who, in doing so, offended the priesthood, the conservatives, and the relations with Rome. He had James, one of the original disciples of Jesus, executed, and had another, Peter, imprisoned for a while.

But then, in 44, after he had reigned only a little over two years, Herod Agrippa died suddenly, presumably of a stroke or heart attack, in the course of games being held in honor of Claudius. His death was an unparalleled disaster for the Jews. Had he lived another twenty years, as he well might have done, his shrewd ability to placate both Jews and Romans might have kept the peace between them, a peace that might then have lasted far beyond his time. As it was, he died leaving a teen-age son, whom Claudius would not trust on the difficult throne of Judea. The land passed under the rule of Roman procurators once more and the moment when all might yet have been well passed forever.

PAUL

If the death of Herod Agrippa I proved a turning point for the Jews, a turning point of quite another sort was soon to take place for the new Jewish sect of Christians — one that was to lead on to a victory no non-Christian could possibly have imagined at the time.

Saul, who had once persecuted the Christians and had been converted to their beliefs, had been forced to retreat to Tarsus, but now he emerged again, arriving in Antioch about 46. The Christians were stronger there than anywhere outside Judea, strong enough to begin to think of sending missionaries to other Jewish communities in the Greek world. It was Saul who, first in conjunction with a companion named Barnabas (bahr′nuh-bas), and later alone, undertook the task.

In three journeys Saul traveled to the island of Cyprus, throughout Asia Minor, to Macedonia and Greece. Everywhere, he found Jewish communities and synagogues in which he could preach of the death and resurrection of Jesus, of his second coming, and of the imminent end of the world. But nearly everywhere the Jews were hostile to the doctrine: Jesus was not their idea of a Messiah.

Almost from the beginning Saul, who had been brought up in a Greek city, realized that if the Jews would not listen, there were Gentiles who would. The classical culture of Greece was long in decay and their gods and rituals no longer satisfied. New beliefs from the east, more mystical, more self-assured, more colorful, and promising life after death, were found much more attractive by the Greeks. As a result, the rites of eastern deities, such as Isis from Egypt, or Cybele from Asia Minor, were rising in favor all over the empire.

Judaism, too, was finding its adherents and there were a surprising number of conversions to that religion. There would have been more, no doubt, but the Jews insisted on the circumcision of every male convert. This is an operation that is embarrassing to many and painful to all, and it took a real believer to accept conversion on those terms. For this reason, most converts to Judaism were women. This, too, served the purpose, however, since the children of Jewish women were counted as

Jews and infant sons could be easily circumcised and be Jews from birth. A second difficulty involved in conversions to Judaism was that a Jew was a member of a nation as well as of a religion. A converted Jew found that the center of his patriotism, as well as of his religion, was supposed to be the Temple at Jerusalem, so that conversion had more than a trace of treason to Rome in it.

Saul seems to have understood these difficulties. To him the matter of messianism was universal and not merely Jewish. To believe in Jesus did not require (in his view) that the political and national aspirations of Judaism be accepted. To him circumcision, in and of itself, was an irrelevant ritual and it was inner belief that counted: ". . . he is a Jew, which is one inwardly; and circumcision is that of the heart, in the spirit, and not in the letter . . ." (Romans 2:29).

Saul, therefore, adopted the Roman name of Paul, and began preaching openly to Gentiles, asking them to accept Jesus without the necessity of circumcision or of following all the minutiae of ritual that had been adopted by the Pharisees. What he was offering was conversion to Judaism without the difficulties involved, and he was extraordinarily successful. Christian communities were established wherever he went, drawing strength from the Gentiles.

The lack of circumcision among the Gentile converts was horrifying to the Jews and a wider gap appeared between them and the Christians as a result. Indeed, even those Jews who accepted Jesus were horrified, so that for a while, Christianity split into two groups: the circumcised Jewish Christians, who accepted the Mosaic Law in full along with their belief in the messianism of Jesus, and the uncircumcised Gentile Christians, who were readier to interpret the teachings of Jesus in the light of Greek philosophy.

The two views clashed head-on in 48 at the Council of Jerusalem. James, a brother of Jesus, led the Jewish-Christian view, and Paul, the Gentile-Christian. The result was a victory foı Paul and Christianity took the road away from national Judaism.

About 57 Paul returned from his third missionary voyage and visited Jerusalem. There he was recognized by the Jews, who viewed him as someone whose teachings ran counter to the law of Moses and who felt that his presence therefore profaned the Temple. Even worse, the rumor spread that he had brought Gentiles into its confines. A riot started, and a lynching seemed sure, until Paul was taken into protective custody by a detachment of Roman soldiers.

The Romans were having the usual troubles with the restive province. A series of procurators had been in power after the death of Herod Agrippa without much luck at controlling the province and since 52 the procurator had been Antonius Felix. He married Drusilla (droo-sil′uh), a daughter of Herod Agrippa I, but that did not keep the situation from continuing to deteriorate.

Paul was brought before Felix on the charge of having profaned the Temple, and Paul defended himself as a Pharisee who merely maintained the resurrection of Jesus — pointing out that resurrection was an important article of pharisaic belief. However, when Paul went on to speak of the imminent end of the world, Felix dismissed him as a crackpot. More to keep the peace than anything else, Felix ordered Paul kept in imprisonment.

There was a new emperor on the throne now, however. In 54 Claudius had been poisoned by his fourth wife, Agrippina (ag″rih-py′nuh), and her young son by a previous marriage, Nero, became Rome's fifth emperor. In 60 Felix, who had been an appointee of Claudius, was relieved and Porcius Festus took his place. Festus, on arriving at his new post in 61, was greeted by Herod Agrippa II.

Herod Agrippa II was the only son of Herod Agrippa I and had been seventeen years old at the time of his father's death.

His uncle, a younger brother of Herod Agrippa I, was reigning over a small region in Lebanon, centered about the city of Chalcis (kal′sis), sixty miles north of the Sea of Galilee. When this uncle, Herod of Chalcis, died in 48, Herod Agrippa II was made king in his place. By 53 his rule was extended over the territory that had once belonged to Philip the Tetrarch and over parts of Galilee as well.

While Herod Agrippa II and Festus were together, the case of Paul came up again and he was brought before the two men. He pleaded his case with such force that Herod Agrippa II said to him, "Almost thou persuadest me to be a Christian."

Paul was a Roman citizen and, expecting nothing but continued imprisonment by a procurator anxious to avoid unnecessary trouble with the Jews, he appealed to the emperor. He was consequently allowed to sail for Rome on what proved to be the fourth and last of his missionary journeys. What happened to Paul afterward is uncertain but he is supposed to have died in Rome about 67.

THE JEWISH REBELLION

Other procurators succeeded Festus and steadily the rumblings in Judea grew worse. There was wanting only a spark to set the whole land on fire. In 66 there were riots in Caesarea, the coastal city where the procurator made his headquarters, and the Jews were driven out. News of this, and also word that the procurator intended to appropriate a large part of the Temple funds for his own purposes, started widespread rioting in Jerusalem.

At the time, Herod Agrippa II and his sister Berenice (ber″-uh-ny′see) happened to be in Jerusalem. Anxiously, they tried to calm tempers, warning that Roman vengeance would be extreme, but the Zealots were in control now and would not listen. They had the precedent of the Maccabean rebellion to think of and the hope on the part of many that a Messiah would arrive. They seized first the Temple, then Jerusalem. The Roman garrison was forced out of the city.

As had been true in the days of the Maccabean revolt, two and a quarter centuries before, the first reaction was on the part of the local governor of the region and he sent inadequate forces hurriedly southward. The Roman legion penetrated to Jerusalem but there met unexpected resistance and retreated. At Beth-horon, twelve miles northwest of Jerusalem, the Jewish forces, which were harrying the retreat, forced him to stand and inflicted a defeat upon him.

That defeat of the Romans convinced even the waverers among the Jews that the days of Maccabean glory had returned, and all the country passed over to the revolt. A rebel government was set up in Jerusalem, the country was divided into military districts, and Galilee, the most northerly and exposed section, was put under the leadership of a young priest named Joseph, better known to us by the Romanized form of the name, Josephus (joh-see′fus).

But if the rebels thought that by defeating a Roman legion they had defeated the Romans, they were wrong. Emperor Nero recognized that he had a major rebellion on his hands, and in 67 he sent no less than three legions to Antioch under the command of Vespasian (ves-pay′zhan), Rome's best general.

Vespasian led his army south and had very little trouble in occupying Galilee. Josephus and some of his men took refuge in the fortress of Jotapata (joh-tap′uh-tuh), seventeen miles west of the Sea of Galilee. This withstood a siege of seven weeks, then fell. Josephus himself managed to escape the slaughter that followed and even worked his way into the regard of Vespasian by shrewdly predicting that the general was fated to become emperor. Josephus, judging the Romans to be irresistible, joined them wholeheartedly thenceforward. For the same reason, Herod Agrippa II did the same, now that his own kingdom was cleared of the rebels.

Vespasian proceeded to clear the Judean seacoast, unopposed by the rebels, who, in the interior, were engaged in the suicidal folly of fighting among themselves with the extremists winning out against anyone who even breathed moderation, however slightly.

In 68 Vespasian began operations in Judea proper. Systematically, province by province, he occupied the land, forcing the Zealots into ever narrower spaces west of the Dead Sea. The Zealots resisted bitterly and, for a while, it might have seemed they had a chance after all, for in the course of the year, a rebellion against Nero rocked Rome. Partly, it was Nero's extravagance and his tyranny over his associates that roused that rebellion; partly, it was the troubles in Judea. In any case, the emperor killed himself rather than face execution.

But that meant a period of anarchy, for no heirs were left of the house of Augustus. The imperial throne was up for grabs; anyone who had a following in the armed forces could enforce that grab. That meant the various generals, of course, and Vespasian felt obliged to allow the fighting to slacken to see what would happen in Rome.

In 69 three different generals each seized the imperial throne temporarily, one after the other, and then in July of that year, the armies in Judea and in Egypt proclaimed Vespasian emperor. By that time Jerusalem was virtually isolated, but Vespasian had to take first things first. He left for Rome (taking with him Josephus, whose prophecy was now apparently coming true) and in 70 defeated his rivals and became emperor.

Vespasian's son Titus (ty′tus) remained in Alexandria, until his father (now emperor) ordered him to proceed to Judea, there to complete the job. In May 70 Jerusalem was placed under siege. Step by step, the walls were broken into; step by step, the defenders fell back. Famine and force did their deadly work and on August 28, the Second Temple was taken and destroyed. Thus ended the Second Temple after six centuries of existence, and a thousand years after Solomon had constructed the first Temple. There has never been a third.

Other parts of the city held out for another month and some fortresses in Judea held out still longer. The last stand was the town of Masada (muh-say′duh) on the western shores of the Dead Sea, thirty-five miles southeast of Jerusalem. It was not until 73 that the Romans could bring it to the point of capture and then, just before the final assault, the last defenders, 960 men, women, and children, killed themselves rather than surrender. The Jewish rebellion was over.

The consequences were serious outside Judea. In Alexandria latent hostility between Greeks and Jews broke out in the open again. With Judea in revolt against Rome, there was no disposition on the part of the government to protect the Alexandrian Jews, as at times they had done in the past. The greatest Jewish temple in Alexandria was destroyed and thousands of Jews were killed.

Alexandrian Jewry never recovered. The only remaining colony of Jews in the Roman Empire that was large and influential after the Judean rebellion was in Cyrene (sy-ree′nee), on the African coast 500 miles west of Alexandria.

Within Judea many thousands of Jews remained and were left to themselves and to a certain amount of religious freedom. They could study their holy books and worship in synagogues, but Jerusalem lay in ruins and by strict government edict the Temple was never to be rebuilt and the high priesthood was to be abolished. What's more, a legion of Roman soldiers was stationed indefinitely in the land.

Herod Agrippa II retained his royal title, but there was nothing much left in his kingdom that he might rule and he was execrated for his Romanizing by the Jews that remained. He therefore left for Rome with his sister, Berenice. In Rome Berenice was the mistress of Titus, son of the emperor and destroyer of the Temple. However, such was the unpopularity of

Jews at this time, that Titus was forced to abandon her by the popular outcry against her.

In 71 Titus and his father, Emperor Vespasian, celebrated a triumph honoring their victories in Judea, and the Arch of Titus, which commemorates that triumph, still stands in Rome. On it are pictured the spoils brought to Rome from the Temple, including the seven-branched candlestick that is now virtually one of the best-known symbols of Judaism.

Conversions to Judaism stopped with the rebellion and Judaism was never again actively to seek conversion. The rebellion had offended Gentiles who were loyal to the empire, and their defeat discouraged those who might otherwise have thought there was something to the messianic hopes of the Jews.

On the other hand, conversions from Judaism to Christianity also stopped. The Christians among the Jews had felt the rebellion marked the beginning of the end and that it heralded the return of Jesus and the beginning of the messianic age. They followed the words of Jesus as given in Matthew 24:16. Speaking of the final days, he had said, "let them which be in Judea flee into the mountains."

The Christians, doing so, took no part in the defense of Jerusalem. For this they were regarded as Romanizers and ostracized. Jewish-Christianity faded and died, and the new religion became entirely Gentile and moved farther and farther away from its Jewish origins.

JUDEA'S LAST STAND

Yet, despite everything, Judaism survived. If Jerusalem no longer existed as the national center, Jewish teachers gathered elsewhere. The center of Jewish learning in Judea after the rebellion was the town of Jamnia (jam′nee-uh) near the coast, some thirty miles west of Jerusalem. There, about 90, Jewish scholars gathered and produced the final edition of the Jewish Bible. They decided which books were to be included and which were to be omitted.*

The scholars who performed this task and who made the final decision on the exact form of those books they accepted called themselves the Masoretes. This is from a Hebrew word meaning "tradition," because these scholars felt themselves to be retaining the ancient tradition and to be removing any later accretions. Their product is therefore the "Masoretic text" and the Hebrew Bible is still supposed to be this text, letter for letter.

The Jewish tradition lingered in the secular world, too. In Rome Josephus remained Jewish and labored to bring the Jewish heritage to the Gentile world. About 77 he had written a history of the Jewish rebellion, and about 90 he wrote a book on Jewish history. The latter, called *The Antiquities of the Jews*, was designed to show that the Jews had as glorious a tradition, and a more ancient one, than the Greeks or Romans. He died some time after 93.

Herod Agrippa II lived till about 100. With him died the last significant remnant of the line of the Maccabees and of the Herods, both of which he represented.

As for Vespasian, he died in 79 and was succeeded by his son Titus. Titus proved a benevolent monarch, generous and affable, but his reign was brief. He died in 81 and was succeeded by his younger brother, Domitian (doh-mish′an), who was much less popular. Domitian, about 90, passed laws that were unfavorable to Jews and Christians. It was not that he had anything against Christians particularly but that they were still viewed by most Romans as merely a kind of Jew. This was the last time that this confusion existed anywhere.

Domitian was assassinated in 96 and was succeeded by an

* The omitted books are still to be found in other versions of the Bible, such as the Septuagint, and make up the "Apocrypha" ("hidden").

aged senator named Nerva (nur′vuh). He was a mild man who lifted restrictions against Jews and Christians and, before he died in 98, saw to it that the next emperor would be the competent general Trajan (tray′jan).

Throughout the first century of the empire, the Roman realm was still expanding, and under Trajan it reached its peak. Trajan added Dacia (the region that now makes up Romania) to the realm between 101 and 107 and then beginning in 113, he marched against the Parthians. He took Armenia in 114 and the Tigris-Euphrates valley in 115 and 116. For a moment, Roman armies actually stood on the Persian Gulf.

But Trajan was an old man by now, well in his sixties. While still far off in the east, he fell sick and rumors of his death began to reach the empire. The Jews in Cyrene, excited perhaps by another messianic hope, burst into rebellion in 116. They massacred all the Gentiles they could seize and were massacred in their turn, even more extensively, when the Roman authorities gained the upper hand. When news of these disorders reached Trajan, he was forced to begin the homeward march. He died on the way back and his cousin and adopted son, Hadrian (hay′dree-an), became emperor in 117. By then the revolt of the Jews in Cyrene had been completely suppressed and the last important Jewish colony in the empire had been wiped out.

In the course of his rule, Hadrian visited the various parts of the empire. In 130 he passed through Judea and was disturbed to find that although Jerusalem had been destroyed sixty years before, its ruins still served as a center of veneration for the Jews. He decided to build a new city on the site, one that was completely Roman and pagan.

When this decision came to be known to the Jews, they were once more stirred to bitter rebellion. The spiritual leader of the new revolt was Akiba ben Joseph (uh-kee′vuh). He was eighty years old and could remember the Second Temple as it was before its destruction. After the destruction, he had been one of the most important of the Judean scholars.

The military leader was Simeon Bar Koziba (bar′koh-zee′vuh). Akiba is supposed to have declared him the Messiah and to have renamed him Bar-Kokhba (bar′kukh′vah), or "son of a star." Akiba is also supposed to have traveled far outside Judea to raise support for the rebellion among the scattered Jews elsewhere.

In the fall of 131 the revolt broke out, and Judea made its last stand. The rebellion had been well organized, much more so than the one in 66, and the Roman forces, utterly surprised, were forced to evacuate their camps near Jerusalem. The Jewish rebels took over what was left of the town, reinstituted sacrifices according to the ancient fashion, issued coins, and attempted to establish a government. One Roman legion, sent into the interior too rashly, never emerged again. Nevertheless, the Romans merely added to their forces and Hadrian himself came to Judea. Methodically, the Romans reestablished their control and by 134 the Jews were forced out of Jerusalem again.

The city which (except for a half-century interval in Chaldean times) had been the Judean capital since David had taken it eleven centuries before, now passed out of Jewish control for what was to be over eighteen centuries (without, however, ever passing out of Jewish thought for even a moment).

Bar-Kokhba took refuge in a fortress seven miles southwest of the city which was taken at the end of the summer of 135, and he himself was killed. The last resistance was then wiped out along the shores of the Dead Sea. Akiba was executed, too. According to tradition, he was flayed alive.

This time it was really the end. The land had been leveled in three years of bitter warfare; most of the towns were destroyed; most of the inhabitants slaughtered. The history of the ancient land of Canaan came to a close, for all the peoples associated with its long and adventurous story were either gone or were reduced to permanent nullity. Many great events yet remained that would take place on its soil, but these would involve men and ideas from outside.

Yet even so Judaism still lived, in Galilee, in many cities of the empire, and, outside the empire, in the Tigris-Euphrates valley. Everywhere it was a small minority, everywhere powerless, everywhere the object of suspicion and hatred; and yet it was to stay alive through eighteen additional centuries of steady, and sometimes incredibly brutal, persecution.

And in a way, it had even been victorious. The land of Canaan, which had contributed so much to the history of civilization — cities, sea trade, pottery, the alphabet — had yet another to make. By fighting off and surviving all its enemies, the Philistines, the Assyrians, the Chaldeans, the Greeks, it might seem that the Jews had in the end finally been wiped out as a nationality by the Romans. Nevertheless, the Jews had kept themselves in being long enough to complete the development of Judaism to the point where Christianity could form from it. And Christianity, stemming from the death of a Jewish preacher and the missionary activity of another Jewish preacher, in the end conquered Rome and all the western world.

A TABLE OF DATES

B.C.	
7800	Oldest traces of human habitation in Jericho
7000	New Stone Age starts in Near East
4500	Copper comes into use in Near East; Byblos founded
4000	Ghassulians enter Canaan
3100	Bronze Age begins in Near East; writing invented in Sumeria
3000	Phoenicians establish themselves in coastal Canaan
2615	Beginning of Old Kingdom in Egypt
2300	Egyptians under Uni invade Canaan; empire of Sargon of Akkad in Tigris-Euphrates
2000	Amorites invade Fertile Crescent
1990	Beginning of Middle Kingdom in Egypt
1900	Time of Abraham
1850	Egyptians under Sesostris III invade Canaan
1700	Empire of Hammurabi in Tigris-Euphrates

B.C.	
1680	Hyksos domination of Egypt; time of Jacob and Joseph
1570	Hyksos driven out of Egypt; New Kingdom established
1469	Thutmose III sole ruler of Egypt
1468	Thutmose III defeats Canaanites at Megiddo
1462	Thutmose III takes Kadesh
1450	Tyre founded
1400	Alphabet in use at Ugarit; Iron Age begins among Hittites; Cretan civilization collapses
1379	Ikhnaton rules Egypt; Hebrew kingdoms established around rim of Canaan
1350	Hittites defeat Mitanni, who disappear from history; Ugarit destroyed by earthquake
1319	Seti I rules Egypt
1304	Rameses II rules Egypt
1298	Rameses II fights drawn battle with Hittites; Canaan remains under

B.C.	
	Egyptian control
1240	Israelites under Joshua cross Jordan and take Jericho
1237	Merneptah rules Egypt
1232	Merneptah defeats Israelite war bands in Canaan
1230	Sea Peoples invade Egypt, defeated by Merneptah
1185	Sea Peoples again invade Egypt, defeated by Rameses III; Philistines establish themselves on Canaanite coast
1150	Barak of Naphtali defeats Canaanites at Mt. Tabor; Song of Deborah
1120	Gideon of Manasseh defeats Midianites
1100	Jephtha of Gilead defeats Ammonites and Ephraimites
1050	Philistines defeat Israelites at Aphek, destroy Israelite sanctuary at Shiloh; time of Samuel
1020	Saul rules Israel; Abibaal rules Tyre
1000	Philistines defeat Saul at Mt. Gilboa; Eshbaal rules Israel; David rules Judah
991	David rules Israel-Judah
990	David takes Jerusalem
970	Revolt of Absalom
969	Hiram rules Tyre
961	Solomon rules Israel-Judah
960	Utica founded by colonists from Tyre
954	Solomon dedicates his Temple at Jerusalem

B.C.	
935	Sheshonk I rules Egypt
930	Rezon establishes rule in Damascus; Jeroboam revolts against Solomon, then flees to Egypt
922	Rehoboam rules Israel-Judah; Israel successfully revolts; Jeroboam rules Israel
917	Sheshonk raids Judah and Israel; sacks Temple
915	Abijah rules Judah
913	Asa rules Judah
901	Nadab rules Israel
900	Nadab killed in army coup; Baasha rules Israel
887	Ithobaal rules Tyre
878	Syrians invade Israel and destroy Dan
877	Elah rules Israel
876	Elah killed in army coup; Omri rules Israel, founds Samaria
873	Jehoshaphat rules Judah
869	Ahab rules Israel with Jezebel as his queen; time of Elijah
859	Shalmaneser III rules Assyria
856	Syrians lay siege to Samaria
855	Ahab defeats Syrians
854	Ahab of Israel and Ben-hadad II of Syria fight drawn battle against Shalmaneser III of Assyria at Karkar
850	Ahab dies in battle; Ahaziah rules Israel; Moab revolts against Israel
849	Jehoram rules Israel, fails to reconquer Moab; the Moabite Stone; Jehoram

B.C.

(a different one) rules Judah; time of Elisha

842 Ahaziah rules Judah, dominated by queen mother, Athaliah; Jehu rebels, kills Jehoram of Israel and Ahaziah of Judah; Jehu rules Israel and has Jezebel executed; Athaliah massacres royal family of Judah and rules Judah; Benhadad II of Syria killed in army coup and Hazael rules Syria; Shalmaneser III of Assyria raids Syria and Israel, Jehu forced to pay tribute

836 Athaliah killed in army coup; Jehoash rules Judah, thanks to the high priest, Jehoiada

814 Jehoahaz rules Israel; Syria under Hazael at peak of power; Carthage founded in North Africa by colonists from Tyre

806 Benhadad III rules Syria; Assyrian army raids Syria and takes Damascus

798 Jehoash (a different one) rules Israel

797 Jehoash of Judah killed in army coup; Amaziah rules Judah

790 Death of Elisha

786 Jehoash of Israel defeats Amaziah of Judah at Beth-Shemesh

783 Jeroboam II rules Israel; Israel reaches peak of power

769 Amaziah killed in army

B.C.

coup; Uzziah rules Judah

760 Amos preaches at Bethel

753 Rome founded

748 Zechariah rules Israel; killed in army coup; Menahem rules Israel

745 Tiglath-pileser III usurps rule of Assyria

738 Tiglath-pileser III defeats western coalition headed by Judah; Pekahiah rules Israel

736 Pekahiah killed in army coup; Pekah rules Israel; Shabaka rules Egypt

734 Jotham rules Judah, dies; Ahaz rules Judah; time of Isaiah

732 Tiglath-pileser III takes Damascus; end of Aramean Syria as independent power; Pekah killed in army coup, Hoshea rules Israel

728 Shalmaneser V rules Assyria

725 Shalmaneser V lays siege to Samaria

722 Shalmaneser V killed in army coup; Sargon II rules Assyria; Samaria falls, end of Israel as independent power; Israelites carried off to exile in Assyria — ten lost tribes; land now occupied by Samaritans

715 Hezekiah rules Judah, strengthens Yahvism

705 Sennacherib rules Assyria

701 Sennacherib lays siege to Jerusalem, but does not

B.C.

take it
687 Manasseh rules Judah
681 Sennacherib assassinated; Esarhaddon rules Assyria
671 Esarhaddon conquers Egypt
669 Ashurbanipal rules Assyria
642 Amon rules Judah
640 Amon assassinated; Josiah rules Judah
627 Ashurbanipal dies; Assyria enters steep decline
622 Discovery of the Book of the Law in the Temple; Yahvism reformed
612 Chaldeans and Medes in alliance take and destroy Nineveh
609 Necho II rules Egypt, defeats and kills Josiah at Megiddo; Jehoahaz rules Judah, deposed by Necho; Jehoiakim rules Judah
605 Nebuchadrezzar rules Chaldea, defeats Necho at Carchemish; time of Jeremiah
597 Nebuchadrezzar lays siege to Jerusalem; Jehoiachin rules Judah; Jerusalem taken by Nebuchadrezzar, Jehoiachin and many others taken off to exile in Babylonia; Zedekiah rules Judah
590 Time of Ezekiel; beginnings of Judaism
587 Nebuchadrezzar lays siege to Jerusalem again, takes Jerusalem, destroys Solomon's Temple, kills

B.C.

Zedekiah and son, more of population carried off into Babylonian Exile; end of Judah as independent kingdom; Nebuchadrezzar lays siege to Tyre
574 Siege of Tyre lifted; Ithobaal III of Tyre deposed; Baal II rules Tyre
561 Amel-Marduk rules Chaldea
559 Amel-Marduk assassinated; Cyrus founds Persian Empire
555 Nabonidus rules Chaldea
546 Cyrus conquers Asia Minor; time of Second Isaiah
540 Carthaginians and Etruscans in alliance defeat Greeks at sea near Corsica; end Greek colonization of western Mediterranean
538 Cyrus takes Babylon; end of Chaldean Empire; Cyrus allows exiled Jews to return to Judea; attempt to restore house of David with Zerubbabel fails
530 Cyrus dies in battle; Cambyses rules Persia
525 Cambyses conquers Egypt
521 Darius I rules Persia
516 Second Temple dedicated in Jerusalem
499 Ionian cities of Asia Minor revolt against Persia
494 Phoenicians defeat Greeks at sea near Miletus; Ionian revolt crushed
490 Athenians defeat Per-

B.C.

sians at Marathon

486 Xerxes I rules Persia

480 Xerxes I leads large force into Greece; defeated by Greeks at naval Battle of Salamis; Greeks defeat Carthaginians at Himera in Sicily

464 Artaxerxes I rules Persia

458 Ezra arrives in Jerusalem; leads religious revival

440 Nehemiah arrives in Jerusalem

437 Walls of Jerusalem rebuilt

415 Athens sends expeditionary force against Syracuse and is disastrously defeated

409 Carthaginians begin successful offensive in Sicily

405 Dionysius I rules Syracuse

404 Artaxerxes II rules Persia

398 Dionysius I takes Carthaginian base at Motya

387 Dionysius I establishes virtual empire in central Mediterranean

379 Carthaginians defeat Dionysius I at Panormus

368 Death of Dionysius I

359 Artaxerxes III rules Persia

356 Philip II rules Macedon

345 Artaxerxes III crushes Phoenician revolt; Tennes of Sidon deposed and executed

344 Timoleon of Corinth arrives in Sicily

343 Artaxerxes III reconquers Egypt

B.C.

339 Timoleon defeats Carthaginians at Crimisus River

338 Philip of Macedon in control of all Greece

336 Philip II assassinated; Alexander III (the Great) rules Macedon

334 Alexander the Great invades Asia

332 Alexander the Great lays siege to Tyre and takes it; end of Tyrian kingship; Alexander takes Judea without a fight; Alexander lays siege to Gaza and takes it; Alexander takes Egypt without a fight and founds Alexandria

323 After conquering all Persian Empire, Alexander the Great dies at Babylon

317 Agathocles rules Syracuse

312 Ptolemy defeats Demetrius at Gaza; Judea under the control of Ptolemy; Seleucus I captures Babylon, founds Seleucia, establishes Seleucid Era

311 Carthaginians lay siege to Syracuse

310 Agathocles invades Africa, threatens Carthage, which lifts the siege of Syracuse

307 Kingdoms established on wreckage of Alexander's empire

301 Antigonus defeated at Ipsus; Alexander's empire permanently disrupted

300 Seleucus I founds Anti-

B.C.

och; Simon I is high priest in Jerusalem
290 Rome in control of all central Italy
289 Agathocles dies; Mamertines established in Messana, Sicily
285 Ptolemy I abdicates; Ptolemy II rules Egypt
283 Ptolemy I dies
281 Pyrrhus brings army into southern Italy; defeats Rome
280 Seleucus I assassinated
277 Pyrrhus takes army into Sicily; defeats Carthaginians
275 Pyrrhus fights Romans one last time; returns to Greece
270 Rome in control of all southern Italy; Hiero of Syracuse defeats Mamertines; Septuagint published in Alexandria
265 Romans defeat Hiero of Syracuse
264 First Punic War begins
256 Romans under Regulus invade Africa; lay siege to Carthage
255 Carthaginians under Xanthippus defeat Regulus
250 Onias II high priest in Jerusalem
247 Hamilcar Barca becomes Carthaginian commander
246 Ptolemy III rules Egypt
241 Carthaginians accept defeat; end of First Punic War; Ptolemy III sacrifices at Temple in Jerusalem
239 Hamilcar Barca defeats and destroys mercenaries threatening Carthage; Rome forces Carthage to give up Sardinia and Corsica
235 Hamilcar Barca goes to Spain
228 Hamilcar Barca dies; Hasdrubal takes over
226 Hasdrubal agrees with Rome to confine his rule to the south of the Iberus River
225 Hasdrubal founds Carthagena on Spanish coast
223 Antiochus III rules Seleucid kingdom
221 Hasdrubal assassinated; Hannibal Barca takes over; Ptolemy IV rules Egypt
219 Hannibal lays siege to Saguntum; Simon II high priest in Jerusalem
218 Second Punic War begins; Hannibal crosses Alps and invades Italy; defeats Romans at the Trebia River and the Ticinus River
217 Hannibal defeats Romans at Lake Trasimene; Ptolemy IV defeats Antiochus III at Raphia
216 Hannibal defeats Romans at Cannae
211 Hannibal marches to the walls of Rome
209 Antiochus III begins reconquest of east
208 Romans defeat Hasdru-

B.C.

bal Barca at Metaurus River; beginning of end for Hannibal

206 Romans under Scipio take Spain

204 Romans under Scipio invade Africa

203 Ptolemy V king of Egypt

202 Romans under Scipio defeat Hannibal at Zama; end of Second Punic War

200 Romans send army into Macedon; Antiochus III defeats Ptolemy V at Paneas, and Judea passes from Ptolemaic to Seleucid control

197 Romans defeat Philip V of Macedon

196 Onias III is high priest in Jerusalem; Romans force Hannibal into exile

195 Hannibal arrives at Tyre; confers with Antiochus III at Ephesus

191 Romans defeat Antiochus III at Thermopylae

190 Romans defeat Antiochus III at Magnesia

187 Antiochus III killed; Seleucus IV rules Seleucid realm

183 Hannibal kills himself

181 Ptolemy VI rules Egypt

175 Seleucus IV assassinated; Antiochus IV rules Seleucid realm and establishes Joshua-Jason as puppet high priest in Jerusalem

172 Onias-Menelaus appointed puppet high priest in Jerusalem

170 Onias III, exiled high

B.C.

priest, killed near Antioch; Antiochus IV invades Egypt, takes Memphis

169 Antiochus IV lays siege to Alexandria; returns to sack Jerusalem

168 Antiochus IV renews siege of Alexandria; forced away by Rome

167 Antiochus IV desecrates Second Temple and decrees end to Judaism; Mattathias and sons begin Maccabean revolt

166 Death of Mattathias; Judas Maccabeus takes command and defeats Seleucid forces at Beth-horon

165 Judas Maccabeus defeats Seleucid forces at Emmaus and Beth-zur; enters Jerusalem, purifies and rededicates Second Temple

163 Antiochus IV dies in east; Antiochus V rules Seleucid realm

162 Seleucid forces defeat Judas Maccabeus at Beth-zechariah; Lysias, Seleucid regent, offers Jews religious freedom; Antiochus V and Lysias killed; Demetrius I rules Seleucid realm

161 Judas Maccabeus killed in battle

159 Elaikim-Alcimus dies; end of Zadokite high priesthood

157 Demetrius I appoints

B.C.

Jonathan, brother of Judas Maccabeus, as governor of Judea
153 Cato heads mission to Carthage and demands it be destroyed
152 Alexander Balas launches civil war against Demetrius I; Jonathan becomes high priest, marking beginning of Maccabean high priesthood
150 Demetrius I killed in battle; Balas rules Seleucid realm
149 Beginning of Third Punic War
147 Jonathan defeats Seleucid army at Azotus
146 Romans take and destroy Carthage forever
145 Demetrius II rules Seleucid realm
143 Tryphon rebels against Demetrius II
142 Tryphon lures Jonathan to Ptolemais and kills him; Simon, his brother, takes over control of Judea and is granted independence by Demetrius II
141 Simon takes Joppa
139 Demetrius II taken prisoner by Parthians
137 Antiochus VII rules Seleucid realm
134 Simon assassinated
133 Antiochus VII takes Jerusalem; makes John Hyrcanus I, son of Simon, ruler of Judea; Rome takes over kingdom of Pergamum in Asia Minor

B.C.

129 John Hyrcanus I destroys Samaritan temple on Mt. Gerizim
125 John Hyrcanus I conquers Idumea; forces Idumeans to accept Judaism
107 John Hyrcanus takes Samaria
104 Aristobulus I rules Judea; conquers Galilee
103 Alexander Jannaeus rules Judea; Maccabean kingdom at peak of power
88 Pontus wars against Rome
76 Salome Alexandra rules Judea; her son John Hyrcanus II is high priest
67 Salome Alexandra dies; her sons, John Hyrcanus II and Aristobulus II, fight over succession
65 Roman general, Pompey, completes defeat of Pontus
64 Pompey dethrones Antiochus XIII, ends Seleucid kingdom; takes Jerusalem and ends Maccabean kingdom; confirms John Hyrcanus II as high priest
53 Parthians defeat Romans under Crassus; Antipater the Idumean keeps Judea loyal to Rome
49 Aristobulus II and his son Alexander released from imprisonment but killed on way back to Judea; Antipater made procura-

B.C.

tor of Judea
48 Julius Caesar defeats Pompey; Pompey flees to Egypt and is killed there
44 Caesar assassinated
43 Antipater the Idumean assassinated
42 Octavian and Mark Antony defeat Caesar's assassins
40 Parthia takes Jerusalem; John Hyrcanus II mutilated; Antigonus Mattathias made high priest
39 Herod, son of Antipater, lands in Judea
37 Herod rules Judea; Antigonus Mattathias executed; Aristobulus III made high priest
36 Aristobulus III executed; end of Maccabean high priesthood
31 Octavian defeats Mark Antony; establishes Roman Empire and rules as Augustus, first emperor
30 John Hyrcanus II executed
29 Mariamne, wife of Herod, executed
6 Sons of Mariamne executed
4 Death of Herod; birth of Jesus

A.D.

6 Herod Archelaus deposed as ethnarch of Judea
14 Tiberius rules as Roman emperor
26 Pontius Pilate rules as procurator of Judea
29 Jesus crucified
31 Martyrdom of Stephen
35 Conversion of Saul on the road to Damascus
37 Caligula rules as Roman emperor; Herod Agrippa I rules over portions of Judea
38 Anti-Jewish riots in Alexandria
40 Caligula decides to put own statue in Temple at Jerusalem; Philo of Alexandria pleads against it; Herod Agrippa I persuades Caligula to change mind
41 Claudius rules as Roman emperor; Herod Agrippa I rules over all Judea
44 Herod Agrippa I dies; Judea returns to rule by procurators
46 Saul begins career as Christian missionary; changes name to Paul; woos Gentiles by eliminating cirumcision
48 Council of Jerusalem, where Paul's version of Christianity wins out; Herod Agrippa II rules in Chalcis
52 Antonius Felix rules as procurator of Judea
53 Herod Agrippa II rules over Iturea and Galilee
54 Nero rules as Roman emperor
57 Paul taken into protective custody
61 Porcius Festus rules as

A.D.	
	procurator of Judea; Paul appeals to emperor and goes to Rome
66	Rebellion breaks out in Judea
67	Roman general, Vespasian, goes to Judea with three legions; takes Jotapata
68	Nero kills himself; anarchy in Rome
70	Vespasian rules as Roman emperor; his son Titus takes Jerusalem, destroys Second Temple, abolishes high priesthood; Alexandrian Jewry destroyed
71	Vespasian and Titus celebrate triumph in Rome
73	Last Jewish holdout at Masada taken
77	Josephus publishes history of Jewish rebellion
79	Titus rules as Roman emperor
81	Domitian rules as Roman emperor
90	Jewish scholars at Jamnia establish Masoretic text of Bible; Domitian passes laws against Jews and Christians; Josephus publishes *Antiquities of the Jews*
96	Domitian assassinated; Nerva rules as Roman emperor, rescinds laws against Jews and Christians
98	Trajan rules as Roman emperor
115	Rome reaches peak of territorial extent, as Trajan takes his army to the Persian Gulf
116	Jews in Cyrene revolt and are wiped out
117	Hadrian rules as Roman emperor
130	Hadrian visits Judea; decides to build pagan city on site of ruined Jerusalem
131	Jews in Judea revolt and take Jerusalem
134	Romans retake Jerusalem
135	Jewish revolt crushed

I — Kings of Israel (all dates B.C.)

1 – LINE OF SAUL (1020–991)

SAUL
(1020–1000)

- Jonathan
- ESHBAAL (1000–991)

2 – LINE OF JEROBOAM (922–900)

JEROBOAM
(922–901)
|
NADAB
(901–900)

3 – LINE OF BAASHA

BAASHA
(900–877)
|
ELAH
(877–876)

4 – LINE OF OMRI (876–842)

OMRI
(876–869)
|
AHAB = *Jezebel*
(869–850) (d. 842)

- AHAZIAH (850–849)
- JEHORAM (849–842)
- ATHALIAH = Jehoram of Judah
  (d. 836)

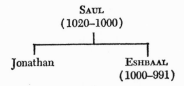

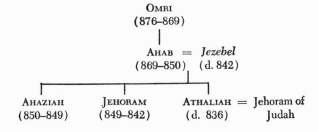

5 – LINE OF JEHU (842–748)

JEHU
(842–814)
|
JEHOAHAZ
(814–798)
|
JEHOASH
(798–783)
|
JEROBOAM II
(783–748)
|
ZECHARIAH
(748)

6 – LINE OF MENAHEM (748–736)

MENAHEM
(748–738)
|
PEKAHIAH
(738–736)

No dynasty:

PEKAH (736–732)

HOSHEA (732–722)

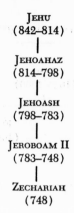

II — Davidic Dynasty of Judah (all dates B.C.)

- **David** (1000–961) = *Bathsheba*
  - **Solomon** (961–922)
    - **Rehoboam** (922–915)
      - **Abijah** (915–913)
        - **Asa** (913–873)
          - **Jehoshaphat** (873–849)
            - **Jehoram** (849–842) = **Athaliah** (842–836) [daughter of Ahab = *Jezebel*]
              - **Ahaziah** (842)
                - **Jehoash** (836–797)
                  - **Amaziah** (797–769)
                    - **Uzziah** (769–734)
                      - **Jotham** (734)
                        - **Ahaz** (734–715)
                          - **Hezekiah** (715–687)
                            - **Manasseh** (687–642)
                              - **Amon** (642–640)
                                - **Josiah** (640–609)
                                  - **Jehoiakim** (609–597)
                                    - **Jehoiachin** (597)
                                  - **Jehoahaz** (609)
                                  - **Zedekiah** (597–587)

III — The Maccabean Family (all dates B.C.)

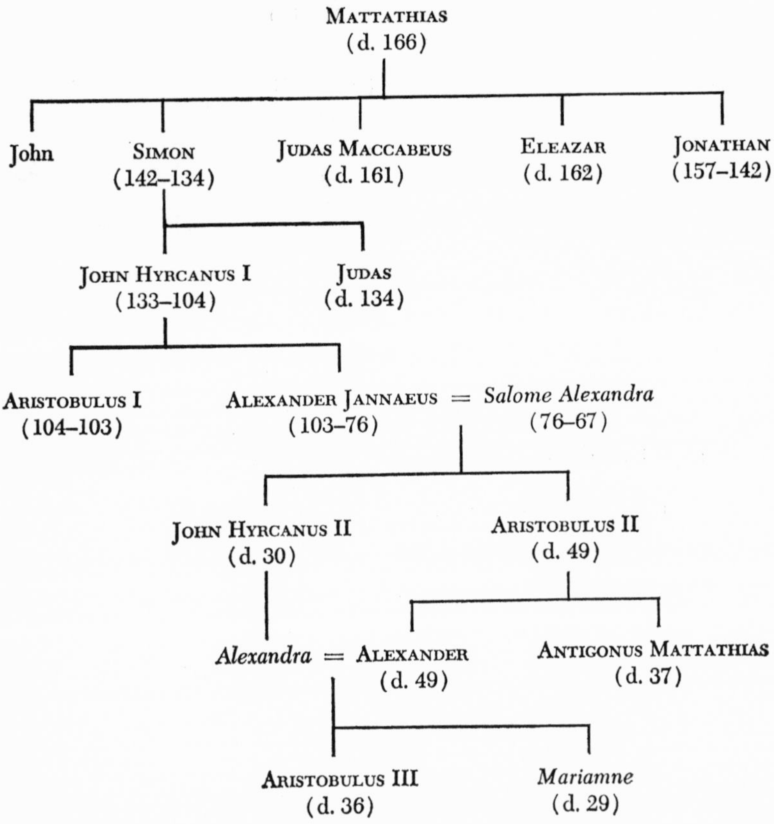

IV — The Family of Herod

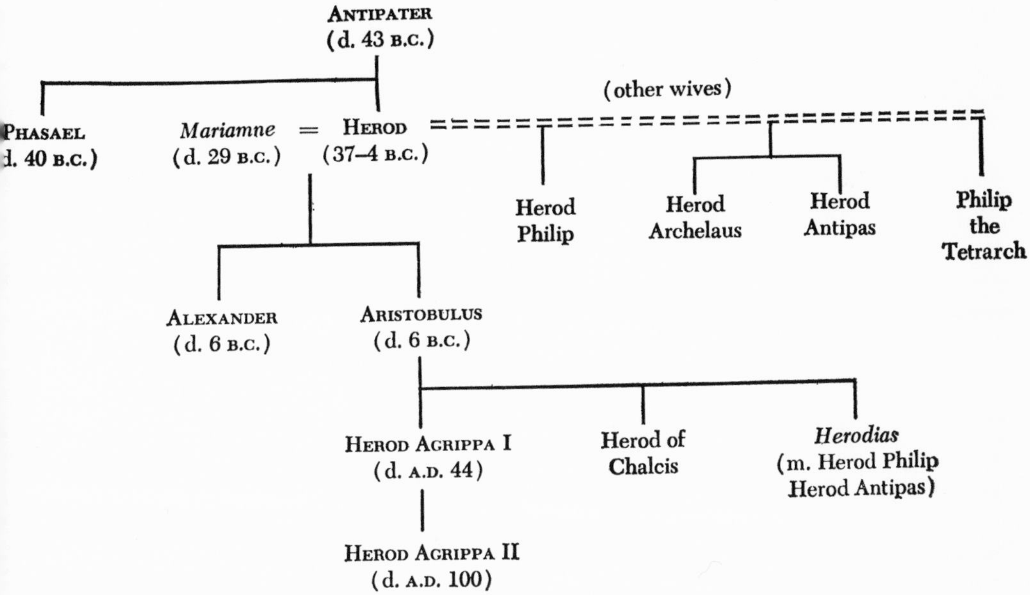

INDEX